Speed Up Your Chine

C000051138

Speed Up Your Chinese is a unique and innovative resource that identifies and explains the common errors that English-speaking learners of Chinese repeatedly make. The book brings together these common errors to offer a valuable insight into the differences between English and Chinese and to reveal the inner workings of the latter allowing students to enhance their understanding and mastery of the Chinese language.

Key features:

- organizes basic principles of Mandarin grammar into coherent categories
- learner-oriented and problem-solving approach analyzes approximately 150 commonly made errors
- highlights and explains differences between Mandarin and English
- 'points to remember' provide vital learning strategies
- exercises with full answer key to reinforce learning
- examples in traditional characters provided in the appendix

Speed Up Your Chinese is the ideal reference for all learners of Chinese.

Shin Yong Robson holds a PhD in Chinese linguistics from the University of Wisconsin at Madison. She has taught at Beloit College since 1992, having initiated its Chinese language program.

SPEED UP YOUR LANGUAGE SKILLS

SERIES EDITOR: Javier Muñoz-Basols, *University of Oxford, UK*

The *Speed Up Your Language Skills* series publishes innovative, high quality textbooks focusing on common errors as an effective tool to improve one's skills in a foreign language. Such errors are often either driven by linguistic transfer from English or caused by common misperceptions about the grammatical structure of a foreign language.

The primary objectives of the series are to explain and illustrate in context the most common errors made by English-speaking students in a foreign language and to classify them in easy-to-reference categories. Students can thus learn the appropriate usage of words and expressions and understand the reasons why they persistently make the same mistakes. The inclusion of exercises, shortcuts, and much-needed strategies, not usually seen in conventional grammar books, facilitates vocabulary acquisition and mastery of essential grammatical elements.

Books in the series are intended as primary or supplementary texts at the intermediate and advanced levels. Due to its self-explanatory approach and user-friendly format, the series is also recommended for self-learners who wish to "speed up" their language skills.

Speed Up Your Chinese

Strategies to avoid common errors

Shin Yong Robson

Routledge
Taylor & Francis Group

LONDON AND NEW YORK

First published 2013
by Routledge
2 Park Square, Milton Park, Abingdon, Oxon OX14 4RN

Simultaneously published in the USA and Canada
by Routledge
711 Third Avenue, New York, NY 10017

Routledge is an imprint of the Taylor & Francis Group, an informa business

British Library Cataloguing in Publication Data
A catalogue record for this book is available from the British Library

Library of Congress Cataloging in Publication Data
A catalog record for this book has been requested

ISBN: 978-0-415-50151-4 (hbk)
ISBN: 978-0-415-50152-1 (pbk)
ISBN: 978-0-203-10098-1 (ebk)

Typeset in Swiss and Zapf Calligraphic
by Graphicraft Limited, Hong Kong

MIX
Paper from
responsible sources
FSC
www.fsc.org   FSC® C004839

Printed and bound in Great Britain by the MPG Books Group

To Art and the memory of my father

Contents

Part III.   Temporal expressions   58

Part IV.   Noun and verb phrases   93

Introduction

Speakers of English wish to see Mandarin Chinese grammar organized in a way that sidesteps the pitfalls of literal translation from their native tongue. Accordingly this book's contents focus on specific problems encountered by English-speaking learners.

While many units in this book address mainstream topics, most organize the issues in new combinations. Many subsections, especially in Parts III–V, explore important grammatical details in ways different from most grammar books. Cross-category examination of items is common in these subsections since they present a series of interlocked topics. For instance, after clarification of the difference between the two types of questions and their structures in §§18–19, §20 demonstrates how these different questions maintain their respective structures as the object clause of the cognitive verb 知道 zhīdào 'know'. §20 thus addresses a common, yet long-overlooked, grammatical confusion. Users do not need to start this book from §1. Plunge into any of the 58 topics that interest you.

Part I addresses simple sentences with one main verb, while **Part II** explains complex sentences or compound clauses. Part II also includes two major types of questions: yes/no questions and those with interrogative words (§§18–19).

Part III concentrates on temporal expressions, an intractable component of Mandarin for English-speakers, since Mandarin is a language without obvious tense markers. Thus Part III offers numerous close comparisons: the difference between chronological time and durational time (§22); how these different time expressions function in a sentence (§24); how Mandarin, without using an a.m./p.m. system, delineates hours of the day (§23); how this seemingly tenseless language expresses past and future time (§§28–30); and how adverbs contribute to this task (§§31–32).

Part IV discusses the different phrase structures: how location words and relative clauses function as modifiers (§§35–36); how Mandarin, without equivalents to the English articles *the* and *a(n)*, handles noun references (§37); and how Mandarin verb complements work (§45). Four of the subsections, §§41–44, are devoted to a multifaceted examination of a unique verb structure—the verb-verb compound—which always challenges English speakers.

Part V focuses on subtle differences between similar words and phrases that may in fact belong to different grammatical categories, or derive from different word formations. The topics of Part V directly address typical errors, and the problems that they demonstrate. These topics also explore grammar details cross-categorically, while explaining differences between Mandarin and English.

Each subsection follows these **steps**: a) states a topic and illustrates the grammatical rules; b) provides examples and again illustrates the rules; c) presents a case-analysis of illustrative errors, along with explanatory corrections; and d) ends with a 'points to remember' note that highlights the core of the discussion. In addition to the subsection exercises, each Part concludes with a review section called *Check Your Grammar*, which lists correct English versions of the typical errors used in that Part. You may wish to translate these English sentences back into Chinese, to check your grasp of the relevant grammar points.

The essence of Mandarin grammar is **phrase/sentence patterns**. Because Mandarin lacks certain structures—such as singular and plural, noun-verb agreement, conjugations, and obvious tense markers—that reality paradoxically makes the grammar easier to grasp. This grammar in a sense emulates mathematics: the phrase/sentence patterns are formulae. Understand them, remember them, and follow them to put the right words in the right places. Then the language works. This is the reason that many sections detail the character of these patterns.

The sample errors in this book come directly from a synthesis of classroom practices and students' written exercises. Far from unique, these samples are highly representative because such mistakes echo across generations. These typical errors are a valuable tool in foreign language study because language learners gain much of their grammatical knowledge from the experience of self-corrected errors. You often learn, and refine, grammar points from such slips. This book aims to address and guide you through such linguistic quandaries.

While the ideal audience of this book, because they know more grammar, is learners who have studied the language for two or more semesters, this book also guides beginners. Those with only a few weeks of Chinese will find familiar details in the subsections. Of course utility grows as beginners progress. On the other hand, the user of this book should have some background in the language since this book does not teach all the details of grammar: it is not a beginning textbook; nor is it comprehensive; rather it serves as a valuable complement to textbooks at all basic levels, and includes only the grammar fundamentally important to your background as an English speaker.

I hope this book provides Chinese language learners with a useful set of tactics for their studies, and I look forward to obtaining feedback from you.

Acknowledgments

I thank the students in my nearly three decades of teaching at the University of Wisconsin and at Beloit College, as well as my students in Beloit's intensive language courses across twelve summers. Those vigorous discussions of grammar with you inspired this book.

I am grateful for a Faculty Grants Award by Beloit College that supported this project.

I thank anonymous reviewers for their valuable feedback, and am especially grateful to my Routledge editor Samantha Vale Noya for her patience, assertiveness, timely feedback, and many useful suggestions. It was a truly pleasant experience working with her. I also thank Javier Muñoz-Basols, the series editor, for his guidance and helpful suggestions. One last, but not least, delight was Cheryl Hutty, the copy-editor, whose sharp queries about notable details improved the text.

Finally, great appreciation goes to my family—my parents for their tireless support, my brother Y.R. and my sister Duan for their humor, their everlasting curiosity about this project, and our insightful exchanges about grammar. My deepest gratitude is reserved for Arthur, my husband, for his understanding and patience, for the hours he spent with me discussing comparative grammar and writing styles, and for sharing my happiness and frustration about this project. His encouragement and inspiration helped to make this book possible.

Website

Complementing this book are supplementary exercises for all subsections at the *Speed Up Your Chinese* website www.routledge.com/cw/robson

Glossary of grammatical terms

A-not-A structure One of the ways to form a yes/no question in Mandarin. The 'A' in the structure may be a descriptive adjective or an action verb. The 'not-A' is the negative form of either one, e.g. 今天冷不冷? *jīntiān lěng-bù-lěng* 'Is today cold (or not)?' 你看没看报? *nǐ kàn-méi-kàn bào* 'Have you read the newspaper (or not)?'

action verbs Verbs that express activities.

adjectives Words that modify nouns. (See also **descriptive adjectives**.)

adverbs Words that modify verbs, adjectives, or other adverbs. In distinction from English, the Mandarin adverb only stands before the word it modifies.

adverbial phrase A phrase that modifies a verb or a descriptive adjective, indicating details such as time, location, manner, and degree. In Mandarin the adverbial phrase may appear before or after the word it modifies.

aspect markers Verb suffixes that indicate how an action is viewed: progressing, continuing, or completed. The three major aspect markers in Mandarin are 了 *-le*, 着 *-zhe*, and 过 *-guò*.

auxiliary verbs Modal verbs that are added before a main verb to indicate ability, probability, willingness, requests, obligation, or wishes. The most common ones in Mandarin are 会 *huì* 'can,' 能 *néng* 'be able to,' 可以 *kěyǐ* 'may,' 应该 *yīnggāi* 'should,' and 得 *děi* 'must.'

clause A group of words that contains a subject and a predicate. A clause that can stand alone as a simple sentence is an independent clause, or the main clause. A clause that cannot stand alone is a dependent clause, also called a subordinate clause.

cognitive verbs Verbs that express the act or process of perceiving or knowing. 知道 *zhīdào* 'know' and 认识 *rènshi* 'recognize' are two common cognitive verbs in Mandarin.

complement In Mandarin a verb complement is another verb or descriptive adjective that, following the main action verb, completes its meaning, as 住 *zhù* 'stay' in 记住 *jì-zhù* 'memorize-stay = to remember'; or 大 *dà* 'big' in 长大 *zhǎng-dà* 'grow-big = to grow up.' A phrase complement usually follows a descriptive adjective to indicate its degree, e.g. 贵得多 *guì-deduō* 'much (too) expensive'; or follows an action verb to indicate the manner of the action, e.g. 来得很晚 *lái-de hěnwǎn* 'come very late.'

complex sentence A sentence that consists of one main clause and one or more subordinate clauses, e.g. 你回来以后，一定给我打电话。 *nǐ huílai yǐhòu, yídìng gěi-wǒ dǎ-diànhuà* 'Please make sure to call me after you return.'

compound sentence A sentence that has two or more independent clauses, e.g. 今天虽然下了雪，却不太冷。 *jīntiān suīrán xià-le-xuě, què bú tài lěng* 'Although it snowed today, it is not too cold.'

conjunctions In Mandarin, coordinating conjunctions are those that join nouns or noun phrases (e.g. 和 *hé* or 跟 *gēn* 'and'), whereas correlative conjunctions are used in pairs to link phrases or clauses (e.g. *both . . . and . . . , either . . . or . . . , not only . . . but also . . . , if . . . then . . . , although . . . but . . .*).

conjunctive adverb An adverb that introduces a clause showing a consequential or temporal relationship with the previous clause in a compound sentence. The most common one in Mandarin is 就 *jiù* '. . . , then . . .'

demonstrative A word that locates a person or thing. In Mandarin it is 这 *zhèi/zhè* 'this' or 那 *nèi/nà* 'that,' preceding or replacing a number before a measure word, e.g. 这一个苹果 *zhèi-yíge-píngguǒ* 'this one apple,' or 那个 苹果 *nèi-ge-píngguǒ* 'that apple.'

descriptive adjectives Words that describe a state of being. Monosyllabic descriptive adjectives modify nouns as English adjectives, e.g. 小溪 *xiǎoxī* 'small stream'; and 短途 *duǎntú* 'short distance.' In a simple sentence whose predicate is a descriptive adjective, the verb of being, 是 *shì*, is not used, e.g. 冬天很冷。 *dōngtiān hěn lěng* 'The winter (is) very cold.'

homonyms Words that have the same pronunciation and the same tone, but different meanings or functions.

interrogative words (interrogatives) Words that are used to ask questions. In English these words usually begin with *wh-* (e.g. what, where, who, when) and introduce a question. In Mandarin the interrogative word occupies the same position in the question as the answer does in the response, e.g. 他姓 什么? *tā xìng shénme?* 'What is his last name?' 他姓王。 *tā xìng wáng* 'His last name is Wang.'

measure word (measure) A word used between a number or demonstrative and a noun, as *slice* in the English phrase 'a/this slice of pie.' The most common measure in Mandarin is 个 *ge* (neutral tone). In Mandarin a measure word is also used between 几/多少 *jǐ/duōshǎo* 'how many' (the question word for a number), 哪 *něi/nǎ* 'which' (the question word for a demonstrative), or 每 *měi* 'each/every' and a noun.

modifiers Words, phrases, or clauses that describe or qualify the meaning of a word, e.g. 热茶 *rè chá* 'hot tea'; 很大 *hěn dà* 'very large'; 仔细地看 *zǐxìde kàn* 'carefully read'; or 刚认识的朋友 *gāng rènshi de péngyou* 'a friend just met.'

noun phrase A phrase that consists of a noun and its modifiers, e.g. 一本中文书 *yì-běn zhōngwén shū* 'a Chinese book.'

nouns with definite/indefinite references A definite reference indicates a particular item (e.g. *the tree* outside my window). The identity of this noun is clear to the reader. An indefinite reference indicates an unspecified noun (e.g. *trees* in the forest). The identity of the noun in this context is not important. Mandarin does not have articles that correspond to *the* and *a(n)* in English. A noun with a definite reference usually gains that specificity from a demonstrative 这 *zhèi/zhè* 'this' or 那 *nèi/nà* 'that'; or is the subject of a sentence, whereas a noun with an indefinite reference is usually not quantified and is the object of a sentence.

objects A direct object is a noun or pronoun that receives the action of a transitive verb. An indirect object is a noun or pronoun that indicates to whom or towards whom the action of a transitive verb is directed, (e.g. The teacher returned *the students* their homework). In Mandarin an indirect object is frequently introduced by the preposition *gěi* in an active-voice sentence, e.g. 我不常给他们打电话，我给他们发短信。 *wǒ bù cháng gěi tāmen dǎ-diànhuà, wǒ gěi tāmen fā-duǎnxìn* 'I don't often call them. I text them.' As shown here, an object may follow its preposition.

potential form Special form of a verb-verb compound in Mandarin. By adding an infix, 得 *-de-* 'able to' or 不 *-bù-* 'unable to,' between the two verbs of the compound, the potential form indicates the (in)ability to accomplish the action.

predicate The part of a sentence that follows the subject and makes a statement about it. A simple Mandarin predicate contains a descriptive adjective (山高。 *shān gāo* 'The mountain (is) tall.') or an action verb (我去。 *wǒ qù* 'I (will) go.') A complete predicate consists of the descriptive adjective or the action verb plus its modifiers, e.g. 山很高。 *shān hěn gāo* 'The mountain (is) very tall.' or 我马上去。 *wǒ mǎshàng qù* 'I (will) immediately go.'

preposition A word that takes a noun or pronoun as its object to form a prepositional phrase, which in Mandarin functions as an adverbial modifier of the main verb, e.g. the preposition 从 *cóng* 'from' takes 中国 *Zhōngguó* 'China' to form the prepositional phrase 从中国 *cóng-Zhōngguó* 'from China.'

This prepositional phrase serves as an adverbial modifier of the main verb in the sentence 他从中国来。*tā cóng-Zhōngguó lái* 'He comes from China.'

pronouns Words that are used in place of nouns. Mandarin usually applies this term to personal pronouns: 我 *wǒ* 'I, me,' 我们 *wǒmen* 'we, us,' 你 *nǐ* 'you (sing.),' 你们 *nǐmen* 'you (pl.);' 他 *tā* 'he, him,' 她 *tā* 'she, her,' and 他们 *tāmen* 'they, them.'

quasi-measures Nouns that can serve as measure words for other nouns, and that do not need a measure when quantified by a numeral or preceded by a demonstrative, e.g. 三杯茶 *sān-bēi-chá* 'three cups of tea,' 一年 *yì-nián* 'one year,' and 那天 *nèi-tiān* 'that day.'

question particle The particle 吗 *ma* (neutral tone), which, added to a statement, changes the statement to a yes/no question.

simple sentence A sentence that consists of a subject and a predicate, e.g. 电影 + 非常有意思 *diànyǐng + fēicháng yǒuyìsi* 'the movie is very interesting.'

subject The noun or noun phrase of a clause or a sentence that identifies the topic or the actor responsible for the action.

subjunctive mood A way of expressing conditions and wishes that are hypothetical rather than actual.

subordinate clause A dependent clause that cannot stand alone as a simple sentence, such as 'before sleeping' in 睡觉以前，我总是喝一点儿牛奶。*shuìjiào yǐqián, wǒ zǒngshi hē yìdiǎnr niúnǎi* 'Before sleeping, I always drink a little milk.' (See also **clause**.)

transitive and intransitive verbs The former are verbs that require a direct object. The latter are verbs that do not take a direct object.

verb phrase In Mandarin it consists of the main verb and its object, or of the main verb and its complements.

Abbreviations

Adj.	adjective
Adv.	adverb
Aux.	auxiliary
DA	descriptive adjective
Dem	demonstrative
DVC	directional verb complement
lit.	literally
Mea	measure (word)
N	noun
Neg.	negation
NP	noun phrase
Num	number
Obj.	object
pl.	plural
RVC	resultative verb complement
sing.	singular
Subj.	subject
V	verb
VC	verb complement
VP	verb phrase
V-V	verb-verb
*	unacceptable, ill-formed
?	questionable

1 Simple sentences

§1. Sentences with a descriptive adjective

For a simple sentence whose predicate is a descriptive adjective, such as 'he is hungry' or 'the movie is interesting,' Mandarin uses the structure shown in 1a.

1a Subj. + Adv. + DA
电影[Subj.]很[Adv.]有意思[DA]。
diànyǐng hěn yǒuyìsi
'The movie is very interesting.'

Similar to English adjectives, Mandarin descriptive adjectives describe states of being, such as 好 *hǎo* 'good,' or 新 *xīn* 'new.' Some textbooks therefore refer to them as **stative verbs**. A Mandarin sentence with a descriptive adjective, however, does not use the verb of being, 是 *shì* 'be.' E.g. 1a literally reads 'movie very interesting.'

In sentences with a descriptive adjective, the adjectives are routinely preceded by an adverbial word/phrase, as *hěn* 'very' in 1a, *fēicháng* 'extraordinarily' in 1b, or *yuèláiyuè* 'more and more' in 1c. The suffix . . . *jí le* 'extremely' is the only adverbial word that follows a descriptive adjective, as shown in 1d, where it may be combined with another adverb *zhēnshì* 'truly' to form a frame around the DA for an even stronger emphasis on the adverbial force of the DA. Note that *zhēnshì* is the only adverb that may form such a frame with . . . *jí le*.

1b 张先生非常忙。
Zhāng xiānsheng **fēicháng** máng
'Mr. Zhang is extraordinarily busy.'

1c   张先生越来越忙。

Zhāng xiānsheng **yuèláiyuè** máng

'Mr. Zhang is getting more and more busy.'

1d   张先生(真是)忙极了。

Zhāng xiānsheng (**zhēnshì**) máng **jí le**

'Mr. Zhang is (truly) extremely busy.'

Negation

The negation, either *bù* 'not,' as in 1e, or *bù zěnme* 'not that . . .' as in 1f, also precedes the descriptive adjective. The negation usually replaces the adverbial word/phrase in the statement.

1e   张先生不忙。

Zhāng xiānsheng **bù** máng

'Mr. Zhang is not busy.'

1f   张先生不怎么忙。

Zhāng xiānsheng **bù zěnme** máng

'Mr. Zhang is not that busy.'

It is necessary to note that an unmodified descriptive adjective, such as *máng* in 1g, implies comparison. Modified by an adverbial word or phrase, on the other hand, sentences such as 1b–f do not have a comparative sense, and merely offer a general statement.

1g   张先生忙。

Zhāng xiānsheng máng

'Mr. Zhang (in comparison to someone else) is busy.'

 The most common error is to use the verb of being, 是 *shì* 'be,' in an isolated, context-free sentence with a descriptive adjective, as in 1h. Sentences such as 1h could occur in oral conversations among native speakers, but only when they mean to stress the fact that Mr. Zhang is in fact really, truly busy (in response to some people's view that he may not be busy). On the other hand, it is ill-formed with the verb 'be', *shì*, in an isolated comment with a descriptive adjective, such as in 1h. To correct the error, one simply uses an adverb to replace *shì*.

1h   ⊗ 张先生*是忙。

Zhāng xiānsheng **shì** máng

✅ 张先生很/太忙。

Zhāng xiānsheng **hěn/tài** máng

'Mr. Zhang is very/too busy.'

Another common error is to use more than one adverb to modify the same descriptive adjective. This mistake usually occurs when suffix . . . *jí le* 'extremely' already attaches to the descriptive adjective, as in error 1i, where another adverb *hěn* 'very' is also used. Remember, the only adverb that can pair with . . . *jí le* is *zhēnshì* 'truly,' as in the correction.

1i　　❌ 这个问题*很难极了。
　　　zhèi-ge wèntí **hěn** nán **jí le**
　　　'This question is ?very extremely difficult.'

　　　✅ 这个问题真是难极了。
　　　zhèi-ge wèntí **zhēnshì** nán **jí le**
　　　'This question is truly extremely difficult.'

> For a simple sentence with a descriptive adjective, such as 'the movie is interesting,' the structure is: Subj. + Adv. + DA. The verb of being, 是 *shì*, is not used.

For related topics, see §§6, 7, and 47.

Exercises

EXERCISE 1. Translate into Chinese.

1　Chinese grammar is very easy.
2　All my friends are extremely tired, but I am not.
3　The weather is getting colder and colder.
4　Milk is not expensive.

§2.　Sentences expressing location and existence

Two structures specify location or existence. One uses the location verb 在 *zài* 'be (located) at' in the structure: (specific) Subj. + 在 *zài*-location phrase; and the other uses the existence verb 有 *yǒu* 'there is/are . . .' in the structure: location phrase + 有 *yǒu*.

The subject of the first pattern, where *zài* is the verb, is a specific noun phrase. The term **specific** indicates that the subject noun (phrase) of this pattern possesses a definite reference, such as a particular person, place, or item, e.g. 'my father' and 'the public library' in 2a–b. A non-specific subject, such as 'three fast-food restaurants' in 2c, is unacceptable with this pattern.

2a   我父亲在家。他刚从德国回来。
wǒ fùqin zài jiā, tā gāng cóng Déguó huílai
'My father is home. He just came back from Germany.'

2b   公共图书馆在第一银行的对面。
gōnggòng túshūguǎn zài dìyī yínháng de duìmiàn
'The public library is across from the First Bank.'

2c   ⊗ *三个快餐店在第一银行的附近。
sān-ge kuàicāndiàn zài dìyī yínháng de fùjìn
'Three fast-food restaurants are near the First Bank.'

Mandarin expresses the idea of 2c in the second structure, where *yǒu* is the verb to describe the existence of a non-specific noun (phrase). This pattern is a close equivalent to the English structure 'there is/are. . . .' See 2d–e below. Note that a **specific** subject should not be used in the *yǒu* pattern. Thus the non-specific *yí-ge gōnggòng túshūguǎn* '**a** public library' in 2e is fine, but the specific *gōnggòng túshūguǎn* '**the** public library' in 2f is unacceptable.

2d   第一银行的附近有三个快餐店。
dìyī yínháng de fùjìn yǒu sān-ge kuàicāndiàn
'There are three fast-food restaurants near the First Bank.'

2e   第一银行的对面有一个公共图书馆。
dìyī yínháng de duìmiàn yǒu **yí-ge** gōnggòng túshūguǎn
'There is a public library across from the First Bank.'

2f   ⊗ 第一银行的对面有*公共图书馆。
dìyī yínháng de duìmiàn yǒu *gōnggòng túshūguǎn
'There is *the public library across from the First Bank.'

Negation

The negation for the *zài* pattern is *bù*, as in 2g; whereas the negation for the *yǒu* pattern is always *méi*, as in 2h.

2g   公共图书馆不在第一银行的对面。
gōnggòng túshūguǎn **bú** zài dìyī yínháng de duìmiàn
'The public library is not across from the First Bank.'

2h   这儿没有很多树。
zhèr **méi**yǒu hěnduō shù
'There are not many trees around here.'

 The most common error is using a non-specific subject in the 在 *zài* structure, such as in 2i. This Mandarin sentence is unacceptable because *wǔ-tiáo-xīnwén* '(any) five items of news' is too general a subject for the verb *zài*. The 有 *yǒu* pattern serves this idea.

2i   *五条新闻在今天的报上。
wǔ-tiáo-xīnwén zài jīntiān de bào-shang
'Five items (of news) are in today's paper.'

今天的报上有五条新闻。
jīntiān de bào-shang **yǒu** wǔ-tiáo-xīnwén
'There are five items (of news) in today's paper.'

> The structure [location + 有 *yǒu* . . .] describes the existence of a non-specific noun phrase, equivalent to 'there is/are . . .'. If a noun phrase is specific, it should be the subject of the pattern [Subj. + 在 *zài*-location].

For related topics, see §§37 and 49.

Exercises

EXERCISE 2. Translate into Chinese.

1 The month of June has 30 days.
2 There is a computer on the desk.
3 Are there six tennis courts near the dorms?
4 The teacher is not in her office.
5 The Yellow River is in northern China.
6 The children are in the park.

§3. When an activity's location is specified

As explained in §2, 在 *zài* 'be (located) at' is the verb for the location of a specific subject, as in the sentence 北京在河北省 *Běijīng zài Héběi shěng* 'Beijing is (located) in Hebei province.' In a sentence where an activity, represented by an action verb, occurs at a location, such as 'they play chess in the park,' Mandarin uses pattern 3a, where *zài* is no longer the verb.

3a Subj. + 在 *zài*-location + VP

In this pattern *zài* and a place word form a location phrase 在 *zài*-location, modifying the main action verb. See examples 3b–d below.

This pattern is a close equivalent to the English expression "someone does/is doing something in/at a certain place." Note that unlike English, in Mandarin the *zài*-location phrase must come **before** the main action verb. And the adverbial word or phrase (if there is one), such as *chángcháng* 'often' in 3c and *měitiān xiàwǔ* 'every afternoon' in 3d, appears before the *zài* phrase.

3b   王先生在大学教书；王太太在银行工作。

Wáng xiānsheng **zài dàxué** jiāo-shū; Wáng tàitai **zài yínháng** gōngzuò

'Mr. Wang teaches at the university; Mrs. Wang works in a bank.'

3c   她常常在超级市场买东西。

tā **chángcháng** zài chāojí shìchǎng mǎi-dōngxi

'She often shops at the supermarket.'

3d   他们每天下午在公园下棋。

tāmen **měitiān xiàwǔ** zài gōngyuán xià-qí

'They play chess in the park every afternoon.'

Negation

In this pattern the negation usually precedes the *zài*-location phrase to stress that the action does not, or not often, occur at the location specified. See example 3e.

3e   她不（常）在超级市场买东西。

tā **bù(cháng)** zài chāojí shìchǎng mǎi dōngxi

'She does not (often) shop at the supermarket.'

Note that while the activity itself could also be negated, as *méi mǎi-dōngxi* 'did not buy anything' in 3f, using the regular negation 不 *bù* to stress directly on the verb could be awkward. Compare 3g with 3c and 3e.

3f   她在超级市场没买东西。

tā zài chāojí shìchǎng **méi** mǎi dōngxi

'She didn't buy anything (when she was) at the supermarket.'

3g   ✗   ?她常常在超级市场不买东西。

tā chángcháng zài chāojí shìchǎng **bù** mǎi dōngxi

'She is often at the supermarket but ?does not buy things.'

One common error is to place the 在 *zài*-location phrase **after** the verb phrase, led by the English word order, while expressing the idea "someone does/is doing something in/at a certain place" in Mandarin. Sentences with this error, such as 3h, are unacceptable in Mandarin. 3h is a word-by-word translation of its English idea, hence producing a non-Mandarin structure. Remember: the pattern expressing such ideas should be: Subj. + 在 *zài*-location + VP (3a).

3h   *我工作在一家汉堡包快餐店。
wǒ gōngzuò zài yì-jiā hànbǎobāo kuàicāndiàn
'I work at a burger joint.'

 我在一家汉堡包快餐店工作。
wǒ **zài yì-jiā hànbǎobāo kuàicāndiàn** gōngzuò

> In a sentence such as 'she works at a bank,' the location phrase 'at a bank' comes **before** the action verb. The structure is: Subj. + 在 *zài*-location + V/VP.

For related topics, see §§4 and 5.

Exercises

EXERCISE 3. Translate into Chinese.

1 The children play in the park every afternoon.
2 Many American students study languages abroad.
3 They planted flowers in the garden.
4 She likes to drink coffee at Starbuck's.
5 We have our lunch at the student cafeteria.

§4. 'Be there' or 'go there': [在 *zài*-location + VP] or [去 *qù* location + VP]

As explained in §3, when an activity's location is specified, the location phrase, introduced by 在 *zài*, appears before the main verb phrase. 4a shows this sentence pattern.

4a Subj. + (Adv. +) 在 *zài*-location + VP
他们（常）在快餐店吃饭。
tāmen (cháng) **zài kuàicāndiàn** chī-fàn
'They (often) eat at fast-food restaurants.'

A pattern similar to this one is 4b, with the verb 去 *qù* 'go' preceding the location. In 4b, the location word after *qù* specifies the destination of the verb phrase that follows. Note in both 4a and 4b, the adverb (if there is one) appears before *zài* or *qù*.

4b Subj. + (Adv. +) 去 *qù* location + VP

李太太（有的时候）去农贸市场买东西。

Lǐ tàitai (yǒude shíhou) **qù** nóngmào shìchǎng mǎi-dōngxi

'Mrs. Li (sometimes) goes to the farmers' market to shop.'

Despite the similarity between 4a and 4b, they use different grammatical structures. 4a has one main verb phrase showing the idea that 'someone does/is doing something in/at a certain place,' whereas 4b uses two verb phrases in succession: the [*qù* + location] 'go to a place' and the second verb phrase that indicates the purpose or reason for going to that place.

4c 他毕业以后去中国工作。

tā bìyè yǐhòu **qù** Zhōngguó **gōngzuò**

'After graduation, he will go to China to work.'

Negation

The negation 不 *bù* or 没 *méi* for pattern 4b usually stands before *qù*, emphasizing the negation of the motion. See examples 4d–e.

4d 他毕业以后不去中国工作。

tā bìyè yǐhòu **bú** qù Zhōngguó gōngzuò

'After graduation, he will not go to China to work.'

4e 他毕业以后没去中国工作。

tā bìyè yǐhòu **méi** qù Zhōngguó gōngzuò

'After graduation, he did not go to China to work.'

 Using both 在 *zài* and 去 *qù* before the location, such as in 4f, is a common error.

4f ✗ 我们今天下午*去 在大湖里游泳。

wǒmen jīntiān xiàwǔ **qù zài** dàhú li yóuyǒng

?'This afternoon, we will go and be at the Big Lake swimming.'

Students need to understand that *zài* means 'be (located) at,' whereas *qù* means 'to go.' While the former indicates that someone or something is located at a given place, the latter involves a motion to some location. Consequently *zài* and *qù* never appear in the same sentence. 4f is erroneous because one may either go to swim at the lake, as in 4g, or be swimming at the lake, as in 4h, but cannot **go** to and **be** at the lake at the same time.

4g 我们今天下午去大湖游泳。

wǒmen jīntiān xiàwǔ **qù** dàhú yóuyǒng

'This afternoon we will go to the Big Lake to swim.'

4h 我们今天下午<u>在</u>大湖里游泳。

wǒmen jīntiān xiàwǔ **zài** dàhú li yóuyǒng

'This afternoon we will be swimming at the Big Lake.'

[在 *zài*-location + VP] expresses the idea 'do something in/at a certain place,' whereas [去 *qù* location + VP] means 'go to a place to do something.' Thus *zài* 'be at' and *qù* 'go' cannot appear in the same sentence.

For related topics, see §§2, 3, and 5.

Exercises

EXERCISE 4. Translate into Chinese.

1 Many American students go to China to study Chinese.
2 Let's go camping in the mountains.
3 I am going to the post office to mail a letter.
4 She often goes to her friend's room to chat.
5 We didn't go to the student cafeteria for lunch today.

§5. Basic word order of an extended [Subj. + VP] sentence

While using adverbial phrases indicating time, location, and/or manner in a Mandarin [Subj. + VP] sentence, 5a shows the basic word order of the extended structure.

5a Subj. + Adv./time(-when) + 在 *zài*-location + VP + time(-spent)

Note that an adverb such as 常常 *chángcháng* 'often,' or 总是 *zǒngshì* 'always,' as well as the chronological time expression (**time-when**), such as 每天晚上 *měitiān wǎnshang* 'every evening,' or 星期天 *xīngqītiān* 'Sunday,' stand before the 在 *zài*-location phrase; and in turn the *zài*-location stands before the main verb phrase of the sentence. On the other hand, the durational time expression (**time-spent**), i.e. the time indicating the length of the activity, stands after the main verb phrase.

The adverbial phrases in the structure 5a, namely, the adverb/time(-when), *zài*-location, and time(-spent), do not necessarily appear in every sentence. Yet whether there is one adverbial phrase as in 5b–e, two adverbial phrases as in 5f–h, or three as in 5i–j, the basic word order of the structure 5a should remain constant. See the following examples. The adverbial forms are marked at the beginning of each example. Pay attention to the word order of adverbial phrases relevant to the main verb phrase.

5b   one adverbial phrase: Time(-when): 'every Friday'
王家每星期五吃饺子。
Wáng jiā **měi xīngqīwǔ** chī-jiǎozi
'Wang's family eats dumplings every Friday.'

5c   one adverbial phrase: Adverb: 'often'
王家常常吃饺子。
Wáng jiā **chángcháng** chī-jiǎozi
'Wang's family often eats dumplings.'

5d   one adverbial phrase: Location: '(at) out'
王先生在外面吃午饭。
Wáng xiānsheng **zài wàimian** chī-wǔfàn
'Mr. Wang has his lunch out.'

5e   one adverbial phrase: Time(-spent): '(eat lunch) for one hour'
王先生吃午饭吃一个小时。
Wáng xiānsheng chī-wǔfàn chī **yí-ge xiǎoshí**
'Mr. Wang eats his lunch for one hour.'

5f   two adverbial phrases: Adverb: 'often'; Location: '(at) out'
王先生常常 在外面吃午饭。
Wáng xiānsheng **chángcháng zài wàimian** chī-wǔfàn
'Mr. Wang often has his lunch out.'

5g   two adverbial phrases: Time(-when): 'every day'; Time(-spent):
      '(eat lunch) for one hour'
王先生每天吃午饭吃一个小时。
Wáng xiānsheng **měitiān** chī-wǔfàn chī **yí-ge xiǎoshí**
'Every day Mr. Wang eats his lunch for one hour.'

5h   two adverbial phrases: Time(-when): 'Wednesday afternoon'; Location:
      'at the supermarket'
王太太星期三下午 在超级市场买菜。
Wáng tàitai **xīngqīsān xiàwǔ zài chāojí shìchǎng** mǎi-cài
'On Wednesday afternoons Mrs. Wang goes grocery shopping at
    the supermarket.'

5i   three adverbial phrases: Adverb: 'always'; Time(-when): 'after dinner';
      Time(-spent): '(take a walk) for a half hour'
王先生王太太总是 晚饭以后散半个钟头步。
Wáng xiānsheng Wáng tàitai **zǒngshì wǎnfàn yǐhòu** sàn **bàn-ge
    zhōngtóu** bù
'Mr. and Mrs. Wang always take a half-hour walk after dinner.'

5j three adverbial phrases: Time(-when): 'every Tuesday'; Location: 'at the university'; Time(-spent): '(attend drawing class) for three hours'

王太太<u>每星期二</u> <u>在大学</u>上<u>三个小时</u>（的）绘画课。

Wáng tàitai **měi xīngqī'èr zài dàxué** shàng **sān-ge xiǎoshí** (de) huìhuà kè

'Every Tuesday Mrs. Wang attends a drawing class at the university for three hours.'

Similar to the problem in §3, common errors arise from the temptation to translate word-by-word from English. This procedure can lead to curious Mandarin sentences.

5k–l demonstrate such errors. The English translations indicate the ideas intended but not realized. These errors appear because the Mandarin word order differs from the English word order.

5k *她工作在学校餐厅每星期五下午四个小时。

tā gōngzuò zài xuéxiào cāntīng měi xīngqīwǔ xiàwǔ sì-ge xiǎoshí

'She works at the school cafeteria every Friday afternoon for four hours.'

✔ 她每星期五下午 [time-when]在学校餐厅 [location]工作 [V]四个小时 [time-spent]。

tā měi xīngqīwǔ xiàwǔ zài xuéxiào cāntīng gōngzuò sì-ge xiǎoshí

5l *我学习每天晚上在图书馆。

wǒ xuéxí měitiān wǎnshang zài túshūguǎn

'I study at the library every evening.'

✔ 我每天晚上 [time-when]在图书馆 [location]学习 [V]。

wǒ měitiān wǎnshang zài túshūguǎn xuéxí

> 5a shows the word order of an extended [Subj. + VP] sentence. While elements of this structure may not appear in every sentence, the basic word order remains constant.

For related topics, see §§3, 22, 23, 24, 36, and 53.

Exercises

EXERCISE 5. Put the parenthetical phrases where they belong in the sentences.

1 我和朋友喝咖啡。（在她家）
2 他们星期五在体育馆打球。（下午）
3 他们昨天吃晚饭。（吃了三个钟头）
4 小马在图书馆工作。（星期二晚上，四个小时）
5 小马每个星期工作。（在图书馆）

6 我去年学了日文。(九个月的)
7 她在电影院看电影。(不常)
8 他们等我呢！(现在，在外面)

EXERCISE 6. Translate into Chinese.

1 That student worked in a supermarket last summer.
2 They usually have a one-hour lunch.
3 We have literature class on Tuesday evenings at 7:00.
4 Every spring they travel for three weeks.
5 She always gets on the train at that subway station.
6 My older sister taught one semester of English in China.

§6. Structures of comparison (i): contrast, with 比 *bǐ*

To contrast differences, as in the sentence 'X is louder than Y,' Mandarin uses the pattern with 比 *bǐ* 'as compared with.' The structure is: X + 比 *bǐ* + Y + DA. In this pattern, X precedes *bǐ* and possesses a comparative relationship, which is described by the descriptive adjective, with Y. The sentence is literally 'X compared to Y is louder.' Note that Y stands before the DA. See examples 6a–b.

6a 咖啡比茶贵。
    kāfēi bǐ **chá guì**
    'The coffee is more expensive than the tea.'

6b 这条街上的房子比邻街的老。
    zhèi-tiáo-jiē shang de fángzi bǐ **línjiē de** lǎo
    'The houses on this street are older than those on the adjacent street.'

The two elements of the comparison, i.e. X and Y, can inhabit varied grammatical structures, such as nouns *kāfēi* 'coffee' and *chá* 'tea' in 6a; or noun phrases such as *zhèi-tiáo-jiē shàng de fángzi* 'the houses on this street' and *línjiē de* 'those on the adjacent street' in 6b. They may also be in verb phrases such as *shuō-zhōngwén* 'speak Chinese' and *xiě-hànzì* 'write Chinese characters,' as in 6c.

6c 说中文比写汉字容易。
    shuō-zhōngwén bǐ **xiě-hànzì** róngyi
    'Speaking Chinese is easier than writing Chinese characters.'

Negation

While it is uncommon, the negation 不 *bù* can be put before *bǐ*. Note that *bù* stands before *bǐ* but never before the descriptive adjective. See example 6d.

6d 说中文<u>不</u>比写汉字容易。

shuō-zhōngwén **bù** bǐ xiě-hànzì róngyi

'Speaking Chinese is not easier than writing Chinese characters.'

Degrees of comparison

There are modifications in the *bǐ* pattern that show degrees of comparison. An expression of measurement normally appears as the complement of the descriptive adjective, such as 一点儿 *yìdiǎnr* 'a little' to show a small difference; or -得多 *-de duō* 'much more' to show a large difference. See examples 6e–f. The idea of 'very' or 'very much' in a comparison is never expressed by using the adverb 很 *hěn* 'very' before the DA, but by adding *-de duō* to the DA. The complement showing degrees of comparison may also be a specific measurement, such as 'ten cents' in 6g. Note that as the complement, the measurement phrase always follows the DA.

6e 手机比座机小<u>一点儿</u>。

shǒujī bǐ zuòjī xiǎo **yìdiǎnr**

'The cell phone is a little smaller than the normal phone.'

6f 她的汽车比我的贵<u>得多</u>。

tāde qìchē bǐ wǒde guì**-de duō**

'Her car is a great deal more expensive than mine.'

6g 咖啡比茶贵<u>一毛钱</u>。

kāfēi bǐ chá guì **yì-máo-qián**

'Coffee costs ten cents more than tea.'

Another modification involves adverbs of degree such as *duō* 'more' (6h)/ *shǎo* 'less'; *zǎo* 'early'/*wǎn* 'late' (6i). These words are used before the verb to indicate the comparative degree of an action. Note that in these cases, a specific measurement, such as *yì-mén-kè* 'one course' in 6h and *liǎng-gè-zhōngtóu* 'two hours' in 6i, is the complement of the verb; so it always follows the verb.

6h 张老师比林老师<u>多</u>教<u>一门</u>课。

Zhāng lǎoshī **bǐ** Lín lǎoshī **duō** jiāo **yì-mén-kè**

'Teacher Zhang teaches one course more than Teacher Lin does.'

6i 我室友比我<u>晚睡</u><u>两个钟头</u>。

    wǒ shìyǒu bǐ wǒ **wǎn** shuì **liǎng-ge-zhōngtóu**

    'My roommate goes to bed two hours later than I do.'

One common error is to use an adverbial word or phrase to modify the descriptive adjective, such as *hěn* 'very' in 6j and . . . *jí le* 'extremely' in 6k. As mentioned in §1, only the unmodified descriptive adjectives in Mandarin imply comparison. In other words, only unmodified descriptive adjectives can appear in a comparative structure. A modified descriptive adjective is incompatible in the 比 *bǐ* pattern. Examples 6j–k therefore are ill-formed.

6j ✖ 很多人认为吃菜比吃肉*<u>很好</u>。

    hěn duō rén rènwéi chī-cài bǐ chī-ròu **hěn** hǎo

    'Many people believe that eating vegetables is *very better than

       eating meat.'

    ✔ 很多人认为吃菜比吃肉<u>好</u>。

    hěn duō rén rènwéi chī-cài bǐ chī-ròu **hǎo**

6k ✖ 他认识的字比我多*<u>极了</u>。

    tā rènshi de zì bǐ wǒ duō **jí le**

    'The characters he recognizes are ?extremely more than I do.'

    ✔ 他认识的字比我<u>多</u>。

    tā rènshi de zì bǐ wǒ **duō**

    'He recognizes more characters than I do.'

    ✔ 他认识的字比我<u>多得多</u>。

    tā rènshi de zì bǐ wǒ **duō-de duō**

    'He recognizes many more characters than I do.'

Another error often occurs with the negation of the *bǐ* pattern. Note that the negation 不 *bù* should precede the comparison word *bǐ*. The negation never occurs before the descriptive adjective. The correct way to express 6l is given at 6d.

6l ✖ *说中文比写汉字<u>不</u>容易。

    shuō-zhōngwén bǐ xiě-hànzì **bù** róngyi

    ?'Speaking Chinese, in comparison to writing Chinese characters, is not easy.'

Finally, the adverb of degree (cf. 6h–i) must appear **before** the verb, whereas the specific measurement is **after** the verb. 6m is unacceptable since the adverb *zǎo* 'early' is put after the verb *lái* 'come.'

6m ✖ 老师比学生*<u>来早</u>十分钟。

    lǎoshī bǐ xuésheng lái **zǎo** shí-fēnzhōng

    'The teacher came ten minutes earlier than the students did.'

    ✔ 老师比学生<u>早来</u>(了)十分钟。

    lǎoshī bǐ xuésheng **zǎo lái** (le) shí-fēnzhōng

The basic pattern is: X + 比 *bǐ* + Y + DA. Adverbs such as 很 *hěn* 'very' never appear in this structure. Degrees of comparison, such as 一点儿 *yìdiǎnr* 'a little' or -得多 *-de duō* 'much more' follow the descriptive adjective.

For related topics, see §§7 and 8.

Exercises

EXERCISE 7. Use the words given to form comparative sentences.

> e.g. 羊肉，鸡肉，一点儿，贵，比 ⇨ 羊肉比鸡肉贵一点儿。

1 日文语法，中文语法，复杂，比
2 箱子，书包，重，比
3 走路，开车，方便，比
4 哥哥，弟弟，一点儿，高，比
5 北京，承德，得多，大，比
6 桔子，苹果，一块钱，贵，比
7 我的室友，我，一个钟头，早起，比
8 他，我，三本书，多看，比

§7. Structures of comparison (ii): similarity

There are three structures that describe similarity/equivalence in Mandarin.

First, to express general similarity between two elements, X and Y, Mandarin uses pattern 7a. The two components are linked by 跟 *gēn* or 和 *hé* 'and' and followed by the adjective 一样 *yíyàng* 'identical, the same.' See examples 7b–c.

7a X + 跟 *gēn*/和 *hé* + Y + 一样 *yíyàng*

7b 这个房间跟那个房间一样。
zhèi-ge fángjiān **gēn** nèi-ge fángjiān **yíyàng**
'This room and that room are alike.'

7c 苹果跟桔子一样吗？
píngguǒ **gēn** júzi **yíyàng** ma
'Are apples the same as oranges?'

Second, to express similarity in specific respects, such as size, length, distance, or other qualities, a descriptive adjective goes after *yíyàng*, as in pattern 7d. In this case, *yíyàng* functions as an adverb meaning 'equally.' See example 7e.

7d   X + 跟 *gēn*/和 *hé* + Y + 一样 *yíyàng* + DA

7e   我妹妹跟我一样<u>高</u>。
wǒ mèimei gēn wǒ yíyàng **gāo**
'My sister and I are the same height.'

Third, to express equivalence between X and Y, Mandarin uses the pattern 7f. Here the word *yǒu* indicates X's comparison to Y regarding the quality expressed by the descriptive adjective, such as *guì* 'expensive' in 7g. An adverb 这么 *zhème* or 那么 *nème* often precedes the DA. These adverbs are generally translated as 'so' or 'as.' *Zhème* 'like this' refers to something close by and *nème* 'like that' to something farther away. See example 7g.

7f   X + 有 *yǒu* + Y (+ 这么 *zhème*/那么 *nème*) + DA

7g   课本<u>有</u>字典那么<u>贵</u>。
kèběn **yǒu** zìdiǎn nème **guì**
'The textbook is as expensive as the dictionary.'

Negation

Negations for the above patterns of similarity/equivalence need clarification.

First, for patterns 7a and 7d, the negation 不 *bù* may precede either *gēn* or *yíyàng* with no difference in meaning, as shown in examples 7h–i below.

7h   我妹妹<u>不</u>跟我一样高。
wǒ mèimei **bù** gēn wǒ yíyàng gāo
'My sister and I are not the same height.'

7i   我妹妹跟我<u>不</u>一样高。
wǒ mèimei gēn wǒ **bù** yíyàng gāo
'My sister and I are not the same height.'

Second, pattern 7f is generally preferred in negating equivalence or similarity. In this pattern the negation 没 *méi* always stands before *yǒu*, indicating that X falls short of Y regarding the quality expressed by the descriptive adjective. See examples 7j–k.

7j   儿子有父亲那么高，可是<u>没</u>有父亲（那么）胖。
érzi yǒu fùqin nème gāo, kěshi **méi**yǒu fùqin (nème) pàng
'The son is as tall as the father, but not as chubby as the father.'

7k　说中文没有写汉字（这么）难。

shuō-zhōngwén **méiyǒu** xiě-hànzì (zhème) nán

'Speaking Chinese is not as difficult as writing Chinese characters.'

Students often mistakenly put the negation 不 *bù* before the descriptive adjective when they mean to express the idea "X is not as . . . as Y.' A sentence such as 7l sounds rather awkward. As the translation shows, it does not express the intended idea but rather its opposite. As explained above, *bù* may either precede 跟 *gēn* or 一样 *yíyàng*, but does not appear before the DA. Or in this case, one may use the negative version of pattern 7f which is preferred in negating similarity.

7l　⊗　?你的电脑跟我的电脑一样不快。

nǐde diànnǎo gēn wǒde diànnǎo yíyàng **bú** kuài

?'Your computer and my computer are the same: neither is fast.'

(Intending to say: 'Your computer and my computer are not equally fast.')

✅ 你的电脑跟我的电脑不一样快。

nǐde diànnǎo gēn wǒde diànnǎo **bù yíyàng kuài**

✅ 你的电脑没有我的电脑快。

nǐde diànnǎo **méiyǒu** wǒde diànnǎo **kuài**

'Your computer is not as fast as mine.'

Another common error is 7m, where the basic pattern, X + 比 *bǐ* + Y + DA, discussed in §6, is mixed with the negation of pattern 7f. As a result 7m does not convey any sensible meaning.

7m　⊗　*南方的冬天比北方的冬天没有那么冷。

nánfāng de dōngtiān **bǐ** běifāng de dōngtiān **méiyǒu** nème lěng

✅ 南方的冬天没有北方的冬天那么冷。

nánfāng de dōngtiān **méiyǒu** běifāng de dōngtiān **nème lěng**

'Winter in the south is not as cold as in the north.'

> The three patterns of similarity/equivalence are 7a, 7d, and 7f. As explained in the text, follow the rules governing their negations.

For related topics, see §§6 and 8.

Exercises

EXERCISE 8. Use the words given to make sentences describing similarity/ equivalence.

e.g. 中文，英文，难，一样　⇨　中文和英文一样难。
姐姐，妹妹，高，没有　⇨　姐姐没有妹妹（那么）高。

1　茶杯，酒杯，大，一样
2　地铁站，汽车站，近，一样
3　蓝色的，绿色的，好看，一样
4　那本书，这本书，有意思，没有
5　中学生，大学生，忙，没有
6　今天，昨天，冷，没有

EXERCISE 9 (§§6–7). Change the sentences to the 比 *bǐ* structure.

e.g. 说中文没有写汉字那么难。　⇨　写汉字比说中文难。

1　钟没有手表贵。
2　旧电脑没有新电脑这么快。
3　桃子没有西瓜好吃。
4　上个星期的功课没有这个星期的这么多。
5　看电视没有看书有意思。
6　滑雪没有滑冰容易学。

§8.　Structures of comparison (iii): behavior

When two parties, X and Y, are compared in their performance of a certain action, as in the sentence 'X swims faster than Y does' or 'X and Y are equally well-read,' an action verb phrase needs to be added to any one of the three comparative patterns discussed in §6 and §7, repeated here as 8a–c.

8a　X + 比 *bǐ* + Y + DA
8b　X + 跟 *gēn* + Y + 一样 *yíyàng* + DA
8c　X + （没）有 *(méi)yǒu* + Y (+ 这么 *zhème*/那么 *nème*) + DA

Generally the action verb phrase is a verb-object compound. In a comparative structure, this verb-object compound must be followed by a repeating verb plus an added -得 *de* in the repetition. The added verb phrase in a comparison then is: V-Obj. + V-得 *de*. For instance, example 8d contains the action *shuō zhōngwén* 'speak Chinese.' In order to compare the abilities of party X and party Y to speak Chinese, one needs to use the phrase [V-Obj. + V-得 *de*]. In this case it is *shuō zhōngwén shuō-de*.

Let us first consider pattern 8a. There are a few variations in this structure, as examples 8d–f illustrate. The duplicated form of [V-Obj. + V 得 *de*] may be before (as in 8d), after (8e), or split by [比 *bǐ* + Y] (8f). Note the descriptive adjective, *hǎo* 'good/well' in this case, functioning as an adverb when the action verb phrase is added, always stands at the end of the comparison.

8d 她说中文说得<u>比</u>我好。

  tā **shuō zhōngwén shuō-de** bǐ wǒ hǎo

  'She speaks Chinese better than I do.'

8e 她比我说中文说得好。

  tā bǐ wǒ **shuō zhōngwén shuō-de** hǎo

8f 她说中文比我说得好。

  tā **shuō zhōngwén** bǐ wǒ **shuō-de** hǎo

The modifications showing degrees of comparison used in the basic *bǐ* pattern also apply to the compared behaviors. They may be an expression of measure such as 一点儿 *yìdiǎnr* 'a little' to show a small difference; or -得多 *-de duō* 'much more' to show a large difference. See example 8g. Again, the measurement phrase always follows the descriptive adjective at the end of the comparison.

8g 她说中文说得比我好<u>一点儿 / 得多</u>。

  tā shuō zhōngwén shuō-de bǐ wǒ hǎo **yìdiǎnr/-de duō**

  'She speaks Chinese a little/much better than I do.'

The various locations for the duplicated form [V-Obj. + V-得 *de*] apply similarly to patterns 8b and 8c. Both are discussed in §7. In structure 8b, the duplicated form [V-Obj. + V-得 *de*] may appear before (as in 8h), after (8i), or split by [跟 *gēn* + Y] (8j). In structure 8c, the duplicated form [V-Obj. + V-得 *de*] may appear before (8k), after (8l), or split by [（没）有 *(méi)yǒu* + Y] (8m). Note that the modifications showing different degrees of measurement in the 比 *bǐ* pattern do not apply in these two patterns.

8h 学生<u>写字写得</u>跟老师一样快。

  xuésheng **xiě-zì xiě-de** gēn lǎoshī yíyàng kuài

  'The student writes Chinese characters as fast as the teacher does.'

8i 学生跟老师<u>写字写得</u>一样快。

  xuésheng gēn lǎoshī **xiě-zì xiě-de** yíyàng kuài

8j 学生<u>写字</u>跟老师<u>写得</u>一样快。

  xuésheng **xiě-zì** gēn lǎoshī **xiě-de** yíyàng kuài

8k 我们<u>看书看得</u>没有他多。

  wǒmen **kàn-shū kàn-de** méiyǒu tā duō

  'We do not read as much as he does.'

8l 我们没有他<u>看书看得</u>多。

  wǒmen méiyǒu tā **kàn-shū kàn-de** duō

8m 我们<u>看书</u>没有他<u>看得</u>多。

  wǒmen **kàn-shū** méiyǒu tā **kàn-de** duō

Students sometimes skip the V-得 *de* part in these comparative patterns. Remember: the V-得 *de* must be used in compared behaviors. While the V-Obj. phrase may be omitted if it is clear from the context, the V-得 *de* part cannot. 8n is unacceptable in Mandarin.

8n　 *我爸爸跟我妈妈<u>做菜</u>一样好。

wǒ bàba gēn wǒ māma **zuò-cài** yíyàng hǎo

'My dad cooks as well as my mom.'

我爸爸跟我妈妈<u>做菜做得</u>一样好。

wǒ bàba gēn wǒ māma **zuò-cài zuò-de** yíyàng hǎo

Another common error is to use an adverbial word or phrase such as *hěn* 'very' (as in 8o) or *fēicháng* 'unusually' (8p) to modify the descriptive adjective in a comparison. Again, only unmodified descriptive adjectives can be used in a comparative structure. Modified descriptive adjectives, such as those in 8o–p, are incompatible with any comparative structure. To correct these mistakes, one needs to remove the adverbs.

8o　老师说中文比学生说得*<u>很</u>快。

lǎoshī shuō-zhōngwén bǐ xuésheng shuō-de **hěn** kuài

'The teacher speaks Chinese ?very faster than the students do.'

老师说中文比学生说得<u>快</u>。

lǎoshī shuō-zhōngwén bǐ xuésheng shuō-de **kuài**

8p　我的同学跟我考试考得*<u>一样非常</u>好。

wǒ de tóngxué gēn wǒ kǎo-shì kǎo-de yíyàng **fēicháng** hǎo

?'My classmate and I tested the same unusually well.'

我的同学跟我考试考得<u>一样好</u>。

wǒ de tóngxué gēn wǒ kǎo-shì kǎo-de **yíyàng hǎo**

> When comparing two parties in their conduct of an action, use the structure: V-Obj. + V-得 *de*. You may add three variations on this structure to each of the comparative patterns 8a–c.

For related topics, see §§6, 7, and 45.

Exercises

EXERCISE 10. The duplicated form of the verb phrase has three patterns. Translate each sentence into Chinese, using all three patterns.

1　My mom sings much better than I do.
2　The younger brother runs as fast as the older brother does.
3　Adults do not sleep as much as children do.

EXERCISE 11 (§§6–8). Translate into Chinese.

1   He is three inches taller than his younger sister.
2   April is a little warmer than March.
3   His cell phone is as new as mine.
4   Shandong cuisine is not as spicy as Sichuan cuisine.
5   The daughter plays chess better than her father.
6   He eats as much as I do. But he is not as chubby as I am.

§9.   The 把 *bǎ* construction (i): its usage

The 把 *bǎ* construction has no direct equivalent in English. To illustrate its function, let us first compare the two ways, shown by 9a–b, of expressing 'he has broken his tea cup' in Mandarin.

9a   The normal word order: Subj. + V + Obj.

他[Subj.]打破了[V]他的茶杯[Obj.]。

tā dǎ-pò-le tāde chábēi

9b   The 把 *bǎ* construction: Subj. + 把-Obj. + V, where 把 *bǎ* transposes
    the object to a position between the subject and the verb.

他[Subj.]把他的茶杯[Obj.]打破了[V]。

tā **bǎ** tāde chábēi dǎ-pò-le

While these two sentences, 9a–b, can be translated identically into English, their different emphases become apparent when one looks at the questions that 9a and 9b answer:

9a answers the question 'What <u>happened</u>?'   ⇨   He <u>broke his tea cup</u>.
9b answers the question 'What did he do to <u>his tea cup</u>?'   ⇨   He <u>broke</u> it.

The Chinese character 把 *bǎ* as a verb means 'grasp; hold.' The *bǎ* construction may be read literally as 'Subj. grasps Obj. and does V (to/with it).' The function of the *bǎ* structure 9b hence emphasizes the result: how the action affects the transposed object.

Based on this function, this construction has two constraints: i) The *bǎ*-Obj., which is also the object of the verb, must be a specific, i.e. definite, noun phrase, such as 他的茶杯 *tāde chábēi* 'his tea cup,' or 那本书 *nèi-běn-shū* 'that book,' etc. Quantified noun phrases, such as 一个茶杯 *yī-ge-chábēi* 'one tea cup' or 五本书 *wǔ-běn-shū* 'five books,' cannot be used as the *bǎ*-Obj. since quantified noun phrases are indefinite in Mandarin (see §37); ii) The verb of the *bǎ* construction must be a transitive action verb. Certain verbs that express motion, emotion, cognition, or existence, such as those in 9c, are therefore incompatible with the *bǎ* construction.

9c   Verbs that cannot be used in the *bǎ* construction
来 *lái* 'come'; 去 *qù* 'go'; 离开 *líkāi* 'depart'; 喜欢 *xǐhuan* 'like'; 怕 *pà* 'fear'; 觉得 *juéde* 'feel'; 像 *xiàng* 'resemble'; 知道 *zhīdào* 'know'; 认识 *rènshi* 'recognize'; 记得 *jìde* 'remember'; 是 *shì* 'be'; 在 *zài* 'be at'; 有 *yǒu* 'there is/are'

The *bǎ* construction is commonplace when:

9d   the sentence contains a directional complement:
他们把书桌搬<u>出去</u>了。
tāmen *bǎ* shūzhuō bān-**chūqu** le
'They moved the desk out.'

9e   the verb takes both direct and indirect objects:
请你把<u>信</u>交给<u>李先生</u>。
qǐng nǐ *bǎ* **xìn** jiāo-gěi **Lǐ xiānsheng**
'Please hand the letter to Mr. Li.'

9f   both an object and a place word are used:
乘客把<u>箱子</u>放在<u>行李架上</u>。
chéngkè *bǎ* **xiāngzi** fàng-zài **xínglijià shang**
'Passengers put their suitcases on the luggage rack.'

9g–j are errors that misuse the 把 *bǎ* construction. Their English translations note what the writers wanted to say. None of these ideas needs to use the *bǎ* construction.

9g   ✗ 他把她的名字 * 知道了。
tā *bǎ* tāde míngzi zhīdào le
   ▶ **Problem**: *zhīdào* 'know' is a verb of cognition rather than action, which does not act upon the *bǎ*-Obj. *tāde míngzi* 'her name.'
   ✓ 他知道了她的名字。
tā zhīdào le tāde míngzi
'He has learned her name.'

9h   ✗ 我 * 把看书觉得很有意思。
wǒ *bǎ* kàn-shū juéde hěn yǒuyìsi
   ▶ **Problems**: i) *kàn-shū* 'read (books)' is a verb phrase which cannot be used as the *bǎ*-Obj.; ii) *juéde* 'feel' is a verb that shows emotions and here it indicates a predicate, *juéde hěn yǒuyìsi* 'feel interesting,' which is a comment and does not directly act upon the *bǎ*-Obj.
   ✓ 我觉得看书很有意思。
wǒ juéde kàn-shū hěn yǒuyìsi
'I think reading is (very) interesting.'

9i ✗ 我很累，想*把今天下午休息休息。

wǒ hěn lèi, xiǎng *bǎ* jīntiān xiàwǔ xiūxi xiūxi

▶ **Problem**: *xiūxi xiūxi* 'rest a bit' is an intransitive verb phrase that certainly does not act upon the time word *jīntiān xiàwǔ* 'this afternoon.'

✓ 我很累，今天下午想休息休息。

wǒ hěn lèi, jīntiān xiàwǔ xiǎng xiūxi xiūxi

'I am tired. I want to rest a bit this afternoon.'

The problem in 9j is the indefinite *bǎ*-Obj. *yí-ge píngguǒ* 'an/one apple.' As mentioned above, the *bǎ*-Obj. must have a definite/specific reference; and in Mandarin quantified noun phrases are indefinite (see §37). A sentence of the normal [Subj. + V + Obj.] word order is a more natural way.

9j ✗ 昨天我*把一个苹果吃了。

zuótiān wǒ *bǎ* yí-ge píngguǒ chī-le

✓ 昨天我吃了一个苹果。

zuótiān wǒ chī-le yí-ge píngguǒ

'Yesterday I ate an apple.'

> The verb of the 把 *bǎ* construction must be a transitive action verb. Verbs that express motion, emotion, cognition, or existence are incompatible with this structure. The *bǎ*-Obj. cannot be a quantified noun phrase.

For related topics, see §§10, 11, and 37.

§10. The 把 *bǎ* construction (ii): other elements and the verb phrase

While the basic form of the 把 *bǎ* construction is [Subj. + 把 *bǎ*-Obj. + V], 10a elaborates the structure and shows that other possible elements, such as a negation, auxiliary verb, adverb, or time phrase, should appear before the *bǎ*-Obj. and that the verb in the *bǎ* construction ought to be a verb phrase.

10a Subj. + (Neg./Aux./Adv./time-when) + 把 *bǎ*-Obj. + VP

In this section, we analyze two structural details: i) the other elements that appear immediately before the *bǎ*-Obj.; and ii) variations in the verb phrase.

First, these are the elements that, if necessary, appear immediately before the *bǎ*-Obj.: negations 不 *bù* or 没 *méi*; auxiliary verbs such as 会 *huì* 'will,' 能 *néng* 'can,' 应该 *yīnggāi* 'should,' or 想 *xiǎng* 'think of'; adverbs such as 立刻 *lìkè* 'immediately,' 也 *yě* 'also,' 先 *xiān* 'first,' or 已经 *yǐjīng* 'already'; and chronological time words such as 下午两点 *xiàwǔ liǎngdiǎn* '2 p.m.,' 星期天 *xīngqītiān* 'Sunday,' etc. See examples 10b–e.

10b　我<u>不</u>把事情办完，不能回家。
　　　wǒ **bù** *bǎ shìqing bàn-wán, bù néng huí-jiā*
　　　'If I don't finish the work, I can't go home.'

10c　你<u>应该</u>把他们送到机场。
　　　nǐ **yīnggāi** *bǎ tāmen sòng-dào jīchǎng*
　　　'You should escort them to the airport.'

10d　我<u>先</u>把事情办完，再回家。
　　　wǒ **xiān** *bǎ shìqing bàn-wán, zài huí-jiā*
　　　'I first finish the work; then I go home.'

10e　她<u>今天上午</u>把数据整理好了。
　　　tā **jīntiān shàngwǔ** *bǎ shùjù zhěnglǐ-hǎo le*
　　　'She sorted out the data this morning.'

Next, let us consider the verb phrase variations. In the *bǎ* construction the main verb cannot stand alone. It must include other elements to form a VP. There are numerous VP variations. 10f–k are common examples of various elements that follow the main verb.

10f　VP = V-RVC compound
　　　老师没把这一章<u>解释清楚</u>。
　　　lǎoshī méi bǎ zhèi-yì-zhāng **jiěshì-qīngchu**
　　　'The teacher didn't explain this chapter clearly.'

10g　VP = V-DVC compound
　　　你可以把东西<u>搬进来</u>。
　　　nǐ kěyǐ bǎ dōngxi **bān-jìnlai**
　　　'You may move your stuff in.'

10h　VP = V + 在 *zài*-location
　　　客人想把他们的车<u>停在路边儿</u>。
　　　kèren xiǎng bǎ tāmen-de chē **tíng zài lùbiānr**
　　　'The guests want to park their cars on the side of the road.'

10i　VP = V + 到 *dào*-location + 去 *qù*/来 *lái*
　　　小王把朋友的自行车<u>骑到学校去</u>了。
　　　Xiǎo Wáng bǎ péngyou-de zìxíngchē **qí dào xuéxiào qù** *le*
　　　'Little Wang rode his friend's bicycle to school.'

10j　VP = V + 给 *gěi*-indirect Obj.
　　　我把功课<u>交给老师</u>了。
　　　wǒ bǎ gōngkè **jiāo gěi lǎoshī** *le*
　　　'I handed my homework to the teacher.'

10k VP = V + verb suffix 了 *le*
我把他的名字忘了。
wǒ bǎ tāde míngzi **wàng le**
'I forgot his name.'

10l–n are common errors. In each case, the asterisk marks the specific problem. The idea that each of these sentences means to express is in parentheses.

10l ✗ 请你填一张表，把你的地址和姓名*清楚。
qǐng nǐ tián yì-zhāng-biǎo, bǎ nǐde dìzhǐ hé xìngmíng **qīngchu**
('Please fill out the form and write your name and address clearly.')
▶ **Problem**: The main verb is missing. *qīngchu* 'clear(ly)' here is the RVC but not the main verb. The verb phrase needs to be a V-RVC: ***xiě**-qīngchu* 'write-clearly.'
✓ 请你填一张表，把你的地址和姓名写清楚。
qǐng nǐ tián yì-zhāng-biǎo, bǎ nǐde dìzhǐ hé xìngmíng **xiě**-qīngchu

10m ✗ 她把她的车*不想借给同学。
tā bǎ tāde chē **bù xiǎng jiè-gěi** tóngxué
('She doesn't want to lend her car to her schoolmate.')
▶ **Problem**: The negative auxiliary phrase *bù xiǎng* 'not want' is misplaced. It should appear before the *bǎ*-Obj., not before the main verb phrase *jiè-gěi* 'lend to.'
✓ 她不想把她的车借给同学。
tā **bù xiǎng** bǎ tāde chē jiè-gěi tóngxué

10n ✗ 我把这个很难的问题*回答不出来。
wǒ bǎ zhèi-ge hěn-nán-de wèntí **huídá-bù-chūlái**
('I can't answer this very difficult question.')
▶ **Problem**: The *bǎ* construction does not take the potential form (see §44) as the verb phrase. In this case the negative potential form *huídá-**bù**-chūlái* 'unable to answer' stresses the impossibility of the action itself and does not affect the *bǎ*-Obj. To express the idea in parentheses, one needs to avoid the *bǎ* construction.
✓ 我回答不出来这个很难的问题。
wǒ **huídá-bù-chūlái** zhèi-ge hěn-nán-de wèntí

A negation, auxiliary verb, adverb, or time phrase appears immediately before the 把 *bǎ*-Obj. The main verb cannot stand alone; it must appear in a verb phrase, as in 10f–k.

For related topics, see §§9, 11, 38, 41, 42, 43, and 44.

Exercises

EXERCISE 12 (§§9–10). If possible, rewrite the sentences using the 把 *bǎ* construction. (Note that some of them cannot be changed to the *bǎ* construction.)

1 我卖了我的旧车。
2 这个练习，你今天一定得做完。
3 这件事，你告诉谁了？
4 我觉得那个故事有趣极了。
5 请你打开电视，好不好？
6 我们今天玩儿得真高兴。
7 如果有问题，请你举起手来。
8 你的功课，你明天交给老师吧。
9 他去年大学毕业了。
10 上课的笔记，我喜欢记在书上。
11 所有的新影碟，他们都借走了。
12 商店送来了老人买的东西。

EXERCISE 13. Translate into Chinese, using the 把 *bǎ* construction.

1 They don't want to open the window.
2 Please move the chairs out.
3 She has already forgotten my phone number.
4 You can't park (your car) here.
5 I saw the problem much too simply.
6 I didn't bring the computer back home.

§11. The passive construction

11a illustrates the structure of a passive sentence in Mandarin. In this structure, one of three prepositions, 被 *bèi*, 让 *ràng*, or 叫 *jiào*, indicates the passive voice. The subject of the sentence is the recipient of the action, or the thing acted upon, whereas the object of the preposition, which is optional for *bèi* but obligatory for both *ràng* and *jiào*, is the agent of the action. 11b–d are examples of the passive construction.

11a Subj.[recipient] + 被/让/叫-Obj.[agent] + VP

11b 衣服被（雨）淋湿了。
yīfu **bèi** (yǔ) lín-shī le
'The clothes are soaked (by the rain).'

11c 钱让贼偷走了。

qián **ràng** zéi tōu-zǒu le

'The money is stolen by the thief.'

11d 老蔡叫老婆骂了一顿。

Lǎo Cài **jiào** lǎopo mà-le yí-dùn

'Old Cài was scolded by his wife.'

The preposition *bèi*, regarded in most grammar books as the main passive marker, usually appears in more formal speech, whereas both *ràng* and *jiào* more frequently occur in colloquial speech. Another difference between *bèi* and *ràng/jiào*, as briefly mentioned earlier, is that when *bèi* is used, the agent of the action does not necessarily need to be clarified, while both *ràng* and *jiào* must take an object as the agent of the action. As shown in examples 11b–d, the agent *yǔ* 'rain' is optional in 11b, whereas both *zéi* 'thief' in 11c and *lǎopo* 'wife' in 11d are obligatory.

The passive construction has three features in common with the 把 *bǎ* construction. First, the verbs used in the passive construction are those that act upon the recipient. Verbs that do not act upon the recipient of the action, such as those that express motion, emotion, or existence, are incompatible with the passive construction (see examples in 9c). Second, the verb in the passive construction cannot stand alone; it must take other elements or complements to form a verb phrase. The passive construction employs the same set of verb phrase variations as the *bǎ* construction (see examples 10f–k). These verb phrases indicate the result of the action upon the recipient. Third, as in the *bǎ* construction, modifying words such as negations, auxiliary verbs, adverbs, and time phrases, as well as the adverb 都 *dōu* 'all,' (see §51) appear before the prepositions *bèi*, *ràng*, or *jiào*. See examples 11e–g.

11e 位子没被占去，我真高兴。

wèizi **méi** bèi zhàn-qù, wǒ zhēn gāoxìng

'The seat was <u>not</u> occupied. I was really happy.'

11f 衣服马上让雨淋湿了。

yīfu **mǎshàng** ràng yǔ lín-shī le

'The clothes were <u>immediately</u> soaked by the rain.'

11g 冰箱里的食物都叫他吃光了。

bīngxiāng-lǐ de shíwù **dōu** jiào tā chī-guāng le

'<u>All</u> the food in the refrigerator was consumed by him.'

Grammarians often contend that the Mandarin passive construction typically refers to an unfortunate hardship suffered by the recipient of the action. In reality, while the passive voice is much less common than the active voice, it is not limited to describing unfavorable events. One may apply the passive construction to a variety of situations. For instance, neither 11h nor 11i refers to an unfortunate event. However, since both contain an agent, the ideas of 11h and 11i can be easily expressed in the *bǎ* construction.

11h 车子叫他洗得干干净净。

chēzi jiào tā xǐ de gāngānjìngjìng

'The car was washed really clean by him.'

11i 走丢了的孩子让警察找回来了。

zǒu-diū-le de háizi ràng jǐngchá zhǎo-huílai le

'The lost child was brought back by the police.'

As a final note, one should bear in mind that in Mandarin the passive construction is much less common than in English. In other words, many English passive sentences, especially those where the agent of the action is not expressed, do not translate into the Mandarin passive construction marked by the preposition *bèi*. The active voice simplifies the sentence and the identification of agency.

 The problem in 11j is that the agent of the action is missing after the preposition 让 *ràng*. Remember, if one chooses to use the preposition 让 *ràng* or 叫 *jiào* in a passive sentence, it must take an object as the agent of the action.

11j ✗ 这些字*让写得很好看。

zhèi-xiē-zì **ràng** xiě-de hěn hǎokàn

'These characters were written very prettily.'

✓ 这些字被写得很好看。

zhèi-xiē-zì **bèi** xiě-de hěn hǎokàn

In 11k, the adverb 都 *dōu* 'all' should appear before the preposition 被 *bèi*, not after it.

11k ✗ 这儿所有的书被*都分了类。

zhèr suǒyǒude shū **bèi dōu** fēn-le-lèi

'All the books here were classified.'

✓ 这儿所有的书都被分了类。

zhèr suǒyǒude shū **dōu** bèi fēn-le-lèi

This construction shares three features with the 把 *bǎ* construction: i) the verb must be transitive; ii) the verb cannot stand alone; iii) modifying words appear before the prepositions 被 *bèi*, 让 *ràng*, or 叫 *jiào*. The object of the preposition is optional for *bèi*, but obligatory for both *ràng* and *jiào*.

For related topics, see §§9, 10, 38, and 51.

Exercises

EXERCISE 14. Rewrite the sentences in the passive construction.

1　小偷偷了他的钱。
2　孩子常常弄坏玩具。
3　他把蛋糕吃了。
4　我没有伞，雨把衣服都淋湿了。
5　他已经把书还给图书馆了。
6　小毛把房间打扫得很干净。

Check your grammar

Translate these sentences into Chinese, and then check to see that you have implemented the relevant grammar points. The parenthetical numbers and letters identify the pertinent subsections and examples.

1　Mr. Zhang is very busy. (§1h)
2　This question is extremely difficult. (§1i)
3　There are five items (of news) in today's paper. (§2i)
4　I work at a burger joint. (§3h)
5　This afternoon we will go to the Big Lake to swim. (§4g)
6　This afternoon we will be swimming at the Big Lake. (§4h)
7　She works at the school cafeteria every Friday afternoon for four hours. (§5k)
8　I study at the library every evening. (§5l)
9　Many people believe that eating vegetables is better than eating meat. (§6j)
10　He recognizes many more characters than I do. (§6k)
11　Speaking Chinese is not easier than writing Chinese characters. (§6l)
12　The teacher came ten minutes earlier than the students did. (§6m)
13　Your computer and mine are not equally fast./Your computer is not as fast as mine. (§7l)
14　Winter in the south is not as cold as in the north. (§7m)
15　My dad cooks as well as my mom. (§8n)
16　The teacher speaks Chinese faster than the students do. (§8o)
17　My classmate and I tested equally well. (§8p)
18　He has learned her name. (§9g)
19　I think reading is (very) interesting. (§9h)
20　I am tired. I want to rest a bit this afternoon. (§9i)
21　Yesterday I ate an apple. (§9j)

22   Please fill out the form and write your name and address clearly. (§10l)
23   She doesn't want to lend her car to her schoolmate. (§10m)
24   I can't answer this very difficult question. (§10n)
25   These characters were written very prettily. (§11j)
26   All the books here were classified. (§11k)

 Notes

2 Complex/compound sentences and questions

§12. Conjunctions linking compound clauses (i): If . . . , then . . .

In the pattern 如果 *rúguǒ*/要是 *yàoshì* . . . 就 *jiù* . . . 'if . . . , then . . .' the pair of complementary words correlate two clauses in a compound sentence. *Yàoshì* is a more colloquial version of *rúguǒ*. The first clause led by *rúguǒ* or *yàoshì* usually expresses a condition, and the second clause containing *jiù* expresses a consequence, as in example 12a. If the entire sentence is a question, as in example 12b, *jiù* is omitted.

12a   如果／要是他有问题，就来问我。
   rúguǒ/yàoshì tā yǒu wèntí, jiù lái wèn wǒ
   'If he has any questions, he will come to ask me.'

12b   如果／要是他不去，谁去？
   rúguǒ/yàoshì tā bú qù, shéi qù
   'If he doesn't go, then who will?'

Rúguǒ or *yàoshì* may be omitted, since in context *jiù* alone implies the first clause expressing a condition. For instance, 12a can be expressed as 12c, where *rúguǒ* or *yàoshì* is omitted. On the other hand, when *rúguǒ* or *yàoshì* is used, *jiù* may be omitted if there is an adverbial modifier for the second clause, e.g. *yídìng* 'certainly' or *yě* 'also,' replaces *jiù* in the second clause in 12d–e.

12c   他有问题，就来问我。
   tā yǒu wèntí, jiù lái wèn wǒ
   'If/when he has any questions, he will come to ask me.'

12d   如果／要是你有问题，一定来问我。
   rúguǒ/yàoshì nǐ yǒu wèntí, **yídìng** lái wèn wǒ
   'If you have any questions, be sure to come ask me.'

12e   如果／要是你有问题，<u>也</u>来问我。
  rúguǒ/yàoshì nǐ yǒu wèntí, **yě** lái wèn wǒ
  'If you have any questions, also come to ask me.'

Note that this structure can be translated into English using either the indicative or the subjunctive mood. See the translations for example 12f.

12f   如果／要是我有钱，就买那条船。
  rúguǒ/yàoshì wǒ yǒu qián, jiù mǎi nèi-tiáo-chuán
  'If I have money, I will buy that boat.'
  'If I had money, I would buy that boat.'

Students need to address two details.

First, in Mandarin 如果 *rúguǒ*/要是 *yàoshì* is a complementary part of this pattern and must appear at the beginning of the compound structure. In other words, Mandarin *rúguǒ/yàoshì* cannot be taken as an isolated equivalent to 'if' or 'whether' in English. Thus examples 12g–h are erroneous. While the English translations of both sentences are fine, the Mandarin sentences are unacceptable because *yàoshì* is misused in both—it is put in the middle of the sentence and treated as if it were simply equivalent to the English word 'whether.'

12g   ✖ *我们都不知道<u>要是</u>这个考试很难。
  wǒmen dōu bù zhīdào **yàoshi** zhèi-ge-kǎoshì hěn nán
  'None of us knows whether this exam is difficult.'
  ✔ 我们都不知道<u>这个考试难不难</u>。(cf. §20 for this grammar point.)
  wǒmen dōu bù zhīdào **zhèi-ge-kǎoshì nán-bù-nán**

12h   ✖ *他问我<u>要是</u>我明年毕业。
  tā wèn wǒ **yàoshi** wǒ míngnián bìyè
  'He asks me whether I will graduate next year.'
  ✔ 他问我明年<u>会不会</u>毕业。
  tā wèn wǒ míngnián **huì-bú-huì bìyè**

Second, *jiù* 'then' in the second clause must follow the subject if there is one in the second clause. See the following examples. 12i is erroneous because *jiù* is put before the subject *wǒmen* 'we' in the second clause.

12i   ✖ 如果没有热水，*<u>就</u>我们不泡茶。
  rúguǒ méiyǒu rèshuǐ, **jiù** wǒmen bú pàochá
  ✔ 如果没有热水，我们<u>就</u>不泡茶。
  rúguǒ méiyǒu rèshuǐ, wǒmen **jiù** bú pàochá
  'If there is no hot water, we will not brew tea.'

如果 *rúguǒ* or 要是 *yàoshì* 'if' must appear **at the beginning** of the compound sentence, whereas 就 *jiù* 'then' should **follow** the subject, if there is one in the second clause.

For related topics, see §§17, 20, 53, and 54.

Exercises

EXERCISE 1. Translate into Chinese.

1   If you have time tonight, we will go to a movie.
2   If I knew, I would tell you.
3   If you forget her name, you will definitely feel embarrassed.

§13.   Conjunctions linking compound clauses (ii): Both . . . and . . .

The pattern 不但 *búdàn* . . . 而且 *érqiě*/并且 *bìngqiě* . . . is equivalent to the English expression 'both . . . and . . .'; or 'not only . . . but also. . . .' Here the complementary words *búdàn* and *érqiě*/*bìngqiě* correlate two clauses in a compound sentence, usually stressing the greater importance of the second clause which follows *érqiě*/*bìngqiě*. *Érqiě* and *bìngqiě* are interchangeable. See examples 13a–b.

13a   我们的功课不但多，而且难。
wǒmen-de gōngkè búdàn duō, érqiě nán
'Our homework is both heavy and difficult.'

13b   张老师不但看书看得多，并且看得很快。
Zhāng lǎoshī búdàn kàn-shū kàn-de duō, bìngqiě kàn-de hěn kuài
'Teacher Zhang not only reads a lot, but also reads quickly.'

The subject of this compound structure usually precedes the conjunction *búdàn*, as *wǒmen-de gōngkè* 'our homework' in 13a and *Zhāng lǎoshī* 'Teacher Zhang' in 13b illustrate. *Búdàn* comes at the beginning of the first clause only when the clauses have different subjects, as in both 13c and 13d. There are two subjects in these sentences: *wǒ* 'I' and *wǒmen quán jiārén* 'the whole family' in 13c; and *gōngyuán-lǐ* 'in parks' and *jiēdào liǎngpáng* 'on curbs' in 13d.

13c 不但<u>我去</u>，而且<u>我们全家人</u>都去。

búdàn **wǒ** qù, érqiě **wǒmen quán jiārén** dōu qù

'Not only will I go, but the whole family will go as well.'

13d 不但<u>公园里</u>，并且<u>街道两旁</u>都种着花。

búdàn **gōngyuán-lǐ**, bìngqiě **jiēdào liǎngpáng** dōu zhòng-zhe huā

'Both in parks and on curbs, flowers are profuse.'

'Both in parks and on curbs, flowers are all over.'

13e is a common error. Here 不但 *búdàn* is put at the beginning of the first clause; yet there is only one subject, *wǒmen* 'we,' for the entire compound structure. Note that while nothing is wrong with the English translation, the Mandarin sentence is awkward.

13e ✗ */?不但<u>我们</u>在宿舍吃饭，并且看电视。

búdàn **wǒmen** zài sùshè chī-fàn, bìngqiě kàn-diànshì

'We both eat and watch television in the dorm.'

✓ <u>我们</u>不但在宿舍吃饭，并且在那儿看电视。

wǒmen búdàn zài sùshè chī-fàn, bìngqiě zài nàr kàn-diànshì

'We both eat in the dorm and watch television there.'

If there is only one subject for the entire compound structure, 不但 *búdàn* 'not only' should **follow** the subject.

For related topics, see §§3, 45, and 51.

Exercises

EXERCISE 2. Translate into Chinese.

1　Students must both attend class and do their homework.

2　She both likes to read stories and to tell us about them.

3　Not only do boys play soccer, but girls do so as well.

§14.　Conjunctions linking compound clauses (iii): Although . . . , (but) . . .

The pair of complementary words 虽然 *suīrán* . . . 可是 *kěshì* . . . 'although . . . , (but) . . .' correlates two clauses that present contrasts. The subject of this compound structure precedes *suīrán* at the beginning of the sentence. See the subjects *zhèi-zhāng-zhuōzi* 'this table' and *Lǎo Wáng* 'Old Wang' in 14a and 14b respectively. The second conjunction *kěshì* appears at the beginning of the second clause, also as shown in 14a–b.

14a 这张桌子虽然小，可是很贵。

    zhèi-zhāng-zhuōzi suīrán xiǎo, kěshì hěn guì

    'Although this table is small, it is expensive.'

14b 老王虽然抽烟，可是不喝酒。

    Lǎo Wáng suīrán chōu-yān, kěshì bù hē-jiǔ

    'Although Old Wang smokes, he doesn't drink.'

If the two clauses of this compound structure have different subjects, one subject appears after *suīrán* in the first clause and the other subject appears after *kěshì* in the second clause, as in 14c.

14c 虽然李太太喜欢看电视，可是李先生不喜欢看。

    suīrán **Lǐ tàitai** xǐhuan kàn diànshì, kěshì **Lǐ xiānsheng** bù xǐhuan kàn

    'Mrs. Li likes to watch television, but Mr. Li doesn't.'

    'Although Mrs. Li likes to watch television, Mr. Li doesn't.'

Note that while no single English sentence contains both 'although' and 'but,' it is grammatically correct to use their equivalents in a single Mandarin sentence, as in 14a–c. Nonetheless it is also grammatically correct to omit *suīrán*, with *kěshì* alone carrying out the basic function of the pattern. 14a, for instance, can be written as 14d. On the other hand, if *suīrán* appears in the first clause, without *kěshì* in the following one, the compound structure sounds rather awkward in most cases, as shown by 14e, even though 14e's English translation is acceptable.

14d 这张桌子小，可是很贵。

    zhèi-zhāng-zhuōzi xiǎo, **kěshì** hěn guì

    'Although this table is small, it is expensive.'

14e ✕ 老王虽然抽烟，?不喝酒。

    Lǎo Wáng **suīrán** chōu-yān, bù hē-jiǔ

    'Although Old Wang smokes, (he) doesn't drink.'

In any case, while a sentence starts with *suīrán*, either *kěshì* or a substitute 但是 *dànshì* 'but' or 却 *què* 'however' ought to be used, as in examples 14f–g. Note that in distinction from the position of *kěshì* or *dànshì*, the Mandarin adverb *què* 'however' must appear **after** the subject of the second clause.

14f 虽然图书馆有不少书，但是字典不多。

    suīrán túshūguǎn yǒu bùshǎo shū, **dànshì** zìdiǎn bù duō

    'Although the library has many books, it doesn't have many

        dictionaries.'

14g 虽然图书馆有不少书，字典却不多。

suīrán túshūguǎn yǒu bùshǎo shū, zìdiǎn **què** bù duō

'Although the library has many books, it doesn't have many dictionaries.'

A common error is to put the adverb 却 *què* 'however' before the subject of the second clause in this compound structure, as in 14h. Remember: if one chooses to use *què* in the second clause and if there is a second subject, *què* must follow that subject. To correct the error in 14h, one can simply drop *wǒ* 'I' in the second clause since the same subject governs both clauses.

14h ⊗ 我虽然很穷，*却 我有很多好朋友。

wǒ suīrán hěn qióng, **què wǒ** yǒu hěn duō hǎo péngyou

'Although I am (financially) poor, I have many good friends.'

✓ 我虽然很穷，却有很多好朋友。

wǒ suīrán hěn qióng, **què** yǒu hěn duō hǎo péngyou

When used to replace 可是 *kěshì* 'but,' the adverb 却 *què* 'however,' must **follow** the subject of the second clause.

For related topics, see §53.

Exercises

EXERCISE 3. Translate into Chinese.

1   Although my friend has a television, he seldom watches it.
2   Although I can speak a bit of Chinese, I don't speak well. (using 却 *què*)
3   Although snow is falling, the weather is not cold. (using 却 *què*)

§15. Sentences expressing simultaneous actions

15a and 15d are two different patterns for expressing simultaneous actions.

15a   Subj. 一边 (儿) *yìbiān(r)* VP₁, 一边 (儿) *yìbiān(r)* VP₂
One subject; two verb phrases
'While doing X, Subj. also does Y.'

一边 (儿) *yìbiān(r)* and 一边 (儿) *yìbiān(r)* in pattern 15a are parallel conjunctions, signifying that two (or even more) actions are happening simultaneously. Note that there is one subject carrying out both (or more) actions at the same time. See examples 15b–c.

15b 我们一边（儿）唱歌，一边（儿）跳舞。
wǒmen yìbiān(r) chàng-gē, yìbiān(r) tiào-wǔ
'We sang as we danced.'/'We sang while dancing.'

15c 他一边（儿）吃饭，一边（儿）喝啤酒，一边（儿）看新闻。
tā yìbiān(r) chī-fàn, yìbiān(r) hē-píjiǔ, yìbiān(r) kàn-xīnwén
'He ate, (and) drank a beer while watching the news.'

While the second pattern, 15d, also contains two simultaneous actions, it is different from 15a because 15d has two subjects.

15d Subj.₁ VP₁ 的时候 *de shíhou*，Subj.₂ 正在 *zhèngzài* VP₂
Two subjects; two verb phrases
'While/when Subj.₁ does X, Subj.₂ is doing Y.'

The first half of this pattern is [Subj.₁ + VP₁] plus the time expression 的时候 *de shíhou* 'while. . . .' This first clause highlights a moment that is secondary to the second clause's continuing action (VP₂). The main clause that follows has the adverb 正在 *zhèngzài* 'in the midst of,' stressing the ongoing action (VP₂) that Subj.₂ is carrying out. The two actions in pattern 15d are interrelated in this way: at the moment when VP₁ occurs, VP₂ is/has been going on. See examples 15e–f.

15e 我给他打电话的时候，他正在睡觉。
wǒ gěi tā dǎ-diànhuà de shíhou, tā zhèngzài shuì-jiào
'When I called him, he was sleeping.'

15f 他到教室的时候，老师正在回答问题。
tā dào-jiàoshì de shíhou, lǎoshī zhèngzài huídá-wèntí
'When he arrived at the classroom, the teacher was answering questions.'

An effective way to use either of these two patterns correctly is to start with the number of subjects—one or two? If there is one subject, use 15a. If there are two subjects, use 15d. This is also a practical method for resolving the problems in this section. The ideas the following erroneous sentences intend to express are in parentheses.

15g (While eating breakfast, I listen to music.)
❌ *我吃早饭的时候，正在听音乐。
wǒ chī-zǎofà de shíhou, zhèngzài tīng-yīnyuè
▶ **Analysis:** There is one subject, 'I,' in this sentence, thus pattern 15a, not 15d, should be used.
✅ 我一边（儿）吃早饭，一边（儿）听音乐。
wǒ **yìbiān(r)** chī-zǎofà, **yìbiān(r)** tīng-yīnyuè

15h (While attending school, many students take part-time jobs.)

 *很多学生念大学的时候，正在打工。

hěnduō xuésheng niàn-dàxué de shíhou, zhèngzài dǎ-gōng

> ▶ **Analysis**: Even though the subject 'many students' refers to a plural noun phrase, this noun phrase represents a single subject. Therefore, it should be pattern 15a, not 15d.

很多学生<u>一边(儿)</u>念大学，<u>一边(儿)</u>打工。

hěnduō xuésheng **yìbiān(r)** niàn-dàxué, **yìbiān(r)** dǎ-gōng

15i (My little sister texted while I was reading a book.)

 *我妹妹一边(儿)给我发短信，我一边(儿)看书。

wǒ mèimei yìbiān(r) gěi wǒ fā-duǎnxìn, wǒ yìbiān(r) kàn-shū

> ▶ **Analysis**: There are two subjects in this sentence, 'my little sister' and 'I.' Thus 15d, not 15a, is the correct pattern for expressing the idea.

我妹妹给我发短信<u>的时候</u>，我<u>正在</u>看书。

wǒ mèimei gěi wǒ fā-duǎnxìn **de shíhou**, wǒ **zhèngzài** kàn-shū.

To express simultaneous actions, if there is one subject, use pattern 15a: [Subj. 一边(儿) *yìbiān(r)* VP₁, 一边(儿) *yìbiān(r)* VP₂]; if there are two subjects, use pattern 15d: [Subj.₁ VP₁ 的时候 *de shíhou*，Subj.₂ 正在 *zhèngzài* VP₂].

For related topics, see §25.

Exercises

EXERCISE 4. Choose the correct Chinese translation of each English sentence.

1 At the party the guests drank and chatted.

    a) 酒会上，客人一边儿喝酒，一边儿聊天。

    b) 酒会上，客人喝酒的时候，正在聊天。

2 He often reads when he eats.

    a) 他常常一边儿吃饭，一边儿看书。

    b) 他常常吃饭的时候，正在看书。

3 When he arrived at school, she was in class.

    a) 他一边儿到学校，她一边儿上课。

    b) 他到学校的时候，她正在上课。

4 Many people talk on their cell phone while driving.

    a) 很多人一边儿开车，一边儿用手机。

    b) 很多人开车的时候，正在用手机。

5 She was driving on the freeway when the rain began.

    a) 雨一边儿下，她一边儿在高速公路上开车。
    b) 开始下雨的时候，她正在高速公路上开车。

6 When you called, I was reading the newspaper.

    a) 你一边儿打电话，我一边儿看报。
    b) 你打电话的时候，我正在看报。

§16. Actions in a sequence: 先 *xiān* VP₁, 再 *zài* VP₂

The pattern for actions in a sequence is: [Subj. 先 *xiān* VP₁, 再 *zài* VP₂]. *Xiān* 'first' precedes the first verb phrase and *zài* 'then' precedes the second one, as in examples 16a–b below. The subject of the sequential actions begins the sentence, as *wǒ* 'I' and *wǒmen* 'we' do respectively in 16a and 16b.

16a 我先洗手，再吃饭。
    wǒ **xiān** xǐ-shǒu, **zài** chī-fàn
    'I will wash my hands before eating.'

16b 我们先学生词，再读课文。
    wǒmen **xiān** xué-shēngcí, **zài** dú-kèwén
    'We will first study the vocabulary, then read the text.'

The second adverb *zài* is interchangeable with 然后 *ránhòu* 'then,' as in example 16c.

16c 她先吃饭，然后看新闻。
    tā **xiān** chī-fàn, **ránhòu** kàn-xīnwén
    'She will first eat, then watch the news.'

When there is a series of actions, *zài* and *ránhòu* may appear before the second and the third verbs as in 16d. Another adverb, 最后 *zuìhòu* 'finally' may be used for the last action, as in 16e.

16d 吃中餐的时候，先吃凉菜，再吃热菜，然后喝汤。
    chī-zhōngcān de shíhou, **xiān** chī-liángcài, **zài** chī-rècài, **ránhòu** hē-tāng
    'In a Chinese meal, one first eats cold dishes, then hot ones, and then
        drinks soup.'

16e 我们先吃凉菜，再吃热菜，然后喝汤，最后吃甜点。
    wǒmen **xiān** chī-liángcài, **zài** chī-rècài, **ránhòu** hē-tāng, **zuìhòu** chī-tiándiǎn
    'We first eat cold dishes, then hot ones, and then drink the soup. Finally
        we enjoy the dessert.'

Regarding their position relative to the subject of the sentence, both *xiān* and *zài* must follow the subject. While both polysyllabic adverbs *ránhòu* and *zuìhòu* could appear before the subject, the sentence sounds smoother if they follow the subject. See example 16f.

16f 先吃凉菜，再吃热菜，我们<u>然后</u>喝汤，我们<u>最后</u>吃甜点。

xiān chī-liángcài, zài chī-rècài, wǒmen **ránhòu** hē-tāng, wǒmen **zuìhòu** chī-tiándiǎn

'First cold dishes, then hot ones, then we drink the soup. Finally we have dessert.'

Most common errors in this pattern occur when students put 先 *xiān* and/or 再 *zài* before the subject. To correct the following mistakes, one should simply remember to put these two monosyllabic adverbs **after** the subject.

16g ✗ *先我做完我的功课，然后我可以跟你去看电影。

xiān wǒ zuò-wán wǒde gōngkè, ránhòu wǒ kěyǐ gēn nǐ qù kàn-diànyǐng

'First I will finish my homework; then I can go watch a movie with you.'

✓ 我先做完我的功课，然后我可以跟你去看电影。

wǒ **xiān** zuò-wán wǒde gōngkè, ránhòu wǒ kěyǐ gēn nǐ qù kàn-diànyǐng

16h ✗ 换旅行支票很麻烦，*先你得有护照，*再你在支票上签字。

huàn lǚxíng zhīpiào hěn máfan, **xiān** nǐ děi yǒu-hùzhào, **zài** nǐ zài zhīpiào shàng qiān-zì

'It is really troublesome to cash traveler's checks. First you need a passport; then you [must] sign each check.'

✓ 换旅行支票很麻烦，你<u>先</u>得有护照，你<u>再</u>在支票上签字。

huàn lǚxíng zhīpiào hěn máfan, nǐ **xiān** děi yǒu-hùzhào, nǐ **zài** zài zhīpiào shàng qiān-zì

Both adverbs 先 *xiān* 'first' and 再 *zài* 'then' should follow the subject.

For related topics, see §53.

Exercises

EXERCISE 5. Put the parenthetical adverbs in the appropriate positions in the sentence.

1 (Learning Chinese, you first study pinyin, then characters.)
学中文，你学拼音，学汉字。(先，再)

2 (Small children first learn how to walk, and then to run.)
小孩子学走路，学跑。(先，再)

3 (First the old passengers get off, then the new passengers get on.)
下车的人下，上车的人上。(先，再)

4 (You sit down first, then we will talk.) 你坐下，我们谈。(先，再)

EXERCISE 6. Translate into Chinese, using the pattern 先 *xiān* VP₁, 再 *zài* VP₂.

1 She decided first to have lunch, then to return home.
2 First you check the map, then go.
3 You speak first, then I will respond.

§17. 'As soon as . . . , then . . .':
一 *yī* VP₁, 就 *jiù* VP₂

The pattern 一 *yī* VP₁, 就 *jiù* VP₂ indicates the immediate connection between the first and the second action, meaning 'as soon as . . . , then . . .' or 'once . . . , then. . . .' *Yī* introduces the first verb phrase, followed by *jiù* and a second verb phrase. The complex sentence may have one or more subjects. See examples 17a–b.

17a One subject: Subj. 一 VP₁ 就 VP₂
他一从国外回来就去看王先生了。
tā yì cóng guówài huí-lai, jiù qù kàn Wáng xiānsheng le
'As soon as he returned from abroad, he went to see Mr. Wang.'

17b Two subjects: Subj.₁ 一 VP₁, Subj.₂ 就 VP₂
电话一响，他就接了。
diànhuà yì xiǎng, tā jiù jiē le
'When the phone rang, he immediately picked it up.'

We may also see this pattern as indicating the consequence of two actions. To a degree the first action functions as the condition producing the second one, as shown by 17c–d.

17c 雨一停，太阳就出来了。
yǔ **yì** tíng, tàiyang **jiù** chū-lai le
'As soon as the rain stopped, the sun came out.'

17d 你开到下一个路口，往右一拐就到了。
nǐ kāi-dào xià yí-ge-lùkǒu, wàng yòu **yì** guǎi **jiù** dào le
'Drive to the next intersection. As soon as you turn right, you will
      be there.'

In this pattern, both *yī* and *jiù* must follow the subject(s), as in 17e–h. The subjects are underlined.

17e 你一打听就知道了。

nǐ yì dǎting jiù zhīdao le

'Once you ask around, you will know.'

17f 她一有钱就给朋友买礼物。

tā yì yǒu-qián jiù gěi péngyou mǎi-lǐwù

'Whenever she has money, she buys gifts for her friends.'

17g 七点一到，电影就开始了。

qīdiǎn yí dào, **diànyǐng** jiù kāishǐ le

'As soon as it was 7 o'clock, the movie began.'

17h 我一敲，你就把门开开。

wǒ yì qiāo, **nǐ** jiù bǎ mén kāi-kai

'Once I knock, you open the door (immediately).'

 Placing 就 *jiù* before Subj.₂ is a common error. Remember: one should always put it **after** the subject.

17i ✖ 你一问完这个问题，*就我回答你。

nǐ yí wèn-wán zhèi-ge-wèntí, jiù wǒ huídá nǐ.

'As soon as you finish this question, *will I answer it.'

✔ 你一问完这个问题，我就回答你。

nǐ yí wèn-wán zhèi-ge-wèntí, wǒ jiù huídá nǐ.

 As shown in patterns 17a–b, both 一 *yī* 'as soon as . . .' and 就 *jiù* 'then' must **follow** the subject of the complex sentence, or their respective subjects if there are two.

 For related topics, see §§53 and 54.

Exercises

EXERCISE 7. Put the parenthetical adverbs in the appropriate positions in the sentence.

1 (Soon after he graduated, he got a very good job.)
他毕业找到一个很好的工作。(一，就)

2 (Today she slept as soon as she returned to the dorm.)
她今天回到宿舍睡觉了。(一，就)

3 (Once the weather becomes cold, it's easy for him to catch a cold.)
天变冷，他容易感冒。(一，就)

4 (The train left as soon as they stepped aboard.) 他们上车，火车开了。(一，就)

EXERCISE 8. Translate into Chinese, using the pattern 一 *yī* VP₁ 就 *jiù* VP₂.

1 Whenever that athlete drinks ice tea, he gets a stomachache.
2 Once she has a little money, she will spend it.
3 Once he explained it, we understood.

§18. Yes/no questions and answers

As the name suggests, a yes/no question requests an answer that is either an agreement "yes," or a disagreement, "no." There are two basic methods to form a yes/no question: either adding the question particle 吗 *ma* to the end of a statement, as in 18a–c; or using both positive and negative forms of the verb/descriptive adjective in the sentence, as in 18d–g.

Method 1

Add the question particle 吗 *ma* to the end of any statement. Without any change in word order, this sentence thereby becomes a yes/no question.

18a	这两个学生明年去中国。
	zhèi liǎng-ge-xuésheng
	  míngniánqù Zhōngguó
	'These two students will
	  go to China next year.'
		⇨	这两个学生明年去中国吗？
			zhèi liǎng-ge-xuésheng
			  míngnián qù Zhōngguó **ma**?
			'Will these two students
			  go to China next year?'

18b	他今天做得完功课。
	tā jīntiān zuò-de-wán
	  gōngkè
	'He is able to finish his
	  homework today.'
		⇨	他今天做得完功课吗？
			tā jīntiān zuò-de-wán
			  gōngkè **ma**?
			'Is he able to finish his
			  homework today?'

18c	新建的机场很大。 xīnjiàn de jīchǎng hěn dà 'The newly built airport is big.'	⇨	新建的机场很大吗？ xīnjiàn de jīchǎng hěn dà **ma**? 'Is the newly built airport big?'

Method 2

Use the "A-not-A" structure. The A in this pattern can be either a verb/VP, as in 18d–f, or a descriptive adjective, as in 18g. When a verb/VP/DA is followed by its negation in the same sentence, the sentence becomes a yes/no question. Note that there is no need to use the question particle 吗 *ma* in the A-not-A structure. Nor should the adverb 很 *hěn* 'very' appear before the DA in this structure, as 18g illustrates.

18d 附近有没有菜市场？

   fùjìn **yǒu-méi-yǒu** càishìchǎng?

   'Is there a vegetable market in the vicinity?'

18e 你们晚上看不看电视？

   nǐmen wǎnshang **kàn-bú-kàn** diànshì?

   'Do you watch TV in the evening?'

18f 你找得到找不到那本书？

   nǐ **zhǎo-de-dào zhǎo-bú-dào** nèi-běn-shū?

   'Are you able to find that book?'

18g 这个箱子重不重？

   zhèi-ge-xiāngzi **zhòng-bú-zhòng**?

   'Is this suitcase heavy?'

If the A in this A-not-A structure is a verb or a verb phrase, there is an alternative way to form the question: put the negation at the end of the sentence. See 18d'–f'.

18d' 附近有菜市场没有？

   fùjìn **yǒu** càishìchǎng **méi-yǒu**?

   'Is there a vegetable market in the vicinity?'

18e' 你们晚上看电视不看？

   nǐmen wǎnshang **kàn** diànshì **bú-kàn**?

   'Do you watch TV in the evening?'

18f' 你找得到那本书找不到？

   nǐ **zhǎo-de-dào** nèi-běn-shū **zhǎo-bú-dào**?

   'Are you able to find that book?'

Answers

Since Mandarin lacks exact counterparts to 'yes' and 'no,' in order to answer a yes/no question, one repeats the verb/VP/DA of the question in its positive or negative form. While the minimal response is the verb/VP that answers the question, elements other than this key word are optional. See example 18h.

18h Q: 他今天做得完功课吗？

   tā jīntiān zuò-de-wán gōngkè **ma**?

   'Is he able to finish his homework today?'

   A: 做得完。

   zuò-de-wán '(He) is able to finish.'

   他做得完。

   tā zuò-de-wán 'He is able to finish.'

他今天做得完。

tā jīntiān zuò-de-wán 'He is able to finish today.'

他今天做得完功课。

tā jīntiān zuò-de-wán gōngkè 'He is able to finish his homework today.'

When the key word for answering a yes/no question is a descriptive adjective, the minimal response can be different degrees of this descriptive adjective. See example 18i.

18i Q: 那个电影有意思吗？

nèi-ge diànyǐng yǒuyìsi **ma**?

'Is that movie interesting?'

A: 有意思。

yǒuyìsi '(It is) interesting.'

很有意思。

hěn yǒuyìsi '(It is) very interesting.'

有意思极了。

yǒuyìsi jí le '(It is) extremely interesting.'

不太有意思。

bú tài yǒuyìsi '(It is) not that interesting.'

18j is erroneous because the question particle 吗 *ma* is added to an A-not-A structure. To form a yes/no question, use either the question particle *ma* or the A-not-A structure. Not both.

18j *他会不会唱歌吗？

tā **huì-bú-huì** chàng-gē **ma**?

'Can he sing?'

✅ 他会唱歌吗？

tā huì chàng-gē **ma**?

✅ 他会不会唱歌？

tā **huì-bú-huì** chàng-gē?

Students sometimes may be confused when using a potential form (cf. §44) in a yes/no question and make an awkward sentence such as 18k, where the A-not-A structure of a simple verb (看不看 *kàn-bú-kàn*) intrudes on a segment of the potential form (-得懂 *de-dǒng*). While some native speakers may admit to hearing such a sentence, 18k, in fact, sounds colloquial and is likely the product of certain dialects. The grammatically standard A-not-A structure for a potential form is: V-得 *de*-V + V-不 *bù*-V. Thus the correct way to ask this question is 18l.

18k ?你看不看得懂中文书？

nǐ **kàn-bú-kàn-de-dǒng** zhōngwén-shū?

181   你看得懂看不懂中文书？

nǐ **kàn-de-dǒng kàn-bù-dǒng** zhōngwén-shū?

'Are you able to read Chinese books?'

> To form a yes/no question, use either the particle 吗 *ma* or the "A-not-A" structure. Not both. The A-not-A structure for a potential form is: V-得 *de*-V + V-不 *bù*-V.

For related topics, see §§1, 2, 20, 41, 44, and 57.

Exercises

EXERCISE 9. Rewrite the yes/no question using the A-not-A structure.

1   樱花很美吗？
2   他的话有道理吗？
3   那个法国人会说英文吗？
4   你喝啤酒吗？
5   你看得懂中文书吗？
6   他们买房了吗？
7   你们周末睡得很晚吗？

EXERCISE 10. Translate into Chinese using either the A-not-A structure or the question particle 吗 *ma*.

1   Can you drive?
2   Do you expect to bump into him this afternoon? (Use the V-V compound 碰到)
3   Did you watch the news last night?
4   Is the soup hot?

§19. Structures with interrogative words: questions and answers

Mandarin interrogative words are listed in 19a.

19a   什么 *shénme* 'what'

什么地方/哪儿 *shénme dìfang/nǎr* 'where'

什么时候 *shénme shíhou* 'when'

哪 *něi(nǎ)* 'which'

多少/几 *duōshǎo/jǐ* 'how many'

多少钱 *duōshǎoqián* 'how much (of money)'

谁 *shéi(shuí)* 'who/whom'
谁的 *shéide(shuíde)* 'whose'
多 *duō* + Adj. 'to what degree of . . .'
为什么 *wèishénme* 'why'
怎么 *zěnme* 'how'

Among these interrogatives, *shénme* 'what' can also combine with a noun to form more specific requests, such as 什么问题 *shénme wèntí* 'what problem?' or 什么工作 *shénme gōngzuò?* 'what (kind of) work?' etc. Two other interrogatives, 'where' and 'when,' are actually formed in this way: 什么 *shénme* + 地方 *dìfang* 'what + place' = 'where'; and 什么 *shénme* + *shíhòu* 时候 'what + time' = 'when.'

Něi(nǎ) 'which' and *duōshǎo/jǐ* 'how many' are usually followed by a measure word and a noun, such as 哪棵树 *něi(nǎ)-kē-shù?* 'which tree?' or 多少/几只鸟 *duōshǎo/jǐ-zhī-niǎo?* 'how many birds?'

Questions that use these Mandarin interrogatives have two notable characteristics: i) They do not use the question particle 吗 *ma*; and ii) the word order of the questions and of their answers is identical. The Mandarin interrogative word occupies the same position in the question as the answer does in the response. This second characteristic applies to all the interrogatives in 19a except for 'why' and 'how.' See the following examples. The interrogatives and their answers are underlined. Note that they appear in the same position in the question and in its answer.

19b	Q:	草上有什么?	⇨	A:	草上有露水。
		cǎo-shàng yǒu **shénme**?			cǎo-shàng yǒu **lùshuǐ**
		'What is on the grass?'			'On the grass is dew.'

19c	Q:	你去哪儿买东西?	⇨	A:	我去农贸市场买东西。
		nǐ qù **nǎr** mǎi-dōngxi?			wǒ qù **nóngmào shìchǎng** mǎi-dōngxi
		'Where do you go shopping?'			'I shop at the farmer's market.'

19d	Q:	你什么时候去?	⇨	A:	我中午去。
		nǐ **shénme shíhou** qù?			wǒ **zhōngwǔ** qù
		'When are you going?'			'I will go at noon.'

19e	Q:	哪杯茶是你的?	⇨	A:	左边这杯是我的。
		něi-bēi-chá shì nǐde?			**zuǒ-biān zhèi-bēi** shì wǒde
		'Which cup of tea is yours?'			'The one on the left is mine.'

19f	Q:	这本字典多少钱?	⇨	A:	这本字典三十块。
		zhèi-běn-zìdiǎn **duōshǎoqián**?			zhèi-běn-zìdiǎn **sānshí-kuài**
		'How much does this dictionary cost?'			'This dictionary costs 30 *yuan*.'

19g Q: 谁去？ ⇨ A: 我去。
　　　　　shéi qù?　　　　　　　**wǒ** qù
　　　　　'Who will go?'　　　　　'I will go.'

19h Q: 他是谁的朋友？ ⇨ A: 他是老张的朋友。
　　　　　tā shì **shéide** péngyou?　　tā shì **Lǎo Zhāng de** péngyou
　　　　　'Whose friend is he?'　　　'He is Old Zhang's friend.'

The last three interrogatives in 19a require separate illustrations.

The answer for [多 *duō* + Adj.] 'to what degree of (length, height, distance, etc.)' usually is a specific measurement, as shown in 19i.

19i Q: 学校离他家多远？ ⇨ A: 学校离他家一英里。
　　　　　xuéxiào lí tā-jiā **duō yuǎn**?　　xuéxiào lí tā-jiā **yì-yīnglǐ**
　　　　　'How far is the school　　　'It is one mile from the
　　　　　　from his home?'　　　　　school to his home.'

Wèishénme 'why' demands an explanation; hence the response starts with 因为 *yīnwèi* 'because,' as in 19j.

19j Q: 他为什么不睡觉？ ⇨ A: 因为他得复习功课。
　　　　　tā **wèishénme** bú shuìjiào?　　**yīnwèi** tā děi fùxí gōngkè
　　　　　'Why hasn't he gone　　　'Because he needs to review
　　　　　　to sleep?'　　　　　　　his work.'

19j′ Q: 他怎么不睡觉？ ⇨ A: 因为他得复习功课。
　　　　　tā **zěnme** bú shuìjiào?　　**yīnwèi** tā děi fùxí gōngkè
　　　　　'How come he hasn't　　　'Because he needs to review
　　　　　　gone to sleep?'　　　　　his work.'

The last interrogative, *zěnme* 'how,' has three related denotations, as in 19k.

19k i) 'how come,' which is similar to *wèishénme* 'why.' See sentence 19j′ above where *zěnme* replaces *wèishénme* and the question basically remains the same.

　　　　ii) 'how,' which seeks corresponding explanations or responses, as in 'how to do something,' e.g. 怎么做 *zěnme-zuò*? 'how does one do . . . ?'; 怎么用 *zěnme-yòng* 'how does one use (it)?'; or 怎么去 *zěnme-qù* 'how does one get to . . . ?' etc.

　　　　iii) 'how is it,' as in the idiomatic phrase 怎么样 *zěnmeyàng*, e.g. 最近怎么样？ *zuìjìn zěnmeyàng*? 'how is everything lately?' or 喝一点儿茶，怎么样？ *hē-yìdiǎnr-chá, zěnmeyàng*? 'how about some tea?' (lit. 'Have some tea, how is it?')

Students tend to make the mistakes illustrated in 19l–m; namely, erroneous word order. The errors exist because they attempt word-by-word translations from English by putting the Mandarin interrogative at the beginning of the question.

19l   ❌ 请问，*什么音乐这张光盘有？我想试听一下。

qǐngwèn, **shénme yīnyuè** zhèi-zhāng guāngpán yǒu? wǒ xiǎng shìtīng-yíxià

(Intending to say: 'Excuse me, what music is on this CD? I'd like to sample it.')

▶ **Analysis**: The interrogative word *shénme yīnyuè* 'what music' should follow the verb *yǒu*. Remember: except for 'why' and 'how,' the Mandarin interrogative occupies the same position in the question as the answer does in the response. For example, we suppose the answer to this question is, 'The CD has Japanese folksongs (on it),' which is 这张光盘有日本民歌 *zhèi-zhāng guāngpán yǒu Rìběn míngē*. Note that as the object of the verb *yǒu*, the answer *Rìběn míngē* 'Japanese folksongs' follows the verb. This is the position where the interrogative word *shénme yīnyuè* 'what music' should therefore be in the question.

✅ 请问，这张光盘上有什么音乐？我想试听一下。

qǐngwèn, zhèi-zhāng guāngpán-shang yǒu **shénme yīnyuè**, wǒ xiǎng shìtīng-yíxià

19m   ❌ *哪儿你喜欢去买东西？

nǎr nǐ xǐhuān qù mǎi-dōngxi

(Intending to say: 'Where do you like to go shopping?'

▶ **Analysis**: The interrogative *nǎr* 'where' is the object of the verb *qù* 'go.' It therefore follows the verb *qù*. Again, this is where the answer is expected to be, e.g. 去商店 *qù shāngdiàn* 'go to store' or 去超市 *qù chāoshì* 'go to supermarket.'

✅ 你喜欢去哪儿买东西？

nǐ xǐhuān qù **nǎr** mǎi-dōngxi

Another common error is to use the unnecessary yes/no question particle 吗 *ma* or the A-not-A structure with the interrogative, as in 19n–o below. Because these two elements pertain to the yes/no question, they should not be used in questions that use interrogatives.

19n   ❌ *你什么时候有中文课吗？

nǐ shénme shíhou yǒu zhōngwénkè **ma**?

(Intending to say: 'When do you have Chinese class?')

✅ 你什么时候有中文课？

nǐ shénme shíhou yǒu zhōngwénkè

19o   ❌ *小李跟谁去不去听演讲？

Xiǎo Lǐ gēn shuí **qù-bú-qù** tīng yánjiǎng?

(Intending to say: 'With whom is Little Li going to listen to the speech?')

✅ 小李跟谁去听演讲？

Xiǎo Lǐ gēn shuí **qù** tīng yánjiǎng?

Except for 'why' and 'how,' an interrogative word occupies the same position in the question as the answer does in the response. Neither the yes/no question particle 吗 *ma* nor the A-not-A structure should be used with any interrogative word.

For related topics, see §§18 and 20.

Exercises

EXERCISE 11. For each of the sentences, ask a question about the underlined segment.

1　那个女孩儿是<u>他妹妹</u>。
2　这是<u>王大夫</u>的电话号码。
3　比尔是<u>加拿大人</u>。
4　我们常常去<u>博物馆</u>。
5　我们<u>星期五中午</u>开会。
6　裙子（卖）<u>三十块</u>。
7　她是<u>历史</u>专业。
8　中文班有<u>五十多个学生</u>。
9　那辆<u>红色的</u>车是老李的。
10　他们<u>坐公交车</u>去机场。

EXERCISE 12. Translate into Chinese.

1　How many days are there in a year?
2　Whose cell phone is this?
3　Where does she often eat dinner?
4　What class do you have today?
5　Which song is your favorite?

§20.　The object clauses of the verb 知道 *zhīdào* 'know'

The cognitive verb 知道 *zhīdào* 'know (about a fact),' either in its positive, negative, or interrogative form, often takes an object clause to elaborate factual knowledge in a sentence such as 'I (don't) know whether he is at home' or 'Do you know when the train arrives?' In Mandarin the object clauses of the verb *zhīdào* by themselves are direct questions. Attached to the verb *zhīdào*, they become indirect questions within the same structure. See 20b–c.

20a 他在家还是出去了？

tā zài-jiā háishì chūqù le?

'Is he home or has he gone out?'

20b 我（不）知道他在家还是出去了。

wǒ (bù) zhīdào **tā zài-jiā háishì chūqù le?**

'I (don't) know whether he is home or has he gone out.'

20c 你知道不知道他在家还是出去了？

nǐ zhīdào bù zhīdào **tā zài-jiā háishì chūqù le?**

'Do you know whether he is home or has he gone out?'

20b could be the answer to the direct question 20a. Note that 20a, as underlined, becomes the object clause of the verb *zhīdào* in 20b. This is also true of the interrogative form of *zhīdào*, in 20c.

As discussed in the previous two sections, there are two other types of direct questions: yes/no questions and questions using interrogative words. Once one grasps their respective structures, the correct way to form an object clause of *zhīdào* follows naturally. See the following two groups.

知道 *zhīdào* + A-not-A structure

The underlined clause is a yes/no question, in the A-not-A structure.

20d 我（不）知道他们喝不喝咖啡。

wǒ (bù) zhīdào **tāmen hē-bù-hē kāfēi**

'I (don't) know whether they drink coffee.'

20e 我（不）知道邮局离这儿远不远。

wǒ (bù) zhīdào **yóujú lí zhèr yuǎn-bù-yuǎn**

'I (don't) know whether the post office is far from here.'

20f 我（不）知道她今天看得完看不完那本书。

wǒ (bù) zhīdào **tā jīntiān kàn-de-wán kàn-bù-wán nèi-běn-shū**

'I (don't) know whether she can finish reading that book today.'

知道 *zhīdào* + interrogative

The underlined clause is a question using an interrogative word.

20g 我（不）知道那个人是谁。

wǒ (bù) zhīdào **nèi-ge-rén shì shéi**

'I (don't) know who that person is.'

20h   我（不）知道<u>你弟弟叫什么名字</u>。

wǒ (bù) zhīdào **nǐ dìdi jiào shénme míngzi**

'I (don't) know what your younger brother is called.'

20i   我（不）知道<u>他们什么时候回来</u>。

wǒ (bù) zhīdào **tāmen shénme shíhou huílai**

'I (don't) know what time they will return.'

20j   我（不）知道<u>你为什么选了这门课</u>。

wǒ (bù) zhīdào **nǐ wèishénme xuǎn le zhèi-mén-kè**

'I (don't) know why you chose this course.'

20k   我（不）知道<u>这种车卖多少钱</u>。

wǒ (bù) zhīdào **zhèi-zhǒng-chē mài duōshǎoqián**

'I (don't) know how much this kind of car costs.'

The cause of these common mistakes is word-by-word translation from English, as shown in 20l–o.

In both 20l and 20m *yàoshì* is directly translated as 'whether/if' and put in the middle of the sentence. To the English sentence 'I don't know whether/if . . . ,' the object clause of the verb 知道 *zhīdào* 'know' should be a yes/no question in the A-not-A structure (see the translations of 20d–f). In the case of 20l, it is 'does his work go smoothly?' *tā gōngzuò shùnlì-bú-shùnlì*? There is no need for the word 'whether/if' in Mandarin. Note also that the erroneous object clause in 20m must be amended to an A-not-A structure.

20l   ✖ 我不知道*<u>要是</u>他工作顺利。

wǒ bù zhīdào **yàoshì tā gōngzuò shùnlì**

✔ 我不知道<u>他工作顺利不顺利</u>。

wǒ bù zhīdào **tā gōngzuò shùnlì-bú-shùnlì**

'I don't know whether his work goes smoothly.'

20m   ✖ 你知道不知道*<u>要是</u>他今天下午在家？

nǐ zhīdào-bù-zhīdào **yàoshì tā jīntiān xiàwǔ zài jiā?**

✔ 你知道不知道<u>他今天下午在不在家</u>？

nǐ zhīdào-bù-zhīdào **tā jīntiān xiàwǔ zài-bú-zài jiā?**

'Do you know whether he is at home this afternoon?'

The object clauses in both 20n and 20o are questions using interrogatives. Again, the problem in 20n–o is that both follow the English word order. Remember: Mandarin interrogatives do not stand at the beginning of the question but in the same position as the answer does in the response (see §19). For example, in the case of 20n, 'what is the teacher saying?' is *lǎoshī shuō shénme?* And this direct question becomes the object clause of *zhīdào*.

20n 上课的时候我不知道*什么老师说。

shàng-kè de shíhòu wǒ bù zhīdào **shénme** lǎoshī shuō

 上课的时候我不知道老师说什么。

shàng-kè de shíhòu wǒ bù zhīdào **lǎoshī shuō shénme**

'In class, I don't know what the teacher is saying.'

20o 我不知道*<u>多少钱</u>那本中文字典卖。

wǒ bù zhīdào <u>**duōshǎoqián**</u> nà-běn zhōngwén zìdiǎn mài

 我不知道那本中文字典卖多少钱。

wǒ bù zhīdào **nà-běn zhōngwén zìdiǎn mài duōshǎoqián**

'I don't know how much that Chinese dictionary sells for.'

> The object clauses after 知道 *zhīdào* are by themselves direct questions. If the idea is 'I (don't) know whether . . . ,' the object clause is an "A-not-A" structured yes/no question; whereas if the idea is 'I (don't) know who/where/when/how . . . ,' the object clause follows the same structure as a question with an interrogative.

For related topics, see §§12, 18, 19, 21, and 58.

Exercises

EXERCISE 13. Translate into Chinese.

1 His parents know whether he likes that job.
2 The students know whether the Final is difficult.
3 We don't know whether the plumber is coming.
4 We also don't know when the plumber is coming.
5 She doesn't know why she took a Chinese course.
6 Do you know whether he drinks tea or coffee?
7 Do you know what (dishes) we should order?

§21. The two *ors*: a question or a statement?

In Mandarin, there are two patterns that structure 'either . . . or . . .' alternatives. One is a question: 'Is it X or Y?' The other is a statement: 'Either (it is) X or Y.'

Question

First, the pattern for questions is: (是 *shì*) . . . 还是 *háishì* . . . ? The conjunctions *shì* (which may be optional) and *háishì* link the two choices, X and Y, one of which will be the answer to the question. The alternatives X and Y can be various grammatical elements. 21a–c are some possibilities.

21a alternatives between subjects:

(是 *shì*) Subj.$_X$ + VP 还是 *háishì* Subj.$_Y$ + VP?

Q: (是)我洗碗还是你洗碗?   A: 我洗。

(shì) **wǒ** xǐ-wǎn háishì **nǐ** xǐ-wǎn?   **wǒ** xǐ.

'Am I going to do the dishes or will you?'   'I will.'

21b alternatives between verb phrases:

Subj. (是 *shì*) VP$_X$ 还是 *háishì* VP$_Y$?

Q: 我们(是)下棋还是看电影?   A: 看电影。

wǒmen (shì) **xià-qí** háishì **kàn-diànyǐng**?   **kàn-diànyǐng**.

'Are we going to play chess or   'Watch a movie.'

watch a movie?'

21c alternatives between objects:

(是 *shì*) Obj.$_X$ 还是 *háishì* Obj.$_Y$?

Q: 我们喝什么? (是)茶还是咖啡?   A: 茶。

wǒmen hē shénme? (shì) **chá** háishì **kāfēi**?   **chá**.

'What are we going to drink? Tea or coffee?'   'Tea.'

For alternative questions, if the verb of the sentence is *shì* 'be,' as in example 21d, the usually optional *shì* at the beginning of this pattern is required, rather than optional.

21d 那是一辆日本车还是一辆法国车?

nèi **shì** yí-liàng Rìběn chē **háishì** yí-liàng Fǎguó chē?

'Is that a Japanese car or a French one?'

Statement

Second, the pattern for the statement 'either (it is) X or Y' is: X 或者 *huòzhě* Y, 都 *dōu*. . . . In this pattern, the conjunction *huòzhě* marks a choice between two or more options; whereas the follow-up adverb *dōu* 'either/all' introduces a complementary phrase as in 'either/all would be fine.' The choices in 'X *huòzhě* Y, *dōu* . . .' also can rely on various grammatical elements. See examples 21e–g, which can likewise be the responses to examples 21a–c respectively if the answers to those questions happen to be 'either would be fine.'

21e 我洗碗或者你洗碗，都可以。

wǒ xǐ-wǎn huòzhě **nǐ** xǐ-wǎn, **dōu** kěyǐ

'I'll wash the dishes, or you do them: either would be OK.'

21f 下棋或者看电影，都行。

xià-qí huòzhě **kàn-diànyǐng**, **dōu** xíng

'Playing chess or watching a movie: either is fine.'

21g 茶或者咖啡，都好。

chá huòzhě **kāfēi**, **dōu** hǎo

'Tea or coffee, either is fine with me.'

Sometimes more than one *huòzhě* is used, depending on the number of choices, as in example 21h.

21h 我们下棋，或者看电影，或者聊天，都行。

wǒmen xià-qí, **huòzhě** kàn-diànyǐng, **huòzhě** liáo-tiān, **dōu** xíng

'We may play chess, watch a movie, or chat: any possibility is fine.'

The bottom line: there are two *or*s in Mandarin: either *háishì* for alternative questions or *huòzhě* for statements of choices. Their functions never switch. The former marks a question, 'Is it X or Y?' And the latter makes a statement, 'Either X or Y would be fine.'

The common error is to use 还是 *háishì*, the "question *or*" for 或者 *huòzhě*, the "statement *or*." This error puzzles listeners because when *háishì* is uttered, a listener would expect a question, but then if a 都 *dōu* 'either/all' appears afterward, the whole sentence sounds very confusing. 21i is such an example, in which *huòzhě*, not *háishì*, should be used.

21i ✗ 对我来说，教书?还是当飞行员，?都是理想的工作。

duì wǒ lái shuō, jiāo-shū **háishì** dāng-fēixíngyuán, **dōu** shì lǐxiǎng de gōngzuò

(Intending to say: 'To me—teaching or being a pilot—either is an ideal job.')

✓ 对我来说，教书或者当飞行员，都是理想的工作。

duì wǒ lái shuō, jiāo-shū **huòzhě** dāng-fēixíngyuán, **dōu** shì lǐxiǎng de gōngzuò

On some occasions, a sentence such as 21j is spoken, which, due to the misuse of *háishì* (the "question *or*"), appears to be a question: 'Next semester, should I study Chinese, or should I study Japanese?' Since this is apparently not meant to be a question, again, it is *huòzhě*, not *háishì*, that should be used.

21j ✗ ?我下学期学中文，还是学日文。

wǒ xià xuéqī xué-zhōngwén, **háishì** xué-rìwén

(Intending to say: 'Next semester, I will study either Chinese or Japanese.')

我下学期学中文，<u>或者</u>学日文。
wǒ xià xuéqī xué-zhōngwén, **huòzhě** xué-rìwén

 There are two patterns that structure 'either . . . or . . .' alternatives. 还是 *háishì* is the 'or' for the question 'Is it X or Y?'; whereas 或者 *huòzhě* is the 'or' for the statement 'Either (it is) X or Y.'

 For related topics, see §§20 and 51.

Exercises

EXERCISE 14. Select 还是 *háishì* or 或者 *huòzhě* from the squared parentheses for each sentence.

1   A: 我坐公共汽车 [还是，或者] 坐地铁去机场？
     B: 你去机场，坐公共汽车 [还是，或者] 坐地铁都很方便。
2   我很渴。请来一杯水 [还是，或者] 一瓶啤酒。
3   你觉得看书有意思 [还是，或者] 看电视有意思？
4   她想买一辆日本车 [还是，或者] 韩国车。

EXERCISE 15. Translate into Chinese.

1   Do you like the red one or the blue one?
2   Which do you think is more expensive, the newspaper or the magazine?
3   You may take this medicine either in the morning or in the evening.
4   She wants to learn an East Asian language, either Chinese or Japanese.
5   Is Mr. Li going to China or India this summer?
6   To me, living in the dorm or off campus is the same.
7   We may eat rice or noodles; either is fine.

Check your grammar

Translate these sentences into Chinese, and then check to see that you have implemented the relevant grammar points. The parenthetical numbers and letters identify the pertinent subsections and examples.

1   None of us knows whether this exam is difficult. (§12g)
2   He asks me whether I will graduate next year. (§12h)
3   If there is no hot water, we will not brew tea. (§12i)
4   We both eat in the dorm and watch television there. (§13e)
5   Although I am (financially) poor, I have many good friends. (§14h)
6   While eating breakfast, I listen to music. (§15g)

7 While attending school, many students take part-time jobs. (§15h)

8 My little sister texted while I was reading a book. (§15i)

9 First I will finish my homework; then I can go watch a movie with you. (§16g)

10 It is really troublesome to cash traveler's checks. First you need a passport; then you (must) sign each check. (§16h)

11 As soon as you finish this question, I will answer it. (§17i)

12 Can he sing? (§18j)

13 Are you able to read Chinese books? (§18k)

14 Excuse me, what music is on this CD? I'd like to sample it. (§19l)

15 Where do you like to go shopping? (§19m)

16 When do you have Chinese class? (§19n)

17 With whom is Little Li going to listen to the speech? (§19o)

18 I don't know whether his work goes smoothly. (§20l)

19 Do you know whether he is at home this afternoon? (§20m)

20 In class, I don't know what the teacher is saying. (§20n)

21 I don't know how much that Chinese dictionary sells for. (§20o)

22 To me—teaching or being a pilot—either is an ideal job. (§21i)

23 Next semester, I will study either Chinese or Japanese. (§21j)

 Notes

3 Temporal expressions

§22. Time phrases (i): *when* (chronological) vs. *how long* (durational)

There are two types of time expressions in Mandarin: chronological time and durational time.

Chronological time

Chronological time expressions identify **time-when**, i.e. a designated time for the occurrence of an action or situation. We can classify these time expressions in the subgroups 22a–h.

22a   year:
二〇〇八年 *èr líng líng bā nián* '2008'
明年 *míng nián* 'next year'

22b   season:
春天 *chūntiān* 'spring'
去年夏天 *qùnián xiàtiān* 'last summer'

22c   month:
二月 *èryuè* 'February'
这个月 *zhèi-ge yuè* 'this month'

22d   week:
星期天 *xīngqītiān* 'Sunday'
上星期二 *shàng xīngqī'èr* 'last Tuesday'

22e day:

十七号 *shíqī hào* 'the 17th day'

昨天 *zuótiān* 'yesterday'

22f period of a day:

早上 *zǎoshang* 'morning'

下午 *xiàwǔ* 'afternoon'

22g clock time:

中午十二点一刻 *zhōngwǔ shí'èr-diǎn yí-kè* '12:15 p.m.'

22h relative time:

从前 *cóngqián* 'before'

刚才 *gāngcái* 'just now'

三天以后 *sān-tiān yǐhòu* 'three days later'

毕业的时候 *bìyè de shíhou* 'when graduating'

Generally, the sequence of chronological time expressions, when they are used together, is from the largest period to the smallest: year-month-date-period of the day-hour-minute; year-season, etc. See examples 22i–k.

22i　二〇一〇年一月一号中午十二点五分

èr líng yī líng nián yīyuè yīhào zhōngwǔ shí'èr-diǎn wǔ-fēn

'12:05 p.m. January 1, 2010'

22j　二〇〇八年夏天

èr líng líng bā nián xiàtiān

'summer 2008'

22k　明年九月

míngnián jiǔyuè

'September of the next year'

Durational time

Durational time expressions refer to **time-spent**, i.e. the length of time an action takes. Durational time expressions usually display the structure: Num + Mea + N. Note that some of the nouns in durational time expressions can be the measures themselves, such as *nián* 'year' (22l), *tiān* 'day' (22p), *yè* 'night' (22q), and *fēnzhōng* 'minute' (22r). In these cases, the structure of the expression is: Num + N. We can classify durational time expressions in the subgroups 22l–s.

22l year:

两年 *liǎng-nián* 'two years'

半年 *bàn-nián* 'half a year'

22m season:

三个夏天 *sān-ge xiàtiān* 'three summers'

22n month:

六个月 *liù-ge yuè* 'six months'

22o week:

四个星期 *sì-ge xīngqī* 'four weeks'

22p day:

三十天 *sānshi-tiān* '30 days'

几天 *jǐ-tiān* 'several days'

22q period of a day:

一（个）上午 *yí (ge) shàngwǔ* 'the whole morning'

一夜 *yí yè* 'the whole night'

22r clock time:

二十四（个）小时 *èrshísì-(ge) xiǎoshí* '24 hours'

三十分钟 *sānshi-fēnzhōng* '30 minutes'

22s indefinite quantities:

一会儿 *yìhǔir* 'a while'

一些日子 *yìxiē rìzi* 'some days'

很久 *hěnjiǔ* 'a long while'

Like chronological time expressions, the sequence for durational time, when compounded, proceeds from the larger period to the smaller one. The character 零 *líng* 'with a little extra' notes the last remnant. See example 22t.

22t 三年三个月零五天   八个小时（零）二十分钟

     sān-nián sān-ge yuè **líng** *wǔ-tiān*   *bā-ge xiǎoshí* **(líng)** *èrshi-fēnzhōng*

     '3 years, 3 months, and 5 days'   '8 hours and 20 minutes'

▶ **Note**: To distinguish the two types of time expressions, one may formulate them as questions. Chronological time expressions answer the question **when?**, i.e. at/during what time the action or situation occurs. Durational time expressions, on the other hand, answer the question **how long?**, i.e. the length of time the action takes.

For example, regarding **when**, the answer may be 三月 *sānyuè* 'March,' while regarding **how long**, the answer should be 三个月 *sān-ge-yuè* 'three months.' Similarly: 这两天 *zhèi-liǎng-tiān* 'these two days' (when) vs. 两天 *liǎng-tiān* 'two days' (how long). The following are some contrasting pairs.

When?	How long?
今年 *jīn nián* 'this year'	一年 *yì-nián* 'one year'
十二月 *shí'èryuè* 'December'	十二个月 *shí'èr-ge-yuè* '12 months'
这个月 *zhèi-ge-yuè* 'this month'	一个月 *yí-ge-yuè* 'one month'
这个星期 *zhèi-ge-xīngqī* 'this week'	一个星期 *yí-ge-xīngqī* 'one week'
一号 *yī hào* 'the 1ˢᵗ'	一天 *yì-tiān* 'one day'
明年秋天 *míngnián qiūtiān* 'next fall'	一个秋天 *yí-ge-qiūtiān* 'one fall'
夜里 *yèlǐ* 'during the night'	一夜 *yí-yè* 'one night'
两点 *liǎng-diǎn* 'two o'clock'	两个钟头 *liǎng-ge-zhōngtóu* '2 hours'
三点一刻 *sān-diǎn yí-kè* '3:15'	一刻钟 *yí-kè-zhōng* '15 minutes'
三点十分 *sān-diǎn shí-fēn* '3:10'	十分钟 *shí-fēn-zhōng* '10 minutes'

Chronological time expressions answer the question **when** the action occurs, whereas durational time expressions answer the question **how long** in time the action takes.

For related topics, see §§23, 24, 31, 33, and 50.

Exercises

EXERCISE 1. Identify the following time phrases as indicating either chronological time or durational time.

1	四十五分钟	5	半个月	9	两天
2	今年春天	6	很久以后	10	三年以前
3	一月一日	7	十个小时	11	星期六晚上九点
4	十五个星期	8	昨天下午	12	四年

§23. Time phrases (ii): periods of the day vs. a.m./p.m.

Chronological time expressions include those expressed by a clock, such as 上午十点 *shàngwǔ shídiǎn* 'ten in the morning.' The structure of this expression is *shàngwǔ* 'morning' + *shídiǎn* 'ten o'clock.' The first word, *shàngwǔ*, clarifies the time as 10 a.m., not 10 p.m.

Unlike English, where a day can be neatly divided into two equal periods: 'a.m.' and 'p.m.,' Mandarin has a set of words that indicate the different periods of a 24-hour day, as shown in 23a–j. These are the words that appear before any particular hour on the clock, such as *shàngwǔ shídiǎn* in the previous paragraph, and 下午三点半 *xiàwǔ sāndiǎnbàn* '3:30 in the afternoon.'

23a 凌晨 *língchén* (before dawn; in the small hours)

23b 清晨 *qīngchén* (early morning)

23c 早晨/早上 *zǎochén/zǎoshang* (morning, from dawn to 8 or 9 a.m.)

23d 上午 *shàngwǔ* (from daybreak to noon; before-noon)

23e 中午 *zhōngwǔ* (midday, around noon)

23f 下午 *xiàwǔ* (afternoon; from noon until sunset)

23g 傍晚 *bàngwǎn* (dusk)

23h 晚上 *wǎnshang* (evening; between sunset and midnight)

23i 夜里 *yèlǐ* (as opposed to 'daytime'; from dusk to dawn)

23j 半夜/午夜 *bànyè/wǔyè* (midnight; around 12:00 a.m.)

As their meanings show, there is not a clear-cut break between any two adjacent time periods represented by these words. Certain parts of the adjacent portions can overlap, and these time periods vary in length. When seasons change, the beginning and end of the periods also vary. For instance, the length of *xiàwǔ* 'afternoon' (23f) varies by season. It could last until 5 p.m. during the winter or until later than 7 p.m. during the summer, since *xiàwǔ* by definition can stretch to sunset and the sun sets at different points in different seasons.

In order to tell time more accurately, one needs these words. Meanwhile one also needs to understand that choosing a word to designate a period of the day in Mandarin depends on common sense. For example, 3 a.m. can be either 夜里三点 *yèlǐ sāndiǎn* 'three during the night' (23i) or 凌晨三点 *língchén sāndiǎn* 'three before dawn' (23a); but it certainly cannot be *上午三点 *shàngwǔ sāndiǎn* 'three in the mid-morning' (23d) or *晚上三点 *wǎnshang sāndiǎn* 'three in the evening' (23h).

Following the 'a.m.' vs. 'p.m.' routine in English, students tend to use only one or two words from the above list to cover the different hours in a 24-hour day. Most commonly used are: 早上 *zǎoshang* (23c), 上午 *shàngwǔ* (23d), 下午 *xiàwǔ* (23f), and 晚上 *wǎnshang* (23h). This practice leads to the following errors in Mandarin.

23k ✖ *上午/下午十二点 (for 12 p.m.)
shàngwǔ/xiàwǔ shí'èr diǎn

> ▶ **Problem:** Neither *shàngwǔ* (23d) nor *xiàwǔ* (23f) matches 'noon.' So the accurate word should be *zhōngwǔ* (23e).

✔ 中午十二点
zhōngwǔ shí'èr diǎn

231   ✖ *早上两点 (for 2 a.m.)
zǎoshang liǎng diǎn

▶ **Problem**: The portion of time that *zǎoshang* (23c) represents is too late for 2 a.m.

✔ 夜里／凌晨两点
yèlǐ/língchén liǎng diǎn

23m   ✖ *下午七点 (for 7 p.m.)
xiàwǔ qī diǎn

▶ **Problem**: The portion of time that *xiàwǔ* (23f) represents usually does not stretch to 7 p.m., although in some parts of the world the sun does not set till after 7 p.m. during the summer. Again, use these words on the basis of common sense.

✔ 晚上七点
wǎnshang qī diǎn

23n   *早上十点 (for 10 a.m.)
zǎoshang shí diǎn

▶ **Problem**: The portion of time represented by *zǎoshang* (23c) usually does not stretch to 10 a.m. *Shàngwǔ* (23d) is more suitable.

✔ 上午十点
shàngwǔ shí diǎn

Unlike the two periods evenly divided by a.m. and p.m., Mandarin has a set of words that indicate the different periods of a 24-hour day. The choice of these words depends on common sense.

For related topics, see §§22, 24, 31, 33, and 52.

Exercises

EXERCISE 2. (§§22–23) Write these time phrases in Chinese.

1 12 p.m.	5 July 14, 1789	9 2:30 in the morning
2 this week	6 half a year	10 one year later
3 two hours & ten minutes	7 five months	11 seven days
4 10 a.m. Monday	8 7:10 p.m.	12 6 a.m. yesterday

§24. Time phrases in a sentence

The two types of time expressions—chronological and durational—occur at different positions in a Mandarin sentence, relative to the main verb.

Chronological time

Chronological time expressions, i.e. **time-when**, indicate the time set for the occurrence or non-occurrence of an action. While this time expression may stand before or (more often) after the subject, it always precedes the main verb of the sentence, as in examples 24a–b. **Time-when** can be a specific point in time, such as *jiǔdiǎn* '(at) nine o'clock' in 24a; or a period of time, such as *shàng-ge xīngqī* 'last week' in 24b.

24a 他们九点上课。
  tāmen **jiǔdiǎn** shàngkè
  'They attend class at nine.'

24b 上个星期我病了，没上班。
  shàng-ge xīngqī wǒ bìng le, méi shàng-bān
  'Last week I was sick and didn't go to work.'

In questions, the interrogative pronoun 什么时候 *shénme shíhou* 'when' always appears after the subject, and precedes the main verb, as in 24c.

24c 你什么时候走？   （我）下个月（走）。
  nǐ **shénme shíhou** zǒu?   (wǒ) xià-ge yuè (zǒu)
  'When are you leaving?'   '(I am leaving) next month.'

The general principle concerning the order of individual time words in the chronological time expression is that larger units precede smaller units (see §22). Examples 24d–e contain chronological time expressions formed by multiple time words.

24d 我姐姐昨天晚上十一点半生了一个女儿。
  wǒ jiějie **zuótiān wǎnshang shíyī-diǎn bàn** shēng-le yí-ge nǚ'er
  'My older sister gave birth to a daughter at 11:30 last night.'

24e 美国一七七六年七月四号宣告独立。
  Měiguó **yī qī qī liù nián qīyuè sì hào** xuāngào dúlì
  'The United States proclaimed its independence on July 4, 1776.'

Durational time

Durational time expressions, i.e. **time-spent**, measure how long an action takes. This time expression stands **after** the main verb. In a sentence, **time-spent** may appear in either of two structures. See examples 24f–g.

24f Subj. + V-Obj. + V + time-spent, where the durational time expression
    immediately follows the repeated main V.
  她看电视看了两个小时。
  tā kàn-diànshì kàn-le **liǎng-ge-xiǎoshí**
  'She watched television for two hours.'

24g Subj. + V + time-spent (的 *de*) + Obj., where the durational time
expression serves as a modifying element with an optional 的 *de*
before the object.

她看了两个小时(的)电视。

tā kàn-le **liǎng-ge-xiǎoshí** (de) diànshì

'She watched television for two hours.'

When the verb is intransitive, i.e. it does not take an object, such as *gōngzuò*
'work' and *xiūxi* 'rest' in example 24h, the durational time expression directly
follows the verb itself.

24h 我们每天工作八个小时，中午休息一个小时。

wǒmen měitiān **gōngzuò** bā-ge-xiǎoshí, zhōngwǔ **xiūxi** yí-ge-xiǎoshí

'Every day we work eight hours and take a one-hour break at noon.'

In questions, the interrogative phrase normally is either 多长时间 *duōcháng
shíjiān* or 多久 *duō jiǔ* 'for how long.' Either interrogative phrase stands in the
time-spent slot, as in either 24i or 24j.

24i 你每天工作多长时间?   八个小时。

nǐ měitiān gōngzuò **duōcháng shíjiān**?   bā-ge xiǎoshí

'How long do you work each day?'   'Eight hours.'

24j 她学中文学了多久了?   (学了)三年了。

tā xué-zhōngwén xué-le **duō jiǔ** le?   (xué-le) sān-nián le

'How long has she studied Chinese?'   '(She has studied) for three
                                              years.'

Combining the two time expressions

A chronological time expression (**time-when**) and a durational time
expression (**time-spent**) may appear in the same sentence, as shown in the
examples 24k–l. Note that the former must stand **before** the main verb,
setting the time zone when the action occurs, whereas the latter must stand
after the main verb, indicating how long the action lasts. E.g. 24k states that
last week (chronological time), the action 'raining' lasted for three days
(durational time).

24k 上个星期这儿下雨下了三天。

shàng-ge xīngqī zhèr xià-yǔ xià-le **sān-tiān**

'Last week it rained here for three days.'

24l 王老师去年夏天教了两个月(的)中文。

Wáng lǎoshī **qù nián xiàtiān** jiāo-le **liǎng-ge yuè** (de) zhōngwén

'Last summer Teacher Wang taught Chinese for two months.'

One common error is for students to follow English word order when they compose a sentence in Mandarin using **time-when** (chronological) expressions. E.g. while nothing is wrong with the English translation of 24m, its Mandarin counterpart is ill-formed because the chronological time *zhèi-ge zhōumò* 'this weekend' is put at the end of the sentence, following the English word order. Remember: the chronological time expression precedes the main verb in Mandarin.

24m ✖ *我去芝加哥这个周末。
  wǒ qù Zhījiāgē **zhèi-ge zhōumò**
  'I will go to Chicago this weekend.'
  ✔ 我这个周末去芝加哥。
  wǒ **zhèi-ge zhōumò** qù Zhījiāgē

Another common mistake is that students often mix the two types of time expressions and misplace them in a sentence. In 24n, the time *yí-ge xuéqī* 'one semester' here is durational time and should be put after the verb phrase *xué-zhōngwén*. 24n is unacceptable since the durational time has been placed before the VP.

24n ✖ 我打算*一个学期到中国去学中文。
  wǒ dǎsuàn **yí-ge xuéqī** dào Zhōngguó qù xué-zhōngwén
  'I plan to go to China to study Chinese for one semester.'
  ✔ 我打算到中国去学一个学期（的）中文。
  wǒ dǎsuàn dào Zhōngguó qù xué **yí-ge xuéqī** (de) zhōngwén

In 24o, the time *liù-diǎn zhōng* 'six o'clock' is chronological time and should be put before the verb phrase *shuì-jiào* 'sleep.' 24o is ill-formed because the chronological time follows the VP. In this case, if one intends to say 'I normally go to bed at six o'clock,' the time *liù-diǎn zhōng* should precede the VP. On the other hand, if one intends to say 'I normally sleep for six hours,' the current time position in 24o is the right place for the durational time, 'six hours.' The time expression for 'six hours,' however, should be *liù-ge zhōngtóu*. Examples 24p–q correctly show the two ideas.

24o ✖ 我平常睡觉睡*六点钟。
  wǒ píngcháng shuì-jiào shuì **liù-diǎn zhōng**
  'I normally sleep for *six o'clock.'

24p 我平常六点钟睡觉。
  wǒ píngcháng **liù-diǎn zhōng** shuì-jiào
  'I normally go to bed at six o'clock.'

24q 我平常睡觉睡六个钟头。
  wǒ píngcháng shuì-jiào shuì **liù-ge zhōngtóu**
  'I normally sleep for six hours.'

Chronological time (when) precedes the main verb of the sentence, whereas durational time (spent) stands after the main verb. 24f and 24g show the two structural forms of durational time expressions.

 For related topics, see §§5, 19, 22, and 23.

 ## *Exercises*

EXERCISE 3. Put the parenthetical time phrase(s) in the appropriate position(s) in each sentence.

1 他出去跑步，风雨无阻。(早上六点)
2 我们休息。(十分钟)
3 张老先生每天打太极拳。(一个钟头)
4 我弟弟过生日。(下个星期六)
5 他昨天太累了，睡了觉。(整整一天)
6 她大学毕业。(明年春天)
7 他们打算结婚。(十月)
8 我们已经认识了？(多久)
9 他们在非洲旅行了。(去年，两个月)
10 几个孩子在外面玩儿了。(今天，三个多小时)
11 他学过中文。(以前，六个星期)
12 邻居请了客。(周末，一天)

EXERCISE 4. Finish each sentence, choosing an appropriate time phrase from the parentheses.

1 小毛 _____ 去了夏令营。(一个夏天，今年夏天)
2 我们 _____ 回家了。(一个星期，上个星期)
3 周末我们打了 _____ 的球。(两个钟头，两点钟)
4 一年有 _____。(十二个月，十二月)
5 现在上午 _____。(九点二十分钟，九点二十分)
6 我室友昨天 _____ 两点才睡。(一夜，夜里)

EXERCISE 5. Translate into Chinese.

1 We watch the news every day at 6 p.m.
2 He gave a 20-minute speech.
3 We have waited here for three hours!
4 The fall semester starts in September.

5　The old man takes a half-hour nap every afternoon.
6　That salesperson works six days a week.

§25.　Time phrase (iii): . . . 的时候 de shíhou

The clause containing the time phrase . . . 的时候 *de shíhou* 'while . . . , when . . .'
complements the action in the main clause. See example 25a.

25a　上中文课的时候，学生一定得说中文。
　　　　shàng-zhōngwénkè de shíhou, xuésheng yídìng děi **shuō-zhōngwén**
　　　　'While attending Chinese class, students must speak Chinese.'

What precedes . . . *de shíhou* has various structures. It is either a verb-object
phrase, as 25a–b, or more commonly a short clause, as 25c–d. The structure
[VP/clause + *de shíhou*] is normally followed by a comma, which means that
the time specified should occur in the first of the two clauses. The subject of
the complex sentence is usually at the beginning of the second clause, as in
25a–c. If there are two subjects, e.g. *māma* 'mom' and *háizi* 'the child'
in 25d, each initiates its respective clause.

25b　讲课的时候，老师用了幻灯图片。
　　　　jiǎng-kè de shíhou, lǎoshī yòng-le huàndēng túpiàn
　　　　'While lecturing in class, the teacher used slides.'

25c　在电影院看电影的时候，很多人吃爆米花。
　　　　zài diànyǐngyuàn kàn-diànyǐng de shíhou, hěnduō rén chī-bàomǐhuā
　　　　'While watching movies in the cinema, many people eat popcorn.'

25d　妈妈不在家的时候，孩子吃了很多巧克力。
　　　　māma bú zàijiā de shíhou, háizi chī-le hěnduō qiǎokèlì
　　　　'When mom was not home, the child ate a lot of chocolate.'

In English a clause led by 'while' may appear in the second half of a
complex sentence. For instance, an alternative translation of 25a is 'Students
must speak Chinese while attending Chinese class.' In Mandarin, however,
the clause with . . . *de shíhou* must be in the first half of the complex
sentence. 25e is unacceptable in Mandarin.

25e　✕ 我常常听音乐，*在图书馆学习的时候。
　　　　wǒ chángcháng tīng-yīnyuè, zài túshūguǎn xuéxí **de shíhou**
　　　　'I often listen to music while studying at the library.'
　　　　✓ 在图书馆学习的时候，我常常听音乐。
　　　　zài túshūguǎn xuéxí **de shíhou**, wǒ chángcháng tīng-yīnyuè

A clause with ... 的时候 *de shíhou* 'while ...' must begin the complex sentence.

For related topics, see §§15 and 39.

Exercises

EXERCISE 6. Translate into Chinese.

1   Some people use a cell phone while driving.
2   He is polite when asking directions.
3   When we first met, she had long hair.
4   While travelling in Africa, I ran into an old schoolmate. (碰到)

§26. Time phrase (iv): 以前 *yǐqián*

The time word 以前 *yǐqián* 'in the past' may appear in either of the following two forms in a Mandarin sentence: i) alone; or ii) placed after another time reference.

First, used alone, *yǐqián* 'in the past, formerly, previously' refers to a time prior to the utterance. It may stand either before or after the subject of a sentence, as in 26a–b respectively. It may also take a noun-phrase position in a comparison, as in 26c.

26a   以前我不懂中文。

   yǐqián wǒ bù dǒng-zhōngwén

   'Previously I didn't understand Chinese.'

26b   他们以前住在费城。

   tāmen **yǐqián** zhù zài Fèichéng

   'They previously lived in Philadelphia.'

26c   我们学校比以前大多了。

   wǒmen xuéxiào bǐ **yǐqián** dà duō le

   'Our school is much larger than it was before.'

Second, *yǐqián* is placed immediately after an expression of chronological time (26d), durational time (26e), a verb phrase (26f), or a clause (26g) to form a specific **time-when** expression, meaning 'before. . . .' Attached to the word, phrase, or clause, *yǐqián* can be shortened to 前 *qián*. The entire expression functions as an adverbial modifier to the main action. The phrase with (以)前 *(yǐ)qián* must precede the main verb phrase in a sentence, whereas the subject of the sentence may stand before or after the phrase with *(yǐ)qián*. See examples 26d–g.

26d 你十点（以）前可以在办公室找到老师。

nǐ **shídiǎn (yǐ)qián** kěyǐ zài bàngōngshì zhǎo-dào lǎoshī

'You may find the teacher in her office before 10 o'clock.'

26e 她两年（以）前还是一个中学生。

tā **liǎng-nián (yǐ)qián** háishì yí-gè zhōngxuéshēng

'She was still a high school student two years ago.'

26f 吃饭（以）前，你应该洗手。

chī-fàn (yǐ)qián, nǐ yīnggāi xǐ-shǒu

'You should wash your hands before dinner.'

26g 我每天去医院上班（以）前遛狗。

wǒ **měitiān qù yīyuàn shàng-bān (yǐ)qián** liù-gǒu

'I walk the dog every day before going to work at the hospital.'

In the case of 以前 *yǐqián*, errors seem to arise from using English as a filter.

26h ✖ *以前练习书法，我需要准备好笔墨和纸。

yǐqián liànxí shūfǎ, wǒ xūyào zhǔnbèi-hǎo bǐ mò hé zhǐ

'?Practicing calligraphy in the past, I need to be ready with brush, ink, and paper.'

▶ **Problem**: When *yǐqián* is not placed after another time reference, it means 'in the past,' or 'previously.' The first phrase therefore means 'when I previously practiced calligraphy,' which is not what the sentence intends to say. To say 'before practicing calligraphy,' one needs to place *yǐqián* **after** the verb phrase *liànxí-shūfǎ* 'to practice calligraphy.'

✔ 练习书法以前，我需要准备好笔墨和纸。

liànxí shūfǎ **yǐqián**, wǒ xūyào zhǔnbèi-hǎo bǐ mò hé zhǐ

'Before practicing calligraphy, I need to be ready with brush, ink and paper.'

26i ✖ 中国人不常排队*以前上车。

Zhōngguórén bùcháng pái-duì **yǐqián** shàng-chē

(Intending to say: 'Chinese people do not often stand in line before getting on buses.')

▶ **Problem**: A phrase-by-phrase translation from an English sentence, the Mandarin verb phrase here creates chaos. Guessing at the intended meaning of 26i, one might say '?Chinese people do not often get on buses before they stand in line'; or '?Chinese people did not often stand in line previously when they tried to get on buses.' Neither guess would work. To express the idea of the English sentence above, place *yǐqián* **after** the VP *shàng-chē* 'get on buses'; then place this entire phrase with *yǐqián* before the main VP *bùcháng pái-duì* 'not often stand in line.' Remember, the phrase with *yǐqián* must precede the main verb phrase.

✔ 中国人上车以前不常排队。

Zhōngguórén **shàng-chē yǐqián** bùcháng pái-duì

26j   我在吃晚饭的＊前，常常相当饿。

wǒ **zài chī-wǎnfàn de qián**, chángcháng xiāngdāng è

'Before dinner I am often hungry.'

▶ **Problem**: The first clause is unacceptable in Mandarin. The shortened word *qián* can never be used as a noun and placed after 的 *de*, and neither *yǐqián* nor *qián* appears in the structure 在 *zài* ... 的 *de* ... 'at. . . .' To fix, simply place *yǐqián* **after** the verb phrase *chī-wǎnfàn* 'to have dinner.'

 我吃晚饭以前常常相当饿。

wǒ chī-wǎnfàn yǐqián chángcháng xiāngdāng è

Used alone, 以前 *yǐqián* is a time word meaning 'in the past.' Used with another time reference, e.g. 'before Friday' or 'before eating,' the other time reference should precede *yǐqián*, and this entire expression must precede the main verb phrase in a sentence.

For related topics, see §§22, 24, 38, and 39.

Exercises

EXERCISE 7. Translate into Chinese.

1 She used to smoke.
2 Please do not call me before 7 a.m.
3 We didn't know each other before.
4 Where did you live before?
5 Before reading the text, we'd better learn the vocabulary first.
6 Do you need to change some money before traveling abroad?

§27. Time phrase (v): 时时刻刻 *shíshíkèkè*

时时刻刻 *shíshíkèkè* 'continuously, always' is a time expression, used as an adverbial modifier to the verb, as in 27a–b.

27a 他时时刻刻提醒自己要冷静。

tā **shíshíkèkè** tíxǐng zìjǐ yào lěngjìng

'He constantly reminds himself to be calm.'

27b 财迷时时刻刻想发财。

cáimí **shíshíkèkè** xiǎng fā-cái

'The miser always wants to get rich.'

While using this expression, however, one needs to understand the literal meaning of this compound phrase since the simple translations 'constantly,' or 'always' easily lead to its misuse. 时 *shí* is 'an hour' and 刻 *kè* is 'a quarter of an hour.' The compound duplicative phrase *shíshíkèkè* literally means 'every single moment of time.' This literal meaning should be grasped as the precise value of translations compressed to 'always' or 'constantly.' Any action using this expression as its adverbial modifier must acknowledge its literal denotation. Keep in mind that only a few actions literally occupy or last '(at) all times.' An adverbial modifier, *shíshíkèkè* always precedes the verb phrase in a sentence, as shown in 27a–b.

 Both 27c and 27d overlook the literal meaning of the phrase 时时刻刻 *shíshíkèkè* 'every single moment of time.' Neither action, *qù jiàn péngyou* 'go to see friends' in 27c or *chī Zhōngguócài* 'eat Chinese food' in 27d, can occupy every single minute. Hence, *shíshíkèkè* cannot apply in these cases. Other adverbs, e.g. 常常 *chángcháng* 'often,' or 总是 *zǒngshì* 'always,' may replace *shíshíkèkè*.

27c ⊗ 他*时时刻刻去见他的中国朋友。
    tā **shíshíkèkè** qù jiàn tāde Zhōngguó péngyou
    ?'He goes to see his Chinese friends at all times.'

    ✅ 他常常去见他的中国朋友。
    tā **chángcháng** qù jiàn tāde Zhōngguó péngyou

27d ⊗ 她真喜欢中国菜，所以她*时时刻刻吃中国饭。
    tā zhēn xǐhuan Zhōngguócài, suǒyǐ tā **shíshíkèkè** chī Zhōngguócài
    'She really likes Chinese food, so she always eats Chinese food.'

    ✅ 她真喜欢中国菜，所以她总是吃中国菜。
    tā zhēn xǐhuan Zhōngguócài, suǒyǐ tā **zǒngshì** chī Zhōngguócài

> Be aware that the simple translation of the time phrase 时时刻刻 *shíshíkèkè* as 'constantly' or 'always' overlooks its literal meaning 'every single moment of time.'

 For related topics, see §24.

Exercises

EXERCISE 8. (§§25–27) Fill the blanks with 的时候 *de shíhou*, 以前 *yǐqián*, or 时时刻刻 *shíshíkèkè*.

1 我 _____ 没听说过这件事。
2 旅行 _____，你最好带着地图。
3 这几天他 _____ 想着她。

4 考试 _____，我们一定得复习。
5 妹妹出国 _____，我们都去机场送她。
6 他 _____ 注意着股票市场的情况。
7 中国人吃饭 _____ 一般用筷子。
8 进门 _____，请你先敲敲门。
9 很久 _____，这里还有很多树。
10 你吃东西 _____，最好不要说话。

§28. V-了 *le*: completed action

The Mandarin aspect marker -了 *le* is a verb suffix. When it attaches to the verb, the structure V-*le* indicates that the action by the verb is completed. The completion of the action signified by -*le* refers to a time either in the past or in the future. See examples 28a–c. Note that sentences with V-*le* may be expressed in English by the past, the present perfect, or the future perfect tenses.

28a   我们昨天去了动物园。
       wǒmen zuótiān qù-**le** dòngwùyuán
       'We went to the zoo yesterday.'

28b   他们买了一个冰箱。
       tāmen mǎi-**le** yí-ge bīngxiāng
       'They have bought a refrigerator.'

28c   明年我的中国朋友毕了业可能回国。
       míngnián wǒde Zhōngguó péngyou bì-**le**-yè kěnéng huíguó
       'My Chinese friend will probably return to her country next year after
          she graduates.'

28c is an example demonstrating that -*le* should not be taken as a past-tense marker because, while it indicates the completion of an action, the occurrence of such action is not limited to past time. In 28c, the time phrase *míngnián* 'next year' clearly sets the action *bìyè* 'graduate' in the future. Yet -*le* is still used in this case to stress that *bìyè* will be a completed action prior to another action, *huíguó* 'return to her country,' i.e. by the time she returns to her country, she will have graduated (a completed action).

The suffix -*le* is not a past-tense marker for an additional reason: some past-tense actions do not need it. E.g. the action 'travel' in 28d is set in the year 1998. Yet the verb in this case does not take -*le* since the sentence does not stress the completion of the action 'traveling.'

28d   我一九九八年在中国旅行。
       wǒ yī jiǔ jiǔ bā nián zài Zhōngguó lǚxíng
       'I traveled/was traveling in China in 1998.'

Negation

In the negation of this structure, the negative adverb 没（有）*méi(yǒu)* 'has not' appears before the verb to express the non-occurrence or incompletion of the action, as in 28e. The suffix -*le* therefore drops out when the negation *méi(yǒu)* takes over.

28e   我没（有）从图书馆借书。
       wǒ **méi(yǒu)** cóng túshūguǎn jiè-shū
       'I didn't check out any books from the library.'

Interrogative forms

The structure V-*le* has three approaches in its yes/no interrogative form, as shown in 28f–h: with question particle 吗 *ma* (28f), in the A-not-A form (28g), and with the negation 没有 *méiyǒu* as the question particle (28h). Note that in both 28f and 28h, -*le* immediately precedes the question particle *ma* or *méiyǒu*. The latter form also allows a variation, 28h′, with -*le* attached to the verb. This variation, however, is not an option for 28f in which *ma* is used. There are, therefore, the following ways (28f–h′) to ask the question: 'Have you watched that movie?'

28f   Subj.+ V + Obj.+ 了 *le* + 吗 *ma*
       你看那个电影了吗？
       nǐ kàn nèi-ge diànyǐng le **ma**?

28g   Subj.+ V-没 *méi*-V + Obj.
       你看没看那个电影？
       nǐ **kàn-méi-kàn** nèi-ge diànyǐng?

28h   Subj.+ V + Obj.+ 了 *le* + 没有 *méiyou*
       你看那个电影了没有？
       nǐ kàn nèi-ge diànyǐng **le méiyou**?

28h′ Subj.+ V-了 *le* + Obj.+ 没有 *méiyou*
       你看了那个电影没有？
       nǐ kàn-**le** nèi-ge diànyǐng **méiyou**?

Examples 28i–l are commonly made errors. In each case, the asterisk marks the specific problem. The idea that each of these sentences intended to express is given in parentheses.

28i   ✗ 你看见李老师了吗？我没看见她*了。
       nǐ kànjiàn Lǐ lǎoshī le ma? wǒ méi kànjiàn tā **le**
       ('Have you seen Teacher Li? I haven't seen her.')
       ▶ **Analysis**: Once the adverb *méi* negates the completion of the action, the suffix -*le* must be dropped.

✅ 你看见李老师了吗？我没看见她。
nǐ kànjiàn Lǐ lǎoshī le ma? wǒ **méi** kànjiàn tā

28j   ✖ 他原来说要来这个学校，其实*不来了。
tā yuánlái shuō yào lái zhèi-ge xuéxiào, qíshí **bù lái le**

('He originally said that he was coming to this school. In fact he didn't come.')

▶ **Analysis**: The negative adverb for this structure should be *méi*, not *bù*; and the suffix -*le* must be dropped in a negation.

✅ 他原来说要来这个学校，其实没来。
tā yuánlái shuō yào lái zhèi-ge xuéxiào, qíshí **méi** lái

28k   ✖ 小孩子吃饭以前*洗了手没洗手？
xiǎo háizi chīfàn yǐqián **xǐ-le-shǒu méi xǐshǒu**?

('Did the little child wash his hands before the meal?')

▶ **Analysis**: cf. 28g. The A-not-A form should be: V-没 *méi*-V + Obj.

✅ 小孩子吃饭以前洗没洗手？
xiǎo háizi chīfàn yǐqián **xǐ-méi-xǐ** shǒu?

28l   ✖ 他*说了我们去芝加哥，我*说了这真是一个好主意。
tā shuō-**le** wǒmen qù Zhījiāgē, wǒ shuō-**le** zhèi zhēn shì yí-ge hǎo zhúyi

('He said we were going to Chicago. I said that was a really good idea.')

▶ **Analysis**: -*le* is erroneously used as a past-tense marker. Neither -*le* is needed here because the emphasis is not on the completed action 'he/I said.'

✅ 他说我们去芝加哥，我说这真是一个好主意。
tā shuō wǒmen qù Zhījiāgē, wǒ shuō zhèi zhēn shì yí-ge hǎo zhúyi

The verb suffix -了 *le* indicates a completed action, and should not be taken as a past-tense marker. The negative form of this structure is 没(有) *méi(yǒu)*. *Méi(yǒu)* and -*le* never appear in the same sentence.

For related topics, see §§18, and 30.

Exercises

EXERCISE 9. Answer each question in both its positive and its negative forms.

e.g. Q: 你昨天上网了吗？ A₁: 我昨天上网了。 A₂: 我昨天没(有)上网。

1 你在咖啡里放牛奶了吗？
2 他的话，你听懂了吗？
3 你说完了没有？
4 进来以前，你敲门了没有？

EXERCISE 10. Translate into Chinese. (Note that not all of them need the verb suffix -了 *le*.)

1 She went to see a doctor two days ago.
2 He didn't watch last evening's news.
3 Last week it rained every day.
4 At dinner, they drank one bottle of red wine.
5 We didn't know you were abroad last year.
6 Has the student finished his homework?

§29. Emphasis on complements: the 是 *shì* . . . 的 *de* pattern

The 是 *shì* . . . 的 *de* pattern only addresses an action that has already occurred. This pattern emphasizes circumstances surrounding the action, such as time, location, means, or purpose, rather than the completed action itself. It asks or answers questions about when, where, with whom, why, or how the action has occurred.

In the *shì* . . . *de* frame, *shì* stands immediately before the emphasized element and *de* always appears after the main verb and usually at the end of the sentence. In an affirmative statement *shì* can be omitted. 29a–f are some examples.

29a Emphasizing time:
　　他们（是）昨天晚上到的。
　　tāmen (shì) **zuótiān wǎnshāng** dào de
　　'They arrived last night.'

29b Emphasizing location:
　　他们（是）从上海来的。
　　tāmen (shì) **cóng Shànghǎi** lái de
　　'They came from Shanghai.'

29c Emphasizing means:
　　我们（是）坐火车来的。
　　wǒmen (shì) **zuò-huǒchē** lái de
　　'We came by train.'

29d   Emphasizing company:

我们（是）跟父母一起来的。

wǒmen (shì) **gēn fùmǔ yìqǐ** lái de

'We came <u>with our parents</u>.'

29e   Emphasizing purpose:

她（是）去那儿学法律的。

tā (shì) qù-nàr **xué-fǎlǜ** de

'She went there <u>to study law</u>.'

29f   Emphasizing the subject:

（是）我锁的门。

(shì) **wǒ** suǒ de mén

'<u>It was I</u> who locked the door.'

While *de* usually stands at the end of the sentence, there is one exception—when the main verb has a noun object, such as *mén* 'door' in 29f or *zhèi-zhāng-huàr* 'this painting' in 29g, *de* normally stands between the verb and its object, as shown in 29f–g. A common variant is to place such an object at the beginning of the sentence as in 29g'.

29g   我是在中国买的这张画儿。

wǒ shì zài Zhōngguó mǎi de **zhèi-zhāng-huàr**

'I bought the painting in China.'

29g'   这张画儿，我是在中国买的。

zhèi-zhāng-huàr, wǒ shì zài Zhōngguó mǎi de

'This painting, I bought it in China.'

The structure of 29g' is not an option if the object is a pronoun, e.g. *tā* 'her' in 29h and 29h'. In such a case *de* may appear at the end of the sentence (29h) or between the verb and its pronoun object (29h').

29h   我是开车去机场接她的。

wǒ shì kāi-chē qù jīchǎng jiē **tā** de

'I went to the airport to pick her up in my car.'

29h'   我是开车去机场接的她。

wǒ shì kāi-chē qù jīchǎng jiē de **tā**

'I went to the airport to pick her up in my car.'

Negation

While *shì* may be omitted in an affirmative statement, it must be retained in a negative statement, and it is always preceded by the negative adverb 不 *bù*. 29d'–f' are the negative counterparts of 29d–f.

29d′   我们<u>不</u>是跟父母一起来的。
wǒmen **bú** shì gēn fùmǔ yìqǐ lái de
'We didn't come with our parents.' (We came alone.)

29e′   她<u>不</u>是去那儿学法律的。
tā **bú** shì qù-nàr xué-fǎlǜ de
'She didn't go there to study law.' (She went there to study medicine.)

29f′   <u>不</u>是我锁的门。
bú shì wǒ suǒ de mén
'It was not I who locked the door.' (Someone else did it.)

Interrogative forms

As discussed in §18, the same two basic methods form a yes/no question with the *shì . . . de* pattern, i.e. either adding the question particle 吗 *ma* to the end of the sentence (29i) or using the A-not-A form, which is always 是不 是 *shì-bú-shì* (29j) in this structure.

29i   他是去年毕业的<u>吗</u>？
tā shì qùnián bì-yè de **ma**?
'Did he graduate last year?'

29j   他<u>是不是</u>去年毕业的？
tā **shì-bú-shì** qùnián bì-yè de?
'Did he graduate last year?'

The same procedure for forming a question that uses an interrogative word also applies to the *shì . . . de* pattern: namely, to place the interrogative word, when, where, who(m), how, etc., in the position that reflects the circumstance emphasized. See examples 29k–m.

29k   Q: 他是<u>什么时候</u>来的？   ⇨   A: 他是<u>昨天</u>来的。
tā shì **shénme shíhou** lái de?   tā shì **zuótiān** lái de
'<u>When</u> did he come?'   'He came <u>yesterday</u>.'

29l   Q: 他是<u>怎么</u>来的？   ⇨   A: 他是<u>坐飞机</u>来的。
tā shì **zěnme** lái de?   tā shì **zuò-fēijī** lái de
'<u>How</u> did he come?'   'He came <u>by plane</u>.'

29m   Q: 他是<u>从哪儿</u>来的？   ⇨   A: 他是<u>从纽约</u>来的。
tā shì **cóng nǎr** lái de?   tā shì **cóng Niǔyuē** lái de
'<u>Where</u> did he come from?'   'He came <u>from New York</u>.'

29n   ✖ 我是十七岁的时候开始工作*。
wǒ shì shíqī-suì de shíhòu kāishǐ gōngzuò
'I started to work when I was 17.'

▶ **Problem**: *de* is missing at the end of the sentence. In the *shì . . . de* pattern, while *shì* may be omitted in an affirmative statement, *de* must always be present.

✅ 我是十七岁的时候开始工作的。
wǒ shì shíqī-suì de shíhòu kāishǐ gōngzuò **de**

29o ❌ 是跟谁*他去打球的？
shì gēn shéi tā qù dǎ-qiú de?
'With whom did he go play ball?'

▶ **Problem**: The subject *tā* 'he' is in the wrong place. It should be at the beginning of the sentence. The *shì . . . de* structure is a frame that emphasizes a particular element of an action, but does not alter the basic word order of the sentence.

✅ 他是跟谁去打球的？
tā shì gēn shéi qù dǎ-qiú de?

29p ❌ 你是*用没用信用卡买这个礼物的？
nǐ shì yòng-méi-yòng xìnyòngkǎ mǎi zhèi-ge-lǐwù de?
'Did you buy this gift with your credit card?'

▶ **Problem**: Ill-formed yes/no question. If one chooses to use the A-not-A structure to form a *shì . . . de* question, the 'A' is always *shì*, not the main verb. In other words, it is always *shì-bú-shì* (cf. 29j).

✅ 你是不是用信用卡买这个礼物的？
nǐ **shì-bú-shì** yòng xìnyòngkǎ mǎi zhèi-ge-lǐwù de?

This pattern emphasizes the complements to a past action, such as time, location, means, or purpose. To form a yes/no question in this structure, either add the particle 吗 *ma* at the end or use 是不是 *shì-bú-shì*. When the complements are interrogatives, the word order remains the same.

For related topics, see §§18, 19, and 30.

Exercises

EXERCISE 11. Change the sentences into the 是 *shì* . . . 的 *de* pattern, emphasizing the underlined segment.

1　她父母<u>昨天晚上</u>回去了。
2　他们<u>坐出租车</u>去郊外了。
3　<u>她妈妈</u>把这件事告诉她了。
4　我去<u>中国</u>学中文了。
5　我<u>上中学的时候</u>去中国学了中文。

6　他花了两千块钱买了新电脑。
7　那个孩子在墨西哥出生了。
8　妹妹从学校回来了。
9　弟弟跟我们一起去滑雪了。

EXERCISE 12. (§§18 & 29) For each sentence, ask a question about the underlined segment.

1　她父母是昨天晚上回去的。
2　他们是坐出租车去郊外的。
3　是她妈妈把这件事告诉她的。
4　我是上中学的时候去中国学的中文。
5　他是花了两千块钱买的新电脑。
6　那个孩子是在墨西哥出生的。
7　妹妹是从学校回来的。
8　弟弟是跟我们一起去滑雪的。

§30.　Completed action vs. its complements: V-了 *le* vs. 是 *shì* . . . 的 *de*

While both the sentence with V-了 *le* and the 是 *shì* . . . 的 *de* pattern describe an already completed action, a fundamental difference lies between their emphases.

A V-*le* sentence emphasizes the completion of the action, whereas the *shì* . . . *de* pattern stresses the particular circumstances related to the action. Compare 30a and 30b. Both sentences refer to a past event of two people getting married. While 30a, with V-*le*, simply states that such an event did occur, 30b, in the *shì* . . . *de* pattern, stresses the time—it was last year—when the event occurred.

30a　他们去年结婚了。
　　　tāmen qùnián jié-hūn **le**
　　　'They got married last year.'

30b　他们是去年结婚的。
　　　tāmen **shì** qùnián jié-hūn **de**
　　　'It was last year when they got married.'

The difference between 30a and 30b may also be captured by considering what question either one may answer. While 30a responds to a question **whether** (or not) the event occurred (30c), 30b stresses the **time** (when) such an event took place (30d). 30c′–d′ are the Mandarin equivalents of 30c–d respectively. Thus the former, 30c′, uses the V-*le* structure, while the latter, 30d′, relies on the *shì . . . de* pattern.

30c	Did they get married last year?	⇨	Yes, they <u>did</u>.
30d	When did they get married?	⇨	They got married <u>last year</u>.

30c′ 他们去年结婚<u>了</u>吗？
tāmen qùnián jié-hūn **le** ma?
'Did they get married last year?'

⇨ 对，他们去年结婚<u>了</u>。(30a)
duì, tāmen qùnián jié-hūn **le**
'Yes (lit. correct), they did.'

30d′ 他们<u>是</u>什么时候结婚<u>的</u>？
tāmen **shì** shénme shíhòu jié-hūn **de**?
'When did they get married?'

⇨ 他们<u>是</u>去年结婚<u>的</u>。(30b)
tāmen **shì** qùnián jié-hūn **de**
'They got married last year.'

We can think about the difference between the V-*le* structure and the *shì . . . de* pattern in this way: the former responds to yes/no questions—whether the event occurred or did not occur, whereas the latter responds to interrogative words that address certain circumstances. In other words, if we intend to stress the occurrence of an action, we use the V-*le* structure. If we need to stress circumstances surrounding the action, we use the *shì . . . de* pattern. See 30e–i.

30e After work, <u>did she do anything</u>? Yes.
她下班以后从办公室开车去机场接先生<u>了</u>。
tā xiàbān yǐhòu cóng bàngōngshì kāi-chē qù-jīchǎng jiē xiānsheng **le**
'After work, she drove from the office to the airport to pick up her husband.'

30f When did she go to the airport?
她<u>是</u>什么时候去机场<u>的</u>？
tā **shì** shénme shíhòu qù-jīchǎng **de**

⇨ She went there <u>after work</u>.
她<u>是</u>下班以后去<u>的</u>。
tā **shì** xiàbān yǐhòu qù **de**

30g From where did she go to the airport?
她<u>是</u>从哪儿去机场<u>的</u>？
tā **shì** cóng nǎr qù-jīchǎng **de**

⇨ She went there <u>from the office</u>.
她<u>是</u>从办公室去<u>的</u>。
tā **shì** cóng bàn′gōngshì qù **de**

30h By what means did she go to the airport?
她<u>是</u>怎么去机场<u>的</u>？
tā **shì** zěnme qù-jīchǎng **de**

⇨ She went there <u>by car</u>.
她<u>是</u>开车去<u>的</u>。
tā **shì** kāi-chē qù **de**

30i For what purpose did she go to the airport?
她<u>是</u>为什么去机场<u>的</u>？
tā **shì** wèishénme qù-jīchǎng **de**

⇨ She went there <u>to pick up her husband</u>.
她<u>是</u>去接先生<u>的</u>。
tā **shì** qù jiē xiānsheng **de**

In the use of either the V-了 *le* structure or the 是 *shì* . . . 的 *de* pattern, the cause of most errors appears to be an incomplete grasp of their respective functions. See the following examples. The idea that each of these sentences means to express is given in parentheses.

30j (How did you go home?   I went home by bus.)

*你怎么回家了?   我坐公车回家。

nǐ zěnme huí-jiā le?   wǒ zuò-gōngchē huí-jiā

▶ **Analysis:** Contrary to what they mean to say, these Mandarin clauses express two unrelated ideas: '?How come you went home?' and 'I go home by bus.' To show the idea in the parentheses, one simply applies the *shì* . . . *de* pattern to both clauses, emphasizing the action's circumstance 'how.' The action *huí-jiā* 'going home,' is achieved by *zuò-gōngchē* 'taking the bus.'

✅ 你是怎么回家的?   我是坐公车回家的。

nǐ **shì** zěnme huí-jiā **de**?   wǒ **shì** zuò-gōngchē huí-jiā **de**

30k (When did you study German?   I studied it last year.)

你是什么时候学德文的?   *我去年学德文。

nǐ **shì** shénme shíhòu xué-déwén de? wǒ qùnián xué-déwén

▶ **Analysis:** The problem here is the second clause, which responds to the question of the first clause, but does not remain in the same grammatical structure. The *shì* . . . *de* pattern solves this problem by emphasizing the temporal circumstance, *qùnián* 'last year.'

✅ 我是去年学的(德文)。

wǒ **shì** qùnián xué **de** (déwén)

30l (We all know that you traveled. But we don't know which month you departed. And we don't know when you returned.)

我们都知道你去旅行了。*可是我们不知道你几月去旅行,*我们也不知道你什么时候回来。

wǒmen dōu zhīdào nǐ qù lǚxíng le. kěshì wǒmen bù-zhīdào nǐ jǐyuè qù lǚxíng, wǒmen yě bù-zhīdào nǐ shénme shíhòu huílai

▶ **Analysis:** In this example, none of the three clauses by itself is ill-formed. While the first clause states clearly, however, that the person has already traveled, the second and third units then, by not using the *shì* . . . *de* pattern, obscure the context. By not using the *shì* . . . *de* pattern, these two clauses mean: 'We don't know which month you will be traveling. Neither do we know when you will return.'

✅ 可是我们不知道你是几月去旅行的,我们也不知道你是什么时候回来的。

kěshì wǒmen bù-zhīdào nǐ **shì** jǐyuè qù lǚxíng **de**, wǒmen yě bù-zhīdào nǐ **shì** shénme shíhòu huílai **de**

V-了 *le* emphasizes the fact of the action's completion. The 是 *shì* ... 的 *de* pattern, on the other hand, stresses the particular circumstances related to a completed action, e.g. at what time, where, by what means, or for what purpose the action occurred.

For related topics, see §§18, 19, 28, and 29.

Exercises

EXERCISE 13. Choose the correct Chinese translation of each English sentence.

1 It was in Italy that they became acquainted.

    a) 他们在意大利认识了。
    b) 他们是在意大利认识的。

2 They became acquainted in Italy.

    a) 他们在意大利认识了。
    b) 他们是在意大利认识的。

3 Grandpa drank three cups of coffee.

    a) 爷爷喝了三杯咖啡。
    b) 爷爷是喝三杯咖啡的。

4 Did you sleep for only five hours yesterday?

    a) 你昨天只睡了五个小时吗？
    b) 你昨天是只睡了五个小时的吗？

5 It was on the second floor that they lived.

    a) 他们住在二楼了。
    b) 他们是住在二楼的。

6 My sister bought this car last year.

    a) 我姐姐去年买了这辆车。
    b) 我姐姐是去年买的这辆车。

7 It was last year that my sister bought this car.

    a) 我姐姐去年买了这辆车。
    b) 我姐姐是去年买的这辆车。

8 The doctor let the patient go home.

   a) 医生让病人回家了。
   b) 医生是让病人回家的。

9 She wore a white blouse today.

   a) 她今天穿了一件白衬衫。
   b) 她今天是穿一件白衬衫的。

10 It was the subway that Mr. Feng took to the city.

   a) 冯先生坐地铁进城了。
   b) 冯先生是坐地铁进城的。

11 Mr. Feng took the subway to the city.

   a) 冯先生坐地铁进城了。
   b) 冯先生是坐地铁进城的。

§31. Adverbs 才 *cái* and 就 *jiù* (i): after a time phrase

When the adverbs 才 *cái* and 就 *jiù* are placed after a time phrase, they are a part of that temporal statement. Here their similarity ends, for in this pattern they are opposites.

Cái implies that the action, identified by the verb that follows it, takes place later than expected, in the sense of 'not until then'; or 'only until then (does the action occur).' This 'then' is the time phrase that precedes *cái*. See example 31a.

Jiù, on the other hand, implies that the action, identified by the verb that follows it, takes place sooner than expected, in the sense of 'as soon/early as (a certain time).' See example 31b. Again, the time phrase that precedes *jiù* is the 'certain time' it refers to.

31a 我明天才回去。 wǒ míngtiān **cái** huíqu 'I won't return until tomorrow.'	**31b** 我明天就回去。 wǒ míngtiān **jiù** huíqu 'I'll return as early as tomorrow.'

Note that 31a and 31b use the same structure, with *cái* and *jiù* each occupying the same position. In most cases, such as in 31a–b and 31d–e, the time phrase before *cái* or *jiù* is chronological time, i.e. it refers to 'until **when**' or 'as early as **when**' the action after *cái* or *jiù* occurs. We formulate the pattern as in 31c.

31c Subj. + chronological time + 才 *cái*/就 *jiù* + VP

If the action is a past occurrence, the sentence with *jiù* ends with the particle 了 *le*, as in 31e. *Le*, however, never appears in a sentence with *cái*, as illustrated in 31d.

31d 电影七点开始，李先生七点一刻才来。

d
diànyǐng qīdiǎn kāishǐ, Lǐ xiānsheng qīdiǎn yíkè **cái** lái

'The movie started at 7:00. Mr. Li didn't arrive until 7:15.'

31e 电影七点开始，王先生六点半就来了。

diànyǐng qīdiǎn kāishǐ, Wáng xiānsheng liùdiǎn bàn **jiù** lái le

'The movie started at 7:00. Mr. Wang arrived early, at 6:30.'

Although not as common, a durational time phrase can also be used before either adverb *cái* or *jiù*, as in examples 31g–h. Durational time phrases refer to **time-spent**. In a sentence with *cái* or *jiù*, durational time indicates the length of time a prior action takes before the consequent second action occurs, i.e. the one that follows *cái* or *jiù*. *Cái* implies that the first action takes a longer time than expected, whereas *jiù* implies that the first action takes a shorter time than expected. The verb phrase representing the second action should come after the adverb *cái* or *jiù*.

31f shows the sentence structure with a durational time phrase. Note that in indicating the completion, the verb suffix *-le* is a necessary complement to the first action (V_1); and stands between V_1 and the durational time phrase. If the first action involves an object, $Obj._1$ comes after the durational time (with an optional 的 *de*), e.g. *duì* 'line' in 31g. This structure may also allow a second subject for the second action (VP_2), e.g. *tā* 'he' in 31h. $Subj._2$ should precede the adverb *cái* or *jiù*.

31f $Subj._1$ + V_1 + 了 *le* + durational time + ((的 *de*) $Obj._1$) + ($Subj._2$)
　　　　才 *cái*/就 *jiù* + VP_2

31g 我排了三个小时（的）队才买到球票。

wǒ pái-le sān-ge-xiǎoshí (de) duì **cái** mǎi-dào qiúpiào

'I had to stand in line three hours for the (baseball) tickets.' (It took that long a time for me to obtain the tickets.)

31h 我等了五分钟他 就来了。

wǒ děng-le wǔ-fēnzhōng **tā jiù** lái le

'I only waited for five minutes before he came.' (I didn't wait long before he showed up.)

Placing the adverbs 才 *cái* or 就 *jiù* after a time phrase, one needs to follow either the pattern in 31c if the time phrase is chronological time; or the pattern in 31f if the time phrase is durational time. Errors such as 31i–j violate the basic rules.

31i ✖ 她*才现在想起来今天是她妹妹的生日。

tā cái **xiànzài** xiǎng-qǐlai jīntiān shì tā mèimei de shēngrì

'Only now does she remember that today is her sister's birthday.'

▶ **Problem**: *Cái* is put before the time word *xiànzài* 'now.' *Cái* should appear after the time phrase.

✔ 她<u>现在</u> <u>才</u>想起来今天是她妹妹的生日。

tā <u>xiànzài</u> <u>cái</u> xiǎng-qǐlai jīntiān shì tā mèimei de shēngrì

31j ✖ 我的室友*<u>三个小时</u>就起来了。

wǒde shìyǒu **sān-ge-xiǎoshí** jiù qǐlai le

'My roommate got up as early as ?three hours.'

▶ **Problem**: The time phrase *sān-ge-xiǎoshí* 'three hours' is durational time. Durational time needs a V-*le* structure when used before *jiù* (cf. 31f). If the idea is 'My roommate got up after having slept for only three hours,' add the verb 睡 *shuì* 'sleep' together with the verb suffix -了 *le* before the durational time. If, on the other hand, the idea is 'My roommate got up as early as three o'clock,' use the chronological time 三点钟 *sān-diǎn zhōng* '3:00.'

✔ 我的室友<u>睡了</u>三个小时就起来了。

wǒde shìyǒu <u>shuì-le</u> sān-ge-xiǎoshí jiù qǐlai le

✔ 我的室友<u>三点钟</u>就起来了。

wǒde shìyǒu <u>sān-diǎn zhōng</u> jiù qǐlai le

Used in identical structures, as in 31c and 31f, the adverbs 才 *cái* and 就 *jiù* in opposed ways cue their respective temporal statements. In either pattern, *cái* or *jiù* stands **after** the time reference and **before** the verb.

For related topics, see §§17, 22, 24, 28, 32, and 54.

Exercises

EXERCISE 14. (§§31–32) Fill in the blanks with 才 *cái* or 就 *jiù*.

1   昨天晚上我们看电视看得很晚，夜里一点 _____ 睡。
2   小马早上起了床以后 _____ 洗澡。
3   他们六月结婚。大家昨天 _____ 知道了，我今天 _____ 知道。
4   爸爸说他七点回家吃晚饭，可是他六点 _____ 回来了。
5   你什么时候去？我现在 _____ 去。
6   那本书，她看了三个星期 _____ 看完。
7   那个孩子三岁了 _____ 会走路。
8   他锁好门 _____ 离开了。

§32. Adverbs 才 *cái* and 就 *jiù* (ii): after a prior action

As a variation of pattern 31f, either adverb 才 *cái* or 就 *jiù* may be placed after a prior action, in the structure outlined in 32a. The prior action is represented by V₁ followed either by the verb complement 完 *wán* 'finish' or by the verb suffix -了 *le*, plus an optional Obj.₁. The adverb *cái* or *jiù* is then followed by another action represented by VP₂. See examples 32b–c.

32a Subj.₁ + V₁ + 完 *wán*/了 *le* + (Obj.₁) + (Subj.₂) 才 *cái*/就 *jiù* + VP₂

32b 孩子洗完/了手才吃饭。
háizi xǐ-wán/le-shǒu **cái** chī-fàn
'Only after the child washes his hands, may he eat.'

32c 孩子洗完/了手就吃饭。
háizi xǐ-wán/le-shǒu **jiù** chī-fàn
'Once the child washes his hands, he will eat.'

In pattern 32a, either the verb complement *wán* 'finish' or the verb suffix *-le* is a required complement to mark the completion of the prior action (V₁). In this structure, *cái* indicates that the completion of the prior action (V₁) is a condition for the action that follows (VP₂), i.e. 'not until the finishing of action V₁, does VP₂ occur.' See 32d–e. Note that if action VP₂ has a different subject, such as *guānzhòng* 'audience' in 32e, it stands before the adverb *cái*.

32d 我看了小说才知道谁是杀手。
wǒ kàn-**le**-xiǎoshuō cái zhīdao shéi shì shāshǒu
'Only after I read the mystery did I know who the killer was.'

32e 她演讲完，观众才开始提问。
tā yǎnjiǎng-**wán**, **guānzhòng** cái kāishǐ tíwèn
'She finished the speech; only then did the audience start asking questions.'

With the adverb *jiù*, pattern 32a is a structure of sequential actions. The adverb *jiù* here indicates 'then' or 'consequently,' introducing VP₂, which takes place after the completion of V₁. *Jiù* hence marks VP₂ as the consequent action upon the completion of the prior action (V₁). Note that the object of V₁, if there is one, comes after *wán* or *-le*, e.g. *xìn* 'letter' in 32f and *wǔfàn* 'lunch' in 32g. And if both actions occur in the past, a second *le* should be added at the end of the sentence, as in 32g.

32f 她写完信就去寄。
tā xiě-wán-**xìn** jiù qù jì
'Once she finishes writing the letter, she will mail it.'

32g 他们吃了午饭就去上课了。

tāmen chī-le-**wǔfàn** jiù qù shàng-kè **le**

'After they'd had lunch, they went to class.'

Summary: when the adverbs *cái* and *jiù* are used **after** a prior action, as in the structure 32a, i) V₁ must be followed either by the verb complement *wán* or by the verb suffix *-le*; ii) *wán* or *-le* precedes Obj₁, if there is one; iii) if there is a Subj.₂, it must precede *cái* or *jiù*; and iv) the sentence particle *le* may appear at the end of a sentence with *jiù*, but never at the end of a sentence with *cái*.

The common errors in this case seem to arise from misplacing the adverb 才 *cái* or 就 *jiù*.

32h 我考完大考*才我的父母来接我。

wǒ kǎo-wán-dàkǎo *cái* **wǒde fùmǔ** lái jiē wǒ

'Only after I take the Final will my parents pick me up.'

▶ **Problem:** *Cái* is put before Subj.₂ *wǒde fùmǔ* 'my parents.' The second subject must precede the adverb *cái*.

✓ 我考完大考我的父母 才来接我。

wǒ kǎo-wán-dàkǎo <u>wǒde fùmǔ</u> <u>cái</u> lái jiē wǒ

32i 我卖了我的旧车*能 就买新车。

wǒ mài-le-wǒde jiù chē **néng jiù** mǎi xīn chē

'Once I have sold my old car, I will be able to buy a new one.'

▶ **Problem:** The auxiliary verb *néng* 'be able to' is put before the adverb *jiù*. The auxiliary verb *néng* is part of VP₂ (see §57) and the entire VP₂ should be modified by the adverb *jiù*. *Jiù* therefore should precede *néng*.

✓ 我卖了我的旧车就 能买新车。

wǒ mài-le-wǒde jiù chē <u>jiù</u> néng mǎi xīn chē

Either 才 *cái* or 就 *jiù* may stand after a prior action, in the structure 32a. *Cái* stresses the completion of the prior action as the condition for the action that follows, whereas *jiù* emphasizes the action that follows as a consequence.

For related topics, see §§17, 28, 31, 41, 54, and 57.

Exercises

EXERCISE 15. (§§31–32) Translate into Chinese, using the grammar pattern given in parentheses.

1   They are not coming until next week. (才)
2   Only when we have the money, will we be able to buy the TV. (才)
3   She had her lunch early, at 11 a.m. (就 . . . 了)
4   Once you pay the bill, we will leave. (就)

§33. Action lasting to a certain point: V-到 *dào* + time phrase

Attached to the main verb, the verb 到 *dào* 'reach, arrive' here functions as a verb complement, meaning 'up to.' The chronological time expression that follows *dào* specifies the moment to which the action leads. The sentence structure is as in 33a, which means '(at the point specified) someone does/did something till. . . .' See examples 33b–d.

33a   Time reference + Subj. + V-Obj. + V-到 *dào* + chronological time

33b   昨天晚上她们聊天儿聊到十二点。
zuótiān wǎnshang tāmen liáo-tiānr **liáo-dào shí'èr diǎn**
'Last night they chatted till 12 o'clock.'

33c   今天下午中文班考试要考到五点。
jīntiān xiàwǔ zhōngwénbān kǎo-shì yào **kǎo-dào wǔ diǎn**
'This afternoon, the Chinese exam will last until 5 o'clock.'

33d   张先生动了手术，得在医院住到星期三。
Zhāng xiānsheng dòng-le shǒushù, děi zài yīyuàn **zhù-dào xīngqīsān**
'After the operation, Mr. Zhang must stay in hospital until Wednesday.'

Note that if the verb phrase is a V-Obj. form, e.g. *liáo-tiānr* 'chat' in 33b and *kǎo-shì* 'take an exam' in 33c, the verb must be repeated, since *dào* as the verb complement only attaches to the verb. In 33d, because the verb *zhù* 'stay' does not involve an object, it need not be repeated.

33e   ✖ 我们上星期六*跳舞到夜里一点。
wǒmen shàng xīngqīliù **tiào-wǔ-dào** yèlǐ yìdiǎn
'Last Saturday we danced until one in the morning.'

► **Problem**: The verb-complement *dào* attaches to the object *wǔ*, which is a noun. Because the verb phrase *tiàowǔ* 'dance' is a V-Obj. structure, the verb *tiào* must be repeated since *dào* only attaches to the verb.

✔ 我们上星期六跳舞跳到夜里一点。
wǒmen shàng xīngqīliù tiào-wǔ **tiào-dào** yèlǐ yìdiǎn

33f   ✖ 昨天我不舒服，因此，我睡觉睡到*十个钟头。
zuótiān wǒ bù shūfu, yīncǐ, wǒ shuì-jiào **shuì-dào shí-ge-zhōngtóu**
'I didn't feel well yesterday, so I slept ?up to ten hours.'

▶ **Problem**: *Shí-ge-zhōngtóu* 'ten hours' is durational time. What follows V-*dào* must be chronological time. If the idea is 'I slept until 10 o'clock (chronological time),' the Mandarin should be:

✅ 我睡觉睡到<u>十点</u>

wǒ shuì-jiào shuì-dào <u>shídiǎn</u>

If, however, the idea is 'I slept for ten hours (durational time),' V-*dào* is not the right phrase to use since this sentence is not concerned with chronological time. Instead, the verb suffix -了 *le* should follow the verb *shuì* and the sentence becomes:

我睡觉<u>睡了</u>十个钟头。

wǒ shuì-jiào <u>shuì-le</u> shí-ge-zhōngtóu

(cf. §§22, 24, and 28)

33g ✗ 我很喜欢看书，有时候会*早上三点*才停看书。

wǒ hěn xǐhuan kàn-shū, yǒushíhou huì **zǎoshang sāndiǎn cái tíng kàn-shū**

'I really like to read. Sometimes it is 3 o'clock in the morning before I stop.'

▶ **Problems**: i) *Zǎoshang* 'morning' is an erroneous way to refer to 3 a.m. (see §23); ii) *Cái tíng kàn-shū* 'only then stop reading' is a literal translation from English. However, it is not an acceptable phrase in Mandarin. Use the [V-*dào* + chronological time] pattern for this sentence.

✅ 我很喜欢看书，有时候会<u>看到夜里三点</u>。

wǒ hěn xǐhuan kàn-shū, yǒushíhou huì <u>kàn-dào yèlǐ sāndiǎn</u>

'I really like to read. Sometimes I read till 3 o'clock in the morning.'

A suffix of the main verb, but not of the verb-object phrase, 到 *dào* 'up to' specifies the moment the action leads to. The time phrase that follows *dào* must represent chronological time (when).

For related topics, see §§22, 23, 24, 28, 38, 39, and 41.

Exercises

EXERCISE 16. Finish each sentence, choosing an appropriate word or phrase from the parentheses.

1   他们等飞机 _____ 夜里十一点多。(等到，到)
2   他昨天工作 _____ 晚上九点。(工到，到)
3   我们星期六晚上玩儿到夜里 _____ 才睡。(两个钟头，两点钟)
4   下雨下到晚上 _____ 才停。(八点，八个多小时)

EXERCISE 17. Translate into Chinese, using the grammar pattern V-到 *dào*.

1   Every Tuesday, we have class till 4 p.m.
2   He waited for you till 9:30.
3   They watched television till 2 in the morning.
4   The winter here is long. It snows until April.

Check your grammar

Translate these phrases/sentences into Chinese, and then check to see that you have implemented the relevant grammar points. The parenthetical numbers and letters identify the pertinent subsections and examples.

1   12 p.m. (§23k)
2   2 a.m. (§23l)
3   7 p.m. (§23m)
4   10 a.m. (§23n)
5   I will go to Chicago this weekend. (§24m)
6   I plan to go to China to study Chinese for one semester. (§24n)
7   I normally go to bed at six o'clock. (§24p)
8   I normally sleep for six hours. (§24q)
9   I often listen to music while studying at the library. (§25e)
10 Before practicing calligraphy, I need to be ready with brush, ink and paper. (§26h)
11 Chinese people do not often stand in line before getting on buses. (§26i)
12 Before dinner I am often hungry. (§26j)
13 He often goes to see his Chinese friends. (§27c)
14 She really likes Chinese food, so she always eats Chinese food. (§27d)
15 Have you seen Teacher Li? I haven't seen her. (§28i)
16 He originally said that he was coming to this school. In fact he didn't come. (§28j)
17 Did the little child wash his hands before the meal? (§28k)
18 He said we were going to Chicago. I said that was a really good idea. (§28l)
19 I started to work when I was 17. (§29n)
20 With whom did he go play ball? (§29o)
21 Did you buy this gift with your credit card? (§29p)
22 How did you go home? I went home by bus. (§30j)
23 When did you study German? I studied it last year. (§30k)
24 We all know that you traveled. But we don't know which month you departed. And we don't know when you returned. (§30l)

25   Only now does she remember that today is her sister's birthday. (§31i)
26   My roommate got up after having slept for only three hours. / My roommate got up as early as three o'clock. (§31j)
27   Only after I take the Final will my parents pick me up. (§32h)
28   Once I have sold my old car, I will be able to buy a new one. (§32i)
29   Last Saturday we danced till one in the morning. (§33e)
30   I didn't feel well yesterday, so I slept until 10 o'clock / for ten hours. (§33f)
31   I really like to read. Sometimes I read till 3 o'clock in the morning. (§33g)

 Notes

4 Noun and verb phrases

§34. Modifier + 的 *de* (i): adjectives as modifiers of nouns

In regard to descriptive adjectives as modifiers of nouns, we recognize three categories: monosyllabic adjectives, polysyllabic adjectives, and monosyllabic adjectives modified by an adverb.

First, most monosyllabic Mandarin adjectives can be used like English adjectives to modify a noun. See those in 34a where the nouns are all modified by monosyllabic adjectives.

34a

高山	大河	小城	好书
gāo shān	**dà** hé	**xiǎo** chéng	**hǎo** shū
'tall mountain'	'big river'	'small town'	'good book'

老人	懒猫	新车	旧地址
lǎo rén	**lǎn** māo	**xīn** chē	**jiù** dìzhǐ
'old people'	'lazy cat'	'new car'	'old address'

Second, most polysyllabic adjectives require a suffix -的 *de* when modifying nouns, as in 34b.

34b

有意思的故事	容易的考试	好看的衣服
yǒuyìsi-de gùshi	**róngyì**-de kǎoshì	**hǎokàn**-de yīfu
'interesting story'	'easy exam'	'good-looking clothing'

舒服的椅子	和蔼的老师	用功的学生
shūfu-de yǐzi	**hé'ǎi**-de lǎoshī	**yònggōng**-de xuésheng
'comfortable chair'	'amiable teacher'	'hard-working student'

Third, when monosyllabic adjectives are modified by adverbs, the descriptive adjective phrases are obviously polysyllabic. Thus modified monosyllabic adjectives likewise require the use of *-de*. See examples in 34c, where the monosyllabic adjectives are modified by negation *bù* 'not,' *hěn* 'very,' *-jíle* 'extremely,' and *zuì* 'the most.'

34c   <u>不重要</u>的事   <u>很忙</u>的人
       bú zhòngyào-de shì   **hěn máng**-de rén
       'unimportant matter'   'very busy people'

       <u>贵极了</u>的东西   <u>最大</u>的河
       guì jíle-de dōngxi   **zuì dà**-de hé
       'extremely expensive things'   'the largest river'

Finally, for idiomatic reasons, in a few phrases polysyllabic adjectives can omit *-de*, as in 34d.

34d   <u>聪明</u>人   <u>有钱</u>人   <u>便宜</u>货
       cōngming rén   **yǒuqián** rén   **piányi** huò
       'intelligent person'   'wealthy people'   'cheap goods'

The most common error in this case is the missing 的 *de* from polysyllabic modifiers such as *bù hǎo* 'not good' in 34e and *nánchī* 'insipid' in 34f.

34e   ✗ 小毛不用功，他是*<u>不好</u>学生。
       Xiǎomáo bú yònggōng, tā shì **bù hǎo** xuésheng
       'Xiaomao does not work hard. He is not a good student.'

       ✓ 小毛不用功，他<u>不是</u>好学生。
       Xiǎomáo bú yònggōng, tā **bú shì** hǎo xuésheng

       ▶ **Note**: While a *de* should be added between the polysyllabic modifier *bù hǎo* and the noun, as in 不好的情况 *bù-hǎo de qíngkuàng* 'bad situation,' or 不好的话 *bù-hǎo de huà* 'unkind remarks,' in this case, the more idiomatic way, as in English, is to negate the verb 是 *shì*, as in this correction.

34f   ✗ 我不要去学校餐厅吃*难吃饭。
       wǒ bú yào qù xuéxiào cāntīng chī **nánchī** fàn
       'I don't want to go to the school cafeteria to eat the insipid food.'

       ✓ 我不要去学校餐厅吃难吃的饭。
       wǒ bú yào qù xuéxiào cāntīng chī **nánchī-de** fàn

Polysyllabic adjectives require a suffix 的 *de* when they modify nouns. This rule also applies to the modified monosyllabic adjectives when they modify nouns.

For related topics, see §§35 and 46.

Exercises

EXERCISE 1. Where necessary, insert 的 *de* between the modifier and the noun.

1	热茶	5	很大城市	9	新汽车
2	干净房间	6	鲜花	10	难题
3	有趣故事	7	短铅笔	11	不甜西瓜
4	旧电脑	8	安静夜晚	12	非常小湖

§35. Modifier + 的 *de* (ii): clauses as modifiers of nouns

English phrases such as "the bicycle *that I bought . . .*" or "my friend *who lives in Boston . . .*" contain a subordinate clause (see italics) that modifies the noun antecedent to the relative pronoun (*that* and *who* in these cases). In contrast to English, a Mandarin subordinate clause that serves as a modifier stands **before** the noun it modifies, linked by 的 *de*. The modified noun phrase uses the structure: Modifier + 的 *de* + N.

The subordinate clause preceding *de* can use multiple structures. See examples 35a–f. In 35a–c, the subject of the subordinate clause is omitted because it is actually the noun being modified, i.e. the one that comes after *de*. In 35d–f, the object of the subordinate clause is the noun being modified.

35a Modifier = V-Obj. phrase:
喝咖啡的人
hē-kāfēi de rén
'the person who drinks/is drinking coffee'

35b Modifier = Aux. + V-Obj. phrase:
会说中文的美国学生
huì-shuō-zhōngwén de Měiguó xuésheng
'American students who can speak Chinese'

35c Modifier = Location + V phrase:
在书店工作的女孩儿
zài shūdiàn-gōngzuò de nǚháir
'the girl who works at the bookstore'

35d Modifier = Subj. + V phrase
她写的信
tā-xiě de xìn
'the letter she wrote'

35e Modifier = Subj. + location + V phrase
我在中国认识的朋友
wǒ-zài Zhōngguó-rènshi de péngyou
'the friend(s) I met in China'

35f Modifier = (Subj. +) time + V phrase
（他们）去年买的房子
(tāmen) qùnián-mǎi de fángzi
'the house (they) bought last year'

The structure [Modifier + 的 *de* + N] remains a noun phrase. This modified noun phrase functions grammatically as a simple noun in a sentence, in spite of containing a subordinate clause. For instance, 35a, *hē-kāfēi de rén* 'the person who drinks/is drinking coffee' can be either the subject of a sentence, as in 35g, or the object, as in 35h.

35g 那个喝咖啡的人是我的朋友。
nèi-ge **hē-kāfēi de rén** shì wǒde péngyou
'The person who is drinking coffee is my friend.'

35h 我认识那个喝咖啡的人。
wǒ rènshi nèi-ge **hē-kāfēi de rén**
'I know the person who is drinking coffee.'

While intending to compose a modified noun with a subordinate clause in Mandarin, some students habitually use English word order. For instance, 35b 'American students who can speak Chinese' may be directly translated to Mandarin as 35i.

35i 美国学生会说中文
Měiguó xuésheng huì shuō-zhōngwén
'American students can speak Chinese.'

The problem here is that although 35i is well-formed, it does **not** create the modified noun phrase 35b that it seeks. 35i is a complete sentence with a subject, *Měiguó xuésheng* 'American students'; an auxiliary, *huì* 'can'; a verb, *shuō* 'speak'; and an object, *zhōngwén* 'Chinese.'

> A subordinate clause that serves as a modifier stands **before** the noun it modifies. The clause and the noun are linked by 的 *de*. The structure of the modified noun phrase is: Modifier (clause) + 的 *de* + N.

For related topics, see §46.

Exercises

EXERCISE 2. Translate into Chinese.

1   the dictionary that she often uses
2   the engineer whose family name is Wang
3   the book I read last week
4   the person who takes the train to work
5   the car he bought recently
6   The car he bought recently is a Toyota (丰田 *fēngtián*).
7   The person who takes the train to work is tall.
8   She really likes the movie we watched last week.

§36. Location phrases

Location phrases indicate place or position. 36a contains basic location words.

36a 东 *dōng* 'east'; 西 *xī* 'west'; 南 *nán* 'south'; 北 *běi* 'north'
上 *shàng* 'above'; 下 *xià* 'below'; 左 *zuǒ* 'left'; 右 *yòu* 'right'
前 *qián* 'front'; 后 *hòu* 'behind'; 里 *lǐ* 'inside'; 外 *wài* 'outside'
对 *duì* 'across from'; 旁 *páng* 'next to'; 中 *zhōng* 'in the middle'

These basic location words may take the suffixes 面 *-miàn*, 边（儿）*-biān(r)*, 头 *-tou*, or 间（儿）*-jiān(r)*. Most of them allow more than one possibility. 36b lists some examples.

36b Location words with their suffixes
东 *dōng*: 东面; 东边（儿） 　　前 *qián*: 前面; 前边（儿）; 前头
西 *xī*: 西面; 西边（儿） 　　后 *hòu*: 后面; 后边（儿）; 后头
南 *nán*: 南面; 南边（儿） 　　里 *lǐ*: 里面; 里边（儿）; 里头
北 *běi*: 北面; 北边（儿） 　　外 *wài*: 外面; 外边（儿）; 外头

上 *shàng*: 上面; 上边（儿）; 上头 　　对 *duì*: 对面
下 *xià*: 下面; 下边（儿）; 下头 　　旁 *páng*: 旁边（儿）
左 *zuǒ*: 左面; 左边（儿） 　　中 *zhōng*: 中间（儿）
右 *yòu*: 右面; 右边（儿）

Some locations words do not take the suffixes above, as 36c illustrates.

36c 附近 *fùjìn* 'near'; 楼上 *lóushàng* 'upstairs'; 楼下 *lóuxià* 'downstairs'
顶上 *dǐngshang* 'top'; 底下 *dǐxia* 'beneath'; 当中 *dāngzhōng* 'in the midst'
东北 *dōngběi* 'northeast'; 东南 *dōngnán* 'southeast'
西北 *xīběi* 'northwest'; 西南 *xīnán* 'southwest'

To point out the specific position, other nouns or pronouns may stand before these location words to form a location phrase. A modifier 的 *de* usually appears between the noun and the location word. Yet this *de* can be omitted. See the examples in 36d.

36d 图书馆（的）对面 *túshūguǎn (de) duìmiàn* 'across from the library'
袋子（的）里边（儿）*dàizi (de) lǐbiān(r)* 'inside the bag'
书柜（的）顶上 *shūguì (de) dǐngshang* 'on top of the bookcase'
床（的）底下 *chuáng (de) dǐxia* 'under the bed'
学校（的）附近 *xuéxiào (de) fùjìn* 'near the school'
城（的）西北 *chéng (de) xīběi* 'to the northwest of the city'

36e lists some idiomatic location phrases where one of the basic location words, usually 上 *shàng* 'above,' 里 *lǐ* 'inside,' or 外 *wài* 'outside,' attaches to its noun to form an abbreviated location phrase. Note that both *shàng* 'above' and *lǐ* are pronounced in the neutral tone when attached to a noun.

36e 桌上 *zhuō-shang* 'on the table'
报上 *bào-shang* 'in the newspaper'
墙上 *qiáng-shang* 'on the wall'
地上 *dì-shang* 'on the floor'
街上 *jiē-shang* 'in the street'
家里 *jiā-li* 'at home'
窗外 *chuāng-wài* 'out the window'

Some students may wish to translate the English location phrases into Mandarin word by word. Thus they produce a phrase that is not a location phrase in Mandarin but a modified noun phrase. For example, 'across from the library' in Mandarin is 图书馆（的）对面 *túshūguǎn (de) duìmiàn*. If one follows the word order in the English phrase, one would have 36f. Nothing is grammatically wrong with 36f, but as the translation shows, it means something else other than 'across from the library.'

36f 对面的图书馆
duìmiàn de túshūguǎn
'the library that is across from (here)'

Comparing 36g with 36h, we receive rather different messages. The difference here is that for location phrases, the modifier noun, i.e. the reference, must stand before the location word (36g, *túshūguǎn (de) duìmiàn*), whereas for a modified noun phrase, the location word stands before the noun and 的 *de* cannot be omitted (36h).

36g 我在图书馆（的）对面等你。
wǒ zài **túshūguǎn (de) duìmiàn** děng nǐ
'I will be waiting for you across from the library.'

36h 我在对面的图书馆等你。

wǒ zài **duìmiàn de túshūguǎn** děng nǐ

'I will be waiting for you at the library that is across from (here).'

In contrast with English, the site specified for a Mandarin location phrase, e.g. 'the school' in 'outside the school,' stands **before** the location word 'outside': 学校(的)外面 *xuéxiào (de) wàimiàn*.

For related topics, see §§34 and 35.

Exercises

EXERCISE 3. Choose the correct Chinese translation of each location phrase.

1 in front of the supermarket

   a) 超级市场的前边(儿)
   b) 前边(儿)的超级市场

2 southeast of the city

   a) 东南的城市
   b) 城市的东南

3 on the second floor of the dorm

   a) 二楼的宿舍
   b) 宿舍的二楼

4 between the two people

   a) 两个人的中间(儿)
   b) 中间(儿)的两个人

5 in the railway station

   a) 里边(儿)的火车站
   b) 火车站的里边(儿)

6 under the chair

   a) 椅子的下面
   b) 下面的椅子

7 across from Starbucks

   a) 星巴克的对面
   b) 对面的星巴克

8   above the jewelry store

  a)   楼上/上面的珠宝店
  b)   珠宝店的楼上/上面

EXERCISE 4. Finish each sentence, using the Chinese terms equivalent to the location phrases in parentheses.

1   _____ 有一个小房子。 (on top of the hill)
2   _____ 到处是花草。 (inside the park)
3   _____ 的位子空着。 (to my left)
4   _____ 是农田。 (next to the highway)
5   _____ 停着很多自行车。 (outside the library)
6   校区就在 _____。 (near the lake)
7   他们在 _____ 装车。 (behind the restaurant)
8   孙子坐在 _____。 (between grandpa and grandma)

§37. Definite and indefinite references of nouns

Mandarin does not have words that correspond to the English articles 'the' and 'a(n).' 37a–e are a few possible combinations of Mandarin noun phrases that coincide with the ideas of 'the' (definite reference) and 'a(n)' (indefinite reference). Let us take the noun 书 *shū* 'book' as an example, and list these combined noun phrases in 37a–e.

37a   N: 书 *shū* '(the) books'
37b   Num + Mea + N: 一本书 *yì-běn-shū* 'one/a book'
37c   Dem + Num + Mea + N: 这十本书 *zhèi-shí-běn-shū* 'these ten books'
37d   Dem + Mea + N: 这本书 *zhèi-běn-shū* 'this book/the book'
37e   Dem + 些 *xiē* (Mea) + N: 这些书 *zhèi-xiē-shū* 'these books/the books'

37a is a simple noun. With neither a demonstrative nor a quantity, it can be either definite (the books) or indefinite (books). 37b, in the structure [Num + Mea + N], shows quantified nouns in Mandarin, e.g. *yì-běn-shū* 'one book'; 两只鸟 *liǎng-zhī-niǎo* 'two birds'; and 十个学生 *shí-ge-xuésheng* 'ten students.'

37c, in the structure [Dem + Num + Mea + N], with a demonstrative 这 *zhèi* 'this' (or 那 *nèi* 'that') appearing before the quantified noun phrase, points specifically to a particular item or a group of items, e.g. *zhèi-yì-běn-shū* 'this (one) book'; *nèi-liǎng-zhī-niǎo* 'those two birds'; and *zhèi-shí-ge-xuésheng* 'these ten students.' With a demonstrative, *zhèi* 'this' (or *nèi* 'that'), when the noun is a single item, the number *yī* 'one' is usually omitted, as in 37d: Dem + Mea + N, e.g. *zhèi-běn-shū* 'this book'; or *nèi-zhī-niǎo* 'that bird.'

In 37e, the suffix *xiē* 'a few' is the measure for a plural noun phrase. Attached to the demonstrative *zhèi* (or *nèi*), *xiē* replaces any other measure to indicate the plurality of the noun phrase, e.g. *zhèi-xiē-shū* 'these (few) books'; or *nèi-xiē-niǎo* 'those (few) birds.'

Using a demonstrative, *zhèi* 'this' (or *nèi* 'that'), the last three illustrations, 37c–e, show noun phrases with definite references. The difference between 37c and 37e is that for 37c we know there are exactly ten books in the group, and the number is deliberately specified, whereas for 37e the number of the books is unspecified.

37a–b represent nouns or noun phrases with indefinite reference. In Mandarin, however, if a noun (or a noun phrase, e.g. *zhōngwén kè*, 'Chinese class') has neither a demonstrative nor a quantity, such as 37a, its definite or indefinite reference is usually determined by its grammatical role in the sentence. As a subject, likely preceding the verb, it is normally definite; as an object, likely in a post-verbal position, it is normally indefinite. See the translations for the noun phrase *zhōngwén kè* 'Chinese classes' in examples 37f–g.

37f 我们学校开中文课。

wǒmen xuéxiào kāi **zhōngwén kè**

'Our school offers Chinese classes.'

37g 中文课不难。

zhōngwén kè bù nán

'The Chinese classes are not difficult.'

A non-quantified noun such as 37a can be the subject of a sentence since it refers to *the books*. On the other hand, it can be completely non-referential when it is the object in a sentence—any *books* in the world. This is not the case for 37b, which, in the structure of [Num + Mea + N], is a quantified noun phrase. A quantified noun phrase such as 37b, *yì-běn-shū* 'one/a book,' with a specified number *yī* 'one,' is not completely non-referential. It refers to *a book*. That is, it has an indefinite reference in two senses: i) it refers to (any) *one* book, but not two or three books; ii) it refers to a certain book whose title is not given. In other words, the quantity defines the noun's clear indefinite reference. A quantified noun phrase therefore cannot be the subject of a sentence.

A very common error is a phrase such as 37h. Note this erroneous phrase has two measures, 些 *xiē* and 个 *ge*. As the plural suffix, *xiē* attaches to the demonstratives 这 *zhèi* 'this' and 那 *nèi* 'that' to form the plural demonstratives

这些 *zhèi-xiē* 'these' and 那些 *nèi-xiē* 'those.' Some students then simply regard *zhèi-xiē* as 'these' and *nèi-xiē* as 'those,' and use them as separate demonstratives, which produces erroneous phrases such as 37h. Remember, *xiē* is a plural suffix, but once used to modify a noun, it **replaces** the measure, and it does not appear in the same phrase with a number (cf. 37c–e).

37h ⊗ *这些十个学生
zhèi-**xiē** shí-**ge**-xuésheng
(intended: 'these ten students')

✓ 这些学生
zhèi-**xiē** xuésheng
'these students'

✓ 这十个学生
zhèi-**shí-ge**-xuésheng
'these ten students'

The problems in 37i and 37j involve the misuse of the quantified noun phrase (Num + Mea + N, 37b). A quantified noun phrase cannot be the subject of a sentence. This is the error in 37i. In this case, one does not need to use the [Num + Mea] *yíliàng*. Without this clarifying number, *qìchē* would be 'cars' with a definite reference since this noun is the subject. And the sentence would work in both Mandarin and English: 'It would be an exceptional situation if **cars** (i.e. not just one car) did not yield to pedestrians.'

37i ⊗ 在美国，*一辆汽车不让行人是很特殊的情况。
zài Měiguó, **yí-liàng**-qìchē bú ràng xíngrén shì hěn tèshū de qíngkuàng
'In America, it would be an exceptional situation if a car didn't yield to pedestrians.'

✓ 在美国，汽车不让行人是很特殊的情况。
zài Měiguó, **qìchē** bú ràng xíngrén shì hěn tèshū de qíngkuàng

The Mandarin sentence 37j is as awkward as its English translation. It sounds as if the person doesn't have one brother but may have more brothers since the number "one" is specified. There is no need in Mandarin to use a quantified object if the verb is negative. 一个 *yí-ge*, even of indefinite reference, still refers to a certain "one." In Mandarin, if a person **doesn't have** an older brother, then he doesn't have any older brothers at all.

37j ⊗ 我没有*一个哥哥。
wǒ méiyǒu **yí-ge**-gēge
?'I don't have one big brother.'

✓ 我没有哥哥。
wǒ méiyǒu gēge
'I don't have big brothers.' (Or: 'I don't have a big brother.' Now you know where the erroneous 37j comes from.)

The demonstratives 这 *zhèi* 'this' and 那 *nèi* 'that' indicate nouns of definite reference. While both quantified nouns (三本书 *sān-běn-shū* 'three books') and non-quantified nouns (书 *shū* 'books') themselves have indefinite reference, the latter becomes a definite reference when it is the subject of a sentence.

For related topics, see §§39 and 49.

Exercises

EXERCISE 5. Complete each noun phrase with the appropriate word.

1 (one) _____ 个苹果	7 (that) _____ 张地图
2 (this one) _____ 个苹果	8 (those) _____ 树
3 (these) _____ 车	9 (those eight) _____ 棵树
4 (these five) _____ 辆车	10 (this) _____ 封信
5 (nine) _____ 件衣服	11 (that one) _____ 份报
6 (which one) _____ 家商店?	12 (which) _____ 条路?

EXERCISE 6. Translate into Chinese.

1 I bought a big map.
2 All three of those cars are blue.
3 This orange is really sweet.
4 Those tourists are Korean.
5 He wants to eat these grapes.
6 There are five small restaurants on this street.
7 She has two children, a daughter and a son.
8 They booked four plane tickets to China.
9 We did not watch that movie.
10 Which dog is yours?

§38. Forms of action verbs

We recognize three forms of action verbs in Mandarin: intransitive verbs, and two derivations of transitive verbs—verb-object compounds and verb-verb compounds.

Intransitive verbs

Intransitive verbs are simple action verbs. They do not take any object, although some of them may take a verb complement. Many of the intransitive verbs are polysyllabic, as in 38a. Used in a sentence they may duplicate, such as *xiūxi-xiūxi* in 38b; be modified by an adverb such as *bùtíngde* 'unceasingly' in 38c or by an adverbial phrase such as *zài dìpíngxiàn shàng* 'above the horizon' in 38d.

38a Intransitive verbs

生长 *shēngzhǎng* 'grow (up)'   工作 *gōngzuò* 'work'

活动 *huódòng* 'exercise'   出现 *chūxiàn* 'appear'

休息 *xiūxi* 'rest'   颤抖 *chàndǒu* 'tremble'

38b 我们现在休息休息。

wǒmen xiànzài **xiūxi-xiūxi**

'Let's take a break now.'

38c 他们在冷风中不停地颤抖。

tāmen zài lěngfēng zhōng **bùtíngde chàndǒu**

'They are trembling non-stop in the cold air.'

38d 朝阳出现在地平线上。

zhāoyáng **chūxiàn zài dìpíngxiàn shang**

'The morning sun rises above the horizon.'

Verb-object compounds

Mandarin transitive verbs commonly appear with an object. Thus they are a form of verb-object compound. The object in a verb-object compound may be a generic one that is not required in the English translation, as in 38e. The object may also be a specific one, as in 38f.

38e V-Obj. compounds with a generic object:

说话 *shuō-huà* (lit. speak-speech) 'speak; talk'

看书 *kàn-shū* (lit. read-book) 'read'

吃饭 *chī-fàn* (lit. eat-rice) 'eat; dine'

38f V-Obj. compounds with a specific object:

说谎 *shuō-huǎng* (lit. speak-lie) 'lie'

看电视 *kàn-diànshì* 'watch television'

吃葡萄 *chī-pútao* 'eat grapes'

The verb and its object can be split by 一会儿 *yìhuǐr* 'a while' or 一点儿 *yìdiǎnr* 'a little,' as in *kàn-yìhuǐr-shū* 'read a while' or *shuō-yìdiǎnr-huǎng* 'tell a little lie.' For more on this topic, see §39.

Verb-verb compounds

Mandarin transitive verbs also appear in the form of verb-verb compounds. In this structure, the first verb represents the action, whereas the second verb, as a verb complement, indicates the resultant state, such as the completion, attainment, or success of the action by the first verb. While being labeled as verb-verb compounds, the majority of the verb complements (the second verb), however, are actually descriptive adjectives. See a few examples in 38g.

38g V-V/DA[complement] compounds

说定 *shuō-dìng* (lit. speak-settle) 'settle; agree on'

看见 *kàn-jian* (lit. look-perceive) 'see'

吃完 *chī-wán* (lit. eat-finish) 'finish eating'

推迟 *tuī-chí* (lit. push-late) 'postpone'

长大 *zhǎng-dà* (lit. grow-big) 'grow up'

解散 *jiě-sàn* (lit. undo-disperse) 'dismiss'

Verb-verb compounds are regarded as action verbs. They may take an object, such as *xíngqī* 'the date of departure' in examples 38h–i. Verb-verb compounds often appear in a 把 *bǎ* construction, as in 38i. (See §9 for the difference in emphasis these sentences indicate.)

38h 王先生推迟了<u>行期</u>。

Wáng xiānsheng tuī-chí le **xíngqī**

'Mr. Wang has postponed his date of departure.'

38i 王先生把<u>行期</u>推迟了。

Wáng xiānsheng bǎ **xíngqī** tuī-chí le

'Mr. Wang has postponed his date of departure.'

 Errors occur when these forms of action verbs go unrecognized, as in 38j–l.

38j ✖ 他一再地喝酒，现在*很<u>喝醉</u>。

tā yízàide hē-jiǔ, xiànzài hěn **hē-zuì**

'He kept drinking (lit. repeatedly drank). Now he is very drunk.'

▶ **Problem**: *Hē-zuì* (lit. drink-drunk) 'be drunk' is a V-V/DA compound, not a descriptive adjective. It therefore cannot be modified by the adverb *hěn* 'very.'

✔ 他一再地喝酒，现在<u>喝醉</u>了。

tā yízàide hē-jiǔ, xiànzài **hē-zuì le**

38k ✖ 今天天气真好，我们应该到外面去*<u>活一会儿动</u>。

jīntiān tiānqì zhēn hǎo, wǒmen yīnggāi dào wàimiàn qù **huó-yìhuǐr-dòng**

'Today's weather is really nice. We should go out to exercise a bit.'

▶ **Problem**: *Huódòng* 'exercise' is a simple intransitive verb. The two characters of this polysyllabic word cannot be split. To correctly express the idea, one can either put *yìhuǐr* 'a while' after the verb *huódòng*, or duplicate the verb.

✔ 我们应该到外面去<u>活动一会儿/活动活动</u>。

wǒmen yīnggāi dào wàimiàn qù **huódòng yìhuǐr/huódòng huódòng**

381   她现在在图书馆＊工作她的学期报告。
tā xiànzài zài túshūguǎn **gōngzuò tāde xuéqī bàogào**
'She is now working on her term paper at the library.'

▶ **Problem**: In Mandarin, *gōngzuò* 'work' is a simple intransitive verb that does not take an object. To correct this error, one needs a different verb, such as 写 *xiě* 'write.'

她现在在图书馆写她的学期报告。
tā xiànzài zài túshūguǎn **xiě** tāde xuéqī bàogào

Intransitive verbs, verb-object compounds, and verb-verb compounds are all action verbs. Intransitive verbs do not take an object. A modifier may split the verb and its object in a verb-object compound. Verb-verb compounds may take an object and often appear in a 把 *bǎ* construction.

For related topics, see §§9, 39, 40, 41, and 42.

 ## *Exercises*

 EXERCISE 7. Identify the following phrases as polysyllabic intransitive verb, verb-object compound, or verb-verb compound.

1	习惯	6	停车	11	喝茶
2	做功课	7	运动	12	听懂
3	记住	8	吃饭	13	以为
4	走路	9	看见	14	学会
5	打开	10	休息	15	请客

§39. Verb-object compounds

In a verb-object compound, an action verb such as 说 *shuō* 'speak' takes a generic object 话 *huà* 'speech' to form the compound 说话 *shuō-huà* (lit. speak-speech). The compound is considered the verb 'speak,' since the generic object is not required in the English translation. 39a gives some common verb-object compounds.

39a 看书 *kàn-shū* 'read-book = read'
写字 *xiě-zì* 'write-character = write'
唱歌 *chàng-gē* 'sing-song = sing'
跳舞 *tiào-wǔ* 'dance-dance = dance'
吃饭 *chī-fàn* 'eat-rice = dine'
做事 *zuò-shì* 'do-thing = work'

画画儿 *huà-huàr* 'paint-picture = paint; draw'
买东西 *mǎi-dōngxi* 'buy-thing = shop'
喝酒 *hē-jiǔ* 'drink-wine = drink (an alcoholic beverage)'
开车 *kāi-chē* 'drive-vehicle = drive'

Mandarin transitive verbs usually do not stand alone. The verb either takes a generic object, as in 39a, or a specific one, as in 39b. The verb-object compounds in 39b have the same action verbs as those in 39a, yet with more specific objects, these compounds represent different activities.

39b 看报 *kàn-bào* 'read a newspaper'
写信 *xiě-xìn* 'write a letter'
唱戏 *chàng-xì* 'act in a traditional drama'
跳水 *diào-shuǐ* 'dive'
吃素 *chī-sù* 'be a vegetarian'
做饭 *zuò-fàn* 'cook'
画图 *huà-tú* 'make a chart; draw designs'
买房子 *mǎi-fángzi* 'buy a house'
喝水 *hē-shuǐ* 'drink water'
开飞机 *kāi-fēijī* 'operate an airplane'

The object in a verb-object compound can be even more elaborate, modified by a quantity, a descriptive adjective, or a modifier clause. See a few examples in 39c.

39c V-Obj. compounds with more elaborate objects:
看两本书 *kàn-**liǎng-běn-shū*** 'read two books'
看德文书 *kàn-**déwén-shū*** 'read German books'
看畅销书 *kàn-**chàngxiāo-shū*** 'read best sellers'
看有趣的书 *kàn-**yǒuqùde-shū*** 'read interesting books'
看昨天买的书 *kàn-**zuótiān mǎide-shū*** 'read the book(s) bought yesterday'

Students sometime mistake verb-object compounds for noun phrases. Remember: no matter how elaborate the object is, the whole compound is a verb phrase, not a noun phrase. See errors 39d–e.

39d ✘ 我的身体天天需要 *一个洗澡。
wǒde shēntǐ tiāntiān xūyào **yí-ge xǐ-zǎo**
'I (lit. my body) need(s) a bath every day.'

▶ **Problem**: The verb-object compound *xǐ-zǎo* 'take a bath' is a verb, not a noun. Thus one cannot use the counter *yí-ge* 'one' before this compound ('*a taking bath'). However, one can place the counter *yí-ge* before the object *zǎo* 'bath' to make it a more elaborate one.

✓ 我的身体天天需要洗一个澡。
wǒde shēntǐ tiāntiān xūyào **xǐ-yíge-zǎo**

39e　　我很喜欢我们的＊中文上课。

wǒ hěn xǐhuan wǒmen-de **zhōngwén shàng-kè**

'I really like our Chinese ?attending class.'

> ▶ **Problem**: The verb-object compound *shàng-kè* 'attend class' is misused as a noun, and is modified by *zhōngwén* 'Chinese.' To correct the mistake, one either uses the noun phrase *zhōngwén kè* 'Chinese class,' or the verb phrase *shàng zhōngwén-kè* 'attend Chinese class.'

　我很喜欢我们的中文课。

wǒ hěn xǐhuan wǒmen-de **zhōngwénkè**

'I really like our Chinese class.'

　我很喜欢上中文课。

wǒ hěn xǐhuan **shàng-zhōngwénkè**

'I really like to attend Chinese class.'

The object in a verb-object compound may be generic (39a), or specific (39b). The object can be modified by a quantity, an adjective, or a modifier clause.

For related topics, see §§34, 35, 37, and 38.

Exercises

EXERCISE 8. Write the noun phrases in Chinese.

1　喝茶:

  a)　drink green tea;
  b)　drink a cup of hot tea;
  c)　drink the tea given (as a gift) by friends

2　坐车:

  a)　take the bus;
  b)　take the taxi;
  c)　take the noon train;
  d)　take the train (that goes) to New York

3　唱歌:

  a)　sing a song;
  b)　sing Japanese songs;
  c)　sing melodic (great-sounding) songs;
  d)　sing the songs written by him;
  e)　sing my favorite songs

4　做菜：

    a)　cook a few dishes;
    b)　cook Chinese dishes;
    c)　cook dishes with regional flavors;
    d)　cook the dishes we like

§40.　When a verb-object compound involves another object

As discussed in §39, the object in a verb-object compound may be generic or more elaborate, as in 40a–b. Either way, the object is a necessary element. In other words, for example, 'drink' (an alcoholic beverage) in Mandarin must be 喝酒 *hē-jiŭ* 'drink-wine.' The verb *hē* itself only appears in a particular context, as in the answer to 你喝酒吗？ *nĭ hē-jiŭ ma* 'Do you drink?' 喝。 *hē* 'Yes, I do.'

40a　The verb has a generic object:
    e.g. 喝<u>酒</u> *hē-jiŭ* 'drink wine = drink'

40b　The verb has a more elaborate object:
    喝<u>法国酒</u> *hē-**Făguó**-jiŭ* 'drink French wine'
    喝<u>一杯酒</u> *hē-**yì-bēi**-jiŭ* 'drink a glass of wine'
    喝<u>朋友送的酒</u> *hē **péngyou sòng de**-jiŭ* 'drink the wine sent by friends'

Verb-object compounds do not take an indirect object. Thus the two sentences in 40c are unacceptable, because the verb-object compound *fā-duănxìn* 'text' takes as its object *wŏde péngyou* 'my friend.'

40c　I often text my friends.
    ⊠ 我常常＊<u>发短信</u>我的朋友。
    wŏ chángcháng **fā-duănxìn** wŏde péngyou
    ⊠ 我常常＊<u>发</u>我的朋友<u>短信</u>。
    wŏ chángcháng **fā** wŏde péngyou **duănxìn**

Yet some verb-object compounds, such as *fā-duănxìn* 'text' in 40c and those in 40d, likely involve another object noun/pronoun, since these activities by definition likely include more than one party.

40d　说话 *shuō-huà* 'speak-speech = converse'
    聊天 *liáo-tiān* 'chat-(about) weather = chat'
    写信 *xiě-xìn* 'write-letter = write a letter'
    打电话 *dă-diànhuà* 'make-phone call = phone'
    开玩笑 *kāi-wánxiào* 'crack-joke = joke'
    结婚 *jié-hūn* 'knot-marriage = get married'

离婚 *lí-hūn* 'leave-marriage = divorce'
上当 *shàng-dàng* 'set-(foolishly) treated = be fooled'
照相 *zhào-xiàng* 'reflect-image = photograph'

To include another object noun/pronoun with the verb-object compound, one must apply different grammatical patterns. The most common way is to employ the adverb 给 *gěi* or 跟 *gēn* to introduce another object to the verb-object compound. In less common cases, the adverb 让 *ràng* is also used. The matching between these adverbs and the verb-object compounds, however, is set. Each of them only works with certain verbs. See examples 40e–g.

40e   Subj. + 给 *gěi* + Obj. + V-Obj. compound:
我常常给父母写信/打电话/发短信/照相。
wǒ chángcháng **gěi** fùmǔ xiě-xìn/dǎ-diànhuà/fā-duǎnxìn/zhào-xiàng
'I often write to/phone/text/take a picture of my parents.'

40f   Subj. + 跟 *gēn* + Obj. + V-Obj. compound:
王先生在跟邻居说话/聊天/开玩笑。
Wáng xiānsheng zài **gēn** línjū shuō-huà/liáo-tiān/kāi-wánxiào
'Mr. Wang is conversing/chatting/joking with his neighbor.'

比尔跟莎丽结婚/离婚了。
Bǐ'ěr **gēn** Shālì jié-hūn/lí-hūn le
'Bill and Sally have married/divorced.'

40g   Subj. + 让 *ràng* + Obj. + V-Obj. compound
那个商人总是让顾客上当。
nèi-ge shāngren zǒngshì **ràng** gùkè shàng-dàng
'That merchant always fools his customers.'

Most errors result from conceiving the verb-object compounds as simple action verbs, and consequently adding another object after the compounds. To correct these errors, follow the patterns in 40e–g, applying the adverbs 给 *gěi*, 跟 *gēn*, or 让 *ràng* accordingly. 40h–k are a few erroneous examples.

40h   ✖ 她总是很忙，来不及*说话她的朋友。
tā zǒngshi hěn máng, láibùjí **shuō-huà** tāde péngyou
('She is always busy, with little time for talking to her friends.')
✔ 她总是很忙，来不及跟她的朋友说话。
tā zǒngshi hěn máng, láibùjí **gēn** tāde péngyou shuō-huà

40i   ✖ 那个古董店的老板*上当我了。
nèi-ge gǔdǒngdiàn-de lǎobǎn **shàng-dàng wǒ** le
('The owner of that antique store fooled me.')
✔ 那个古董店的老板让我上了当。
nèi-ge gǔdǒngdiàn-de lǎobǎn **ràng** wǒ shàng-le-dàng

40j ❌ 我*打交道了他很多次。

wǒ **dǎ-jiāodào le tā** hěnduō cì

('I have contacted him quite a few times.')

✓ 我跟他打了很多次交道。

wǒ **gēn** tā dǎ-le hěnduō-cì jiāodào

40k ❌ 她一*离婚了她的先生，就*结婚了别的男人。

tā yì **lí-hūn le tāde xiānsheng**, jiù **jié-hūn le biéde nánren**

('As soon as she divorced her husband, she married another man.')

✓ 她一跟她的先生离了婚，就跟别的男人结了婚。

tā yì **gēn** tāde xiānsheng lí-le-hūn, jiù **gēn** biéde nánren jié-le-hūn

One needs to apply patterns 40e–g to activities that by definition involve more than one party. In these patterns an adverb such as 给 *gěi* or 跟 *gēn* introduces another object to the verb-object compound.

For related topics, see §39.

Exercises

EXERCISE 9. (§§39–40) Translate into Chinese.

1 Mom made a fruitcake.
2 We have listened to five speeches this week.
3 That child is learning how to paint.
4 Mr. Li checked out two books from the library today.
5 They only buy goods made in the United States.
6 We ordered her favorite dishes.
7 My little sister rarely writes to my parents. She always calls them.
8 She really wants to marry him.
9 Sales people deal with customers every day. (打交道)
10 He likes to joke with friends.

§41. Simple verbs vs. verb-verb compounds

As introduced in §38, Mandarin transitive verbs usually function in one of two structures: either as verb-object compounds or as verb-verb compounds. Because the latter can also take an object, 41a illustrates these three structures with the same verb 写 *xiě* 'write.'

41a　V-Obj. compound: 写信 *xiě-xìn* 'write a letter'
　　　　V-V compound: 写完 *xiě-wán* (lit. write-finish) 'finish writing'
　　　　V-V compound + Obj.: 写完信 *xiěwán-xìn* 'finish writing a letter'

The translations show that with the simple verb *xiě* 'write,' the verb-object compound 写信 *xiě-xìn* only specifies the action 'writing a letter.' To indicate that the letter is actually finished by its writer, we need to use the verb-verb compound, i.e. we need to add the second verb 完 *wán* 'finish' onto the first verb *xiě* to specify the idea 'finish writing the letter.'

Thus there is a difference between a simple verb and a verb-verb compound formed by the same action verb and its verb complement (the second verb). 41b–g offer more examples.

41b　看 *kàn* 'look' vs. 看见 *kàn-jian* (lit. look-see) 'see'
41c　看 *kàn* 'read' vs. 看懂 *kàn-dǒng* (lit. read-comprehend) 'understand (by
　　　　reading)'
41d　找 *zhǎo* 'look for' vs. 找到 *zhǎo-dào* (lit. look for-reach) 'find'
41e　买 *mǎi* 'buy' vs. 买到 *mǎi-dào* (lit. buy-reach) 'be able to buy'
41f　喝 *hē* 'drink' vs. 喝完 *hē-wán* (lit. drink-finish) 'finish drinking'
41g　带 *dài* 'bring' vs. 带回 *dài-huí* (lit. bring-return) 'bring back'

A simple verb and a verb-verb compound therefore convey different meanings. Now compare 41h, which contains the simple verb *zhǎo*, with 41i, which has the verb-verb compound *zhǎo-dào*.

41h　我们得去<u>找</u>李先生。
　　　　wǒmen děi qù **zhǎo** Lǐ xiānsheng
　　　　'We must go to look for Mr. Li.'

41i　我们得去<u>找到</u>李先生。
　　　　wǒmen děi qù **zhǎo-dào** Lǐ xiānsheng
　　　　'We must go to find Mr. Li.'

The choice of using either a simple verb or a verb-verb compound depends on what one intends to express.

41j　我们八点就开始<u>找</u>李先生，到十点才<u>找到</u>。
　　　　wǒmen bādiǎn jiù kāishǐ **zhǎo** Lǐ xiānsheng, dào shídiǎn cái **zhǎo-dào**
　　　　'We started to <u>look for</u> Mr. Li at 8 o'clock; we didn't <u>find</u> (him) until 10
　　　　o'clock.'

When students misuse the verb-verb compound, the ideas they tend to express are confusing. See the following examples.

41k   ✗ 我昨天没?看他。

wǒ zuótiān méi **kàn** tā

?'I didn't look at him yesterday.'

▶ **Analysis**: The simple verb *kàn* only means 'look at.' One needs to use the verb-verb compound *kàn-jian* '(look and) see.'

✓ 我昨天没看见他。

wǒ zuótiān méi **kàn-jian** tā

'I didn't see him yesterday.'

41l   ✗ 如果你常常练习，你就能?记很多汉字。

rúguǒ nǐ chángcháng liànxí, nǐ jiù néng **jì** hěn duō hànzì

'If you practice often, you will ?memorize many Chinese characters.'

▶ **Analysis**: The simple verb *jì* means 'memorize.' One needs to use the verb-verb compound *jì-zhù* (lit. memorize-stay) 'remember.'

✓ 你就能记住很多汉字。

nǐ jiù néng **jì-zhù** hěn duō hànzì

'You will remember many Chinese characters.'

A simple verb, e.g. 找 *zhǎo* 'look for,' and a verb-verb compound formed by the same action verb and its verb complement, e.g. 找到 *zhǎo-dào* 'find,' express different meanings. Some activities need to be described by the latter.

For related topics, see §§38 and 42.

Exercises

EXERCISE 10. (§§41–42) Finish each sentence, choosing an appropriate verb/verb compound from the parentheses.

1 现在不少美国人在 _____ 中文。(学，学会)

2 他用了三个月才 _____ 游泳。(学，学会)

3 我真没 _____ 他也来了。(想，想到)

4 他们 _____ 在湖边买房子。(想，想到)

5 这个周末他们去城外 _____ 朋友。(看，看见)

6 那个电影，你 _____ 了吗？(看，看见)

7 我们在报上 _____ 了这个消息。(看，看到)

8 你们一定得把菜 _____。(吃，吃完)

9 我们已经 _____ 了第十五课。(完，学完)

10 真冷。我们 _____ 窗子吧。(关，关上)

11 昨天，我看见你在 _____ 衣服。(洗，洗干净)

12 李大明没把那个字 _____。(写，写清楚)

§42. Verb complements (i): resultative

Verb complements refer to the second verb of verb-verb compounds, such as 到 *dào* 'reach' in 找到 *zhǎo-dào* (lit. look for-reach) 'find.' As the name suggests, the verb complement in a verb-verb structure expresses the resultant state, such as the completion, attainment, or success of the action by the first verb (找 *zhǎo* 'look for' in this case).

Commonly used verb complements generally fall into two categories: resultative verb complements (this section) and directional verb complements (see §43). The former category includes a large number of descriptive adjectives, as in 42a.

42a Commonly used RVCs (underlined):
听见 *tīng-jiàn* 'listen-<u>perceive</u> = hear'
唱完 *chàng-wán* 'sing-<u>finish</u> = finish singing'
够着 *gòu-zháo* 'reach toward-<u>touch</u> = attain'
想到 *xiǎng-dào* 'think-<u>reach</u> = think of'
抓住 *zhuā-zhù* 'grab-<u>stay</u> = hold onto'
长成 *zhǎng-chéng* 'grow-<u>become</u> = grow into'
做好 *zuò-hǎo* 'do-<u>good</u> = satisfactorily done'
猜对 *cāi-duì* 'guess-<u>right</u> = guess correctly'
听错 *tīng-cuò* 'listen-<u>wrong</u> = mishear'
写清楚 *xiě-qīngchu* 'write-<u>clear</u> = write clearly'

The verb-verb compound, formed by a simple action verb and a resultative verb complement, should be regarded as one verb and may take an object. Compare examples 42b and 42c. 42b has the simple verb *xǐ*, whereas 42c contains the verb-verb compound *xǐ-gānjing*, both taking the object *yīfu* 'clothes.'

42b 她总是星期六上午洗衣服。
tā zǒngshì xīngqīliù shàngwǔ **xǐ**-yīfu
'She always does her laundry on Saturday mornings.'

42c 她星期六一定得洗干净衣服才能做别的事。
tā xīngqīliù yídìng děi **xǐ-gānjing**-yīfu cái néng zuò biéde shì
'On Saturdays she can't do anything else until her clothes are (washed) clean.'

▶ **Note**: While regarding a Mandarin verb-verb compound as one verb, it is necessary to remain conscious of its two-part V-RVC structure. In other words, one must keep in mind the meanings of both the action verb and its verb complement. For example, the meaning of the verb-verb compound 够着 *gòu-zháo* 'reach toward-touch = attain' only means 'touch an actual object by reaching over.' One cannot use *gòu-zháo* to express the idea 'he has attained a goal.' Considering only the combined meaning of a verb-verb compound and overlooking the meaning of the action verb may lead to grammatical errors.

Using the resultative verb complement as the main verb is a common error, as shown in 42d–e. The underlined words are RVCs that cannot function as main verbs. In both cases, an action verb needs to precede the RVC.

42d ✖ 我已经*完了我的功课。
wǒ yǐjīng **wán**-le wǒde gōngkè
'I have already finished my homework.'

✔ 我已经做完 ('do-finish') 了我的功课。
wǒ yǐjīng **zuò-wán**-le wǒde gōngkè

42e ✖ 考试的时候，学生没*清楚问题。
kǎo-shì de shíhou, xuésheng méi **qīngchu** wèntí
'During the exam, the student didn't clear? the question.'

✔ 考试的时候，学生没看清楚 ('read-clear') 问题。
kǎo-shì de shíhou, xuésheng méi **kàn-qīngchu** wèntí

42f shows what happens when students simply translate the English verb 'see' into 看见 *kàn-jian*. In Mandarin, this verb-verb compound, with the verb *kàn* 'look' and the verb complement *jiàn* 'perceive,' specifies concrete visual perception, not 'visit (someone),' as was the apparent intent in 42f. To correct this error, one can use *jiàn* 'see, perceive' as the main verb.

42f ✖ 李明忘了去*看见他的老师，他很不好意思。
Lǐ Míng wàng-le qù **kàn-jian** tāde lǎoshī, tā hěn bùhǎoyìsi
'Li Ming forgot to go to see his teacher. He is embarrassed.'

✔ 李明忘了去见他的老师，他很不好意思。
Lǐ Míng wàng-le qù **jiàn** tāde lǎoshī, tā hěn bùhǎoyìsi

In a V-RVC compound, the initial verb expresses the action, whereas its verb complement (the second verb) describes the resultant state of the action. The meanings of both verbs are important.

For related topics, see §§38 and 41.

§43. Verb complements (ii): directional

Directional verb complements follow an action verb or a placement verb and indicate the direction of an action, such as 回 *huí* 'return' in 送回 *sòng-huí* 'send back' or 出去 *chūqù* 'out' in 搬出去 *bān-chūqù* 'move out.' Mandarin directional verb complements can be basically sorted into three groups: simple (43a and 43b); and compound (43d).

43a Simple DVCs (1)

-来 *lái* 'come'	e.g. 飞来 *fēi-lái* 'fly here'	
-去 *qù* 'go'	e.g. 送去 *sòng-qù* 'send over'	

来 *lái* 'come' and 去 *qù* 'go' as simple verbs respectively indicate a motion toward or away from the speaker. While serving as directional verb complements to other active verbs, they likewise indicate the direction of the action. As the examples in 43a show, the verb-verb compound *fēi-lái* (DVC = *lái*) indicates the motion of 'flying' is toward the speaker, whereas the verb-verb compound *sòng-qù* (DVC = *qù*) shows the motion of 'sending' is away from the speaker.

43b Simple DVCs (2)

-上 *shàng* 'ascent-up'	e.g. 提上 *tí-shàng* 'lift up'
-下 *xià* 'descend-down'	e.g. 放下 *fàng-xià* 'put down'
-进 *jìn* 'enter-in'	e.g. 搬进 *bān-jìn* 'move in'
-出 *chū* 'exit-out'	e.g. 卖出 *mài-chū* 'sell out'
-起 *qǐ* 'rise-up'	e.g. 拿起 *ná-qǐ* 'pick up'
-回 *huí* 'return-back'	e.g. 收回 *shōu-huí* 'collect back'
-过 *guò* 'cross-over'	e.g. 推过 *tuī-guò* 'push over'

The members of the 43b group may also function as active verbs, taking *lái* or *qù* as their directional verb complement. In other words, the verbs from 43b followed by *lái* or *qù* from 43a form the following V-DVC compounds in 43c.

43c

上来 *shànglái* 'come up here'	上去 *shàngqù* 'go up there'
下来 *xiàlái* 'come down here'	下去 *xiàqù* 'go down there'
进来 *jìnlái* 'come in here'	进去 *jìnqù* 'go in there'
出来 *chūlái* 'come out here'	出去 *chūqù* 'get out (of here)'
起来 *qǐlái* 'get up'	
回来 *huílái* 'come back here'	回去 *huíqù* 'go back there'
过来 *guòlái* 'come over here'	过去 *guòqù* 'go over there'

All the members of 43c may also serve in turn as compound directional verb complements to other active verbs. See the examples in 43d. In each of these cases, the first element, i.e. a member from the 43b group, shows the direction of the motion: up or down, in or out, etc.; and the second element, i.e. *lái* 'come' or *qù* 'go,' shows whether the direction of the action is toward or away from the speaker.

43d Compound DVCs

-上来 / -上去   e.g. 送上来/上去 *sòng-shànglái/-shàngqù*
          'send up here/there'

-下来 / -下去   e.g. 拿下来/下去 *ná-xiàlái/-xiàqù* 'take down here/there'

-进来 / -进去   e.g. 走进来/进去 *zǒu-jìnlái/-jìnqù* 'walk in here/there'

-出来 / -出去   e.g. 搬出来 / 出去 *bān-chūlái/-chūqù*
          'move out (from there/here)'

-起来   e.g. 站起来 *zhàn-qǐlái* 'stand up'

-回来 / -回去   e.g. 跑回来/回去 *pǎo-huílái/-huíqù* 'run back here/there'

-过来 / -过去   e.g. 跳过来/过去 *tiào-guòlái/-guòqù* 'jump over here/there'

Like the V-RVC compounds, V-DVC compounds may take an object, as in 43e. And they often appear in a 把 *bǎ* construction, as in 43f.

43e   姐姐拿出一条漂亮的围巾。

jiějie ná-chū **yì-tiáo piàoliang de wéijīn**

'The older sister took out a pretty scarf.'

43f   学生把中文字典带来了。

xuésheng bǎ **zhōngwén zìdiǎn** dài-lái le

'The student brought the Chinese dictionary here.'

When a V-DVC structure takes a compound directional verb complement, i.e. those from the 43d group, its object may appear either after the whole V-DVC structure (43g) or before *lái* or *qù* (43h).

43g   马先生送过来一瓶酒。

Mǎ xiānsheng sòng-guòlái **yì-píng-jiǔ**

'Mr. Ma sent over a bottle of wine.'

43h   马先生送过一瓶酒来。

Mǎ xiānsheng sòng-guò **yì-píng-jiǔ** lái

'Mr. Ma sent over a bottle of wine.'

If, however, the direction of the motion involves a location, such as *chéng* 'the city' in 43i, this location word must appear just before the final ending *lái* or *qù*. Now compare 43i with 43i' below; the latter is grammatically unacceptable.

43i   他把车开回城去了。

tā bǎ chē kāi-huí **chéng**-qù le

'He drove the car back to the city.'

43i′   *他把车开回去城了。
tā bǎ chē kāi-huíqù **chéng** le

 A common error is the misplaced location word. See the ill-formed example 43j. Remember: if the direction of the motion involves a location, *túshūguǎn* 'the library' in this case, the location word must appear immediately **before** the final ending *lái* or *qù*.

43j   图书馆员说学生不能把字典*借<u>出</u>去图书馆。
túshūguǎnyuán shuō xuésheng bùnéng bǎ zìdiǎn jiè-**chūqù** túshūguǎn
'The librarian says that students can't check the dictionaries out of the library.'

   ...学生不能把字典借<u>出</u>图书馆去。
xuésheng bùnéng bǎ zìdiǎn jiè-**chū** túshūguǎn **qù**

> While not in the 把 *bǎ* construction, the object of a V-DVC compound may appear either after the whole V-DVC structure (43g) or before 来 *lái* or 去 *qù* (43h). The latter, however, is the only choice for an object that is a location (43i).

 For related topics, see §§9, 38, 41, and 42.

Exercises

EXERCISE 11. Fill in the blanks with directional complements 下，进，出，回，起，来 or 去, using each only once.

1   请进！请坐 _____ 吧！
2   她不喜欢这儿，所以搬 _____ 以前的宿舍去了。
3   天气真好。我们出 _____ 走走吧？
4   上课以前，学生走 _____ 教室。下课以后，学生走 _____ 教室。
5   聚餐的时候，他带 _____ 一个新朋友。
6   他忽然想 _____ 一件事。

§44. Verb-verb compounds: actual and potential forms

Verb-verb compounds appear in a sentence in one of two forms: the **actual** or the **potential**. The actual form addresses the occurrence or non-occurrence of the compound's action, e.g. whether a person actually heard (听见了 *tīngjiàn le*) or did not hear (没听见 *méi tīngjiàn*). The potential form addresses the ability to accomplish the action, e.g. whether the person is able or unable to hear.

Actual form

The actual form of a verb-verb compound, as shown in 44a–b, functions as a simple verb. The occurrence of the V_{action} + V_{result} is indicated by the verb suffix -了 *le* following the compound, and its non-occurrence by the negation 没(有) *méi(yǒu)* preceding the compound.

44a The action has succeeded. (Positive: V-V + 了 *le*)

警察抓到了小偷。

jǐngchá **zhuā-dào le** xiǎotōu

'The police caught the thief.'

44b The action has not succeeded. (Negative: 没（有） *méi(yǒu)* + V-V)

警察没（有）抓到小偷。

jǐngchá **méi(yǒu) zhuā-dào** xiǎotōu

'The police didn't catch the thief.'

Because verb-verb compounds in their actual form usually occur in the 把 *bǎ* construction (see §§9–10), note this slight difference regarding the position of the verb suffix -了 *le*: while it must follow the resultative verb complement (44c), with the V-DVC structure there are two choices: -*le* either follows the directional verb complement or the action verb (44d–d').

44c 警察把小偷抓到了。(V-RVC-了)

jǐngchá bǎ xiǎotōu zhuā-dào **le**

'The police caught the thief.'

44d 警察把小偷带回来了。(V-DVC-了)

jǐngchá bǎ xiǎotōu dài-huílai **le**

'The police brought back the thief.'

44d' 警察把小偷带了回来。(V-了-DVC)

jǐngchá bǎ xiǎotōu dài-**le**-huílai

'The police brought the thief back.'

Potential form

The potential form of verb-verb compounds, on the other hand, uses infixes. Inserting 得 *de* for the positive form or 不 *bù* for the negative form between the action verb and its verb complement indicates the potential capacity to accomplish the action. For example, if the actual verb-verb compound is 抓到 *zhuā-dào* 'grab-reach (catch),' the positive potential form is 抓得到

zhuā-de-dào 'be able to catch (the thief)'; and the negative potential form is 抓<u>不到</u> *zhuā-bú-dào* 'unable to catch (the thief).' See a few examples in 44e.

44e   V-V compounds in potential form
Positive
看得完 *kàn-de-wán* 'able to finish (reading)'
做得好 *zuò-de-hǎo* 'able to do well'
回得来 *huí-de-lái* 'able to return here'
Negative
看不完 *kàn-bù-wán* 'unable to finish (reading)'
做不好 *zuò-bù-hǎo* 'unable to do well'
回不来 *huí-bù-lái* 'unable to return here'

▶ **Note:** Two points about the actual and potential forms are important.

First, when an action verb takes a resultative verb complement or a directional verb complement, it does not follow that both actual and potential forms are commonly used. For instance, a verb-verb compound with the resultative verb complement 了 *liǎo* for 'possibility'—such as 吃不了 *chī-bù-liǎo* 'impossible to eat' in 我们吃<u>不了</u>这么多菜 *wǒmen chī-bù-liǎo zhème duō cài* 'We can't possibly eat so much food'—by definition only appears in the potential form, and never in the actual.

Second, as we have established that only the actual form of a verb-verb compound is used with the *bǎ* construction, compare 44f with 44g. The latter is unacceptable because it uses the verb-verb compound's potential form.

44f   请你把话说<u>清楚</u>。
qǐng nǐ bǎ huà **shuō-qīngchu**
'Please speak clearly.'

44g   ⊗ 请你把话*说<u>得清楚</u>。
qǐng nǐ bǎ huà **shuō-de-qīngchu**
?'Please be able to speak clearly.'

44h   ⊗ 中文的生词太多，我常常*<u>不能记得住</u>。
zhōngwén de shēngcí tài duō, wǒ chángcháng **bùnéng jì-de-zhù**
'There are too many Chinese words. I often can't remember (them).'

▶ **Problem**: The sentence introduces an unnecessary negation *bùnéng* 'cannot' to the verb-verb compound's potential form *jì-de-zhù* 'be able to remember.' One should simply use the negative equivalent *jì-bú-zhù* 'unable to remember.'

✓ 中文的生词太多，我常常记不住。
zhōngwén de shēngcí tài duō, wǒ chángcháng **jì-bú-zhù**

44i 我今天一定得把功课都*做得完。

wǒ jīntiān yídìng děi bǎ gōngkè dōu **zuò-de-wán**

'Today I must finish all the homework.'

▶ **Problem:** The potential form does not go with the 把 *bǎ* construction. To correct the mistake, simply use the actual form.

 我今天一定得把功课都做完。

wǒ jīntiān yídìng děi bǎ gōngkè dōu **zuò-wán**

44j 美英把头发*剪了短。

Měiyīng bǎ tóufa **jiǎn-le-duǎn**

'Měiyīng has cut her hair short.'

▶ **Problem:** The verb suffix -*le* splits the action verb *jiǎn* 'to scissor' and its resultative verb complement *duǎn* 'short.' Since the verb-verb compound functions like a simple verb, -*le* should attach to the resultative verb complement (cf. 44c).

 美英把头发剪短了。

Měiyīng bǎ tóufa **jiǎn-duǎn le**

The actual form of a verb-verb compound appears as [V-V + 了 *le* (positive)] and [没(有) *méi(you)* + V-V (negative)]. The potential form of a verb-verb compound uses infixes: [V-得 *de*-V (positive)] and [V-不 *bù*-V (negative)].

For related topics, see §§9, 10, 28, 41, 42, and 43.

Exercises

EXERCISE 12. (§§42–44) Fill in the blanks with verb complements 见 *jiàn*, 懂 *dǒng*, 到 *dào*, 住 *zhù*, 完 *wán*, 下 *xià*, 起来 *qǐlái*, or 出去 *chūqù*. You need to put the potential infix 得 *de* (able to) or 不 *bù* (unable to) before each complement according to the context. Some complements may be used more than once.

1　我没学过法文，法国电影我看 _____(understand)。
2　餐厅很大，坐 _____(contain) 一百个客人。
3　菜太多了，我们吃 _____(finish)。
4　坐在后面的人听 _____(hear) 吗？
5　我忘了她姓什么，我想 _____(recall) 了。
6　我们记 _____(register) 这么多的生词。
7　老师说中文说得不快，学生都听 _____(understand)。
8　想看球赛的人很多，我买 _____(obtain) 票。
9　东西很小，她搬 _____(out)。
10　功课不多，我们做 _____(finish)。

EXERCISE 13. (§§42–44) Translate the sentences into Chinese, using the verb-verb compound given in parentheses. Note that some of these compounds need to be in the actual form, and some are in the potential form.

1 We did not see him return.（看见）
2 Can you finish this book today?（看完）
3 The door is broken; it can't be closed.（关上）
4 Today they bought fresh fish.（买到）
5 Mrs. Zhang is not able to read English.（看懂）
6 The whole family has heard this news.（听到）
7 This topic is very complicated. One cannot explain it easily.（说清楚）
8 Nurse Wang has already moved out.（搬出去）
9 Sorry, I didn't understand what you said.（听懂）
10 This is the address. Do you think we can find him here?（找到）
11 You are right: she really is my sister.（说对）
12 He ordered too much food. We didn't finish.（吃完）

§45. To describe an action's manner or degree

To describe an action's manner or degree, we use pattern 45a, where the duplicated verb takes 得 *de* to introduce a complement. The verb 说 *shuō* in the verb-object compound 说话 *shuō-huà* 'speak' must be repeated when it takes 得 *de*.

45a Subj. + V-Obj. + V-得 *de* + complement
王老师说话<u>说</u>得很快。
Wáng lǎoshī shuō-huà **shuō**-de hěn kuài
'Teacher Wang speaks fast.'

The complement after *de* is actually a modified descriptive adjective phrase, functioning as an adverbial phrase, to indicate the manner or the degree of the action.

45b 她妹妹唱歌唱得<u>真是好极了</u>。
tā mèimei chàng-gē chàng-de **zhēnshì hǎo-jíle**
'Her younger sister sings really well.'

45c 我昨天喝咖啡喝得<u>太多</u>，晚上睡不着。
wǒ zuótiān hē-kāfēi hē-de **tài duō**, wǎnshang shuì-bù-zháo
'Since I drank too much coffee yesterday, I wasn't able to sleep last night.'

When the context makes the point clear, the verb-object segment (**not** the V-*de*) in pattern 45a can be omitted. For example, the answer to the question 老师说话说得快吗？ *lǎoshī shuō-huà shuō-de kuài ma?* 'Does the teacher speak fast?' naturally is 她说得很快。 *tā shuō-de hěn kuài* 'Yes, (she speaks) very fast.' The verb-object compound *shuō-huà* 'speak' does not need to be repeated in the answer since it is clearly stated in the question.

Alternatively, the object in the verb-object segment may be at the beginning of the sentence, as in 45d. There is no need for the duplication of the verb in this structure.

45d　那首歌，她唱得不错。

　　　　nèi-shǒu-gē, tā chàng-de búcuò

　　　　'That song, she sings rather well.'

When the verb is intransitive, i.e. when it is not a verb-object compound, such as *xiūxi* 'rest' in 45e and *lái* 'come' in 45f, there is no need for duplication. The particle *de* directly attaches to the verb itself, as shown in these examples.

45e　天气太热，我们休息得不好。

　　　　tiānqì tài rè, wǒmen **xiūxi-de** bù hǎo

　　　　'The weather is too hot. We didn't rest well.'

45f　你来得不巧，她刚走。

　　　　nǐ **lái-de** bù qiǎo, tā gāng zǒu

　　　　'You came at the wrong time. She just left.'

The interrogative form for this pattern usually focuses on the complement, as shown in 45g–h. The phrase 怎么样？ *zěnmeyàng* 'how is . . . ?' is commonly used in the complement position, as in 45h.

45g　你看书看得多不多？

　　　　nǐ kàn-shū kàn-de **duō-bù-duō**

　　　　'Do you read much?'

45h　他学中文学得怎么样？

　　　　tā xué-zhōngwén xué-de **zěnmeyàng**

　　　　'How are his Chinese studies going?'

▶ **Summary**: These details are essential for pattern 45a: Subj. + V-Obj. + V-得 *de* + complement. i) The verb of the verb-object compound must be duplicated before taking *de*. ii) The duplication can only be omitted when the verb is intransitive or when the object occurs at the beginning of the sentence. iii) When the context makes the point clear, the verb-object segment can be omitted; but the V-*de* segment can never be omitted. iv) The complement after *de* most likely is a descriptive adjective phrase functioning as an adverbial modifier. Other kinds of phrases such as noun phrases, verb phrases, or time expressions do not fit in this position. v) The interrogative form focuses on the complement, not on the verb.

The following are a few common errors that in one way or another violate the details of pattern 45a.

45i   ✖ 我妈妈*做菜得好吃极了。
wǒ māma **zuò-cài-de** hǎochī jíle
'My mom cooks delicious dishes.' (She cooks exceedingly well.)

  ▶ **Problem**: The verb is not duplicated.

  ✔ 我妈妈做菜做得好吃极了。
wǒ māma **zuò-cài zuò-de** hǎochī jíle

45j   ✖ 中国的现代化*进行进得很快。
Zhōngguó-de xiàndàihuà **jìnxíng jìn-de** hěn kuài
'China's modernization is moving very fast.'

  ▶ **Problem**: Part of the polysyllabic intransitive verb is duplicated.

  ✔ 中国的现代化进行得很快。
Zhōngguó-de xiàndàihuà **jìnxíng-de** hěn kuài

45k   ✖ 我每天睡觉*睡得五个小时。
wǒ měitiān shuì-jiào **shuì-de wǔ-ge xiǎoshí**
'I sleep five hours every day.'

  ▶ **Problem**: A time expression is used as the complement.

  ✔ 我每天睡觉睡得很少。(I sleep very little every day.)
wǒ měitiān shuì-jiào shuì-de **hěn shǎo**

  ✔ 我每天睡觉睡五个小时。(A different pattern. See §24.)
wǒ měitiān shuì-jiào **shuì wǔ-ge xiǎoshí**

45l   ✖ 中文课，老师*讲不讲得很清楚？
zhōngwénkè, lǎoshī **jiǎng-bu-jiǎng** de hěn qīngchu
'Does the teacher teach the Chinese class clearly?'

  ▶ **Problem**: The interrogative focuses not on the complement but on the verb.

  ✔ 中文课，老师讲得清楚不清楚？
zhōngwénkè, lǎoshī **jiǎng-de qīngchu bù qīngchu**

45a is the pattern for describing an action's manner or degree. Here V-得 *de* introduces a complement, which is normally a descriptive adjective.

For related topics, see §46.

Exercises

EXERCISE 14. Complete the sentences, using the structure [V-Obj. + V-得 *de* + complement].

1   (The teacher writes Chinese characters beautifully.) 老师写字 _____ 。
2   (The old gentleman rises early.) 老先生起来 _____ 。
3   (Does Dad drink much beer?) 爸爸喝啤酒 _____ ?
4   (You type very slowly!) 你打字 _____ !
5   (I don't swim that well.) 我游泳 _____ 。
6   (The older sister walks quickly.) 姐姐走路 _____ 。
7   (How well does the chef cook?) 大厨做菜 _____ ?
8   (You don't eat enough fruit.) 你吃水果 _____ 。

Check your grammar

Translate these phrases/sentences into Chinese, and then check to see that you have implemented the relevant grammar points. The parenthetical numbers and letters identify the pertinent subsections and examples.

1   Xiaomao does not work hard. He is not a good student. (§34e)
2   I don't want to go to the school cafeteria to eat the insipid food. (§34f)
3   American students who can speak Chinese (§35b)
4   the library that is across from (here) (§36f)
5   these ten students (§37h)
6   In America, it would be an exceptional situation if a car didn't yield to pedestrians. (§37i)
7   I don't have big brothers. (§37j)
8   He kept drinking (lit. repeatedly drank). Now he is very drunk. (§38j)
9   Today's weather is really nice. We should go out to exercise a bit. (§38k)
10   She is now working on her term paper at the library. (§38l)
11   I (lit. my body) need(s) a bath every day. (§39d)
12   I really like our Chinese class. / I really like to attend Chinese class. (§39e)
13   She is always busy, with little time for talking to her friends. (§40h)
14   The owner of that antique store fooled me. (§40i)
15   I have contacted him quite a few times. (§40j)
16   As soon as she divorced her husband, she married another man. (§40k)
17   I didn't see him yesterday. (§41k)
18   If you often practice, you will remember many Chinese characters. (§41l)
19   I have already finished my homework. (§42d)
20   During the exam, the student didn't quite understand (didn't read clearly) the question. (§42e)
21   Li Ming forgot to go to see his teacher. He is embarrassed. (§42f)

22   The librarian says that students can't check the dictionaries out of the library. (§43j)
23   There are too many Chinese words. I often can't remember (them). (§44h)
24   Today I must finish all the homework. (§44i)
25   Meiying has cut her hair short. (§44j)
26   My mom cooks delicious dishes. (She cooks exceedingly well.) (§45i)
27   China's modernization is moving very fast. (§45j)
28   I sleep very little every day. / I sleep five hours every day. (§45k)
29   Does the teacher teach the Chinese class clearly? (§45l)

 Notes

5 Usage comparison of words and phrases

§46. Distinguishing the three homonyms: 的 *de*₁, 地 *de*₂, and 得 *de*₃

Each of these three characters, 的, 地, and 得, each pronounced *de* (neutral tone), has its own grammatical function.

First, the modification of nouns, indicated by 的 *de*₁. The structure: Modifier-的 *de*₁ + N. The word/phrase that precedes *de*₁ modifies the noun that stands after it. 46a illustrates the modifiers (see §§34–35).

46a The modifier is a noun:
老师的办公室 *lǎoshī-de*₁ *bàngōngshì* 'the teacher's office'
图书馆的书 *túshūguǎn-de*₁ *shū* 'the library's books'

The modifier is a pronoun:
她的房间 *tā-de*₁ *fángjiān* 'her room'
我们的主意 *wǒmen-de*₁ *zhúyi* 'our idea'

The modifier is a polysyllabic descriptive adjective, or a monosyllabic one modified by an adverb:
成功的商人 *chénggōng-de*₁ *shāngren* 'successful businessman'
很新的电脑 *hěnxīn-de*₁ *diànnǎo* 'a very new computer'

The modifier is a clause:
我昨天买的车 *wǒ zuótiān mǎi-de*₁ *chē* 'the car I bought yesterday'
他讲的故事 *tā jiǎng-de*₁ *gùshi* 'the story he told'

Second, the modification of verbs, indicated by 地 *de*₂. The structure: DA-地 *de*₂ + V. That is, DA-*de*₂ becomes an adverbial phrase modifying the verb. The suffix *de*₂ attaches either to a polysyllabic descriptive adjective, or a monosyllabic one modified by an adverb, such as 很 *hěn* 'very' or 非常 *fēicháng* 'exceptionally.' DA-*de₂* precedes the verb to modify the verb's manner of action. See the examples in 46b.

46b DA + 地 *de₂* / adverb-DA + 地 *de₂* ⇨ adverbial phrase (V)
高兴 *gāoxìng* 'happy' + 地 *de₂* ⇨ 高兴地(唱) 'happily (singing)'
仔细 *zǐxì* 'careful' + 地 *de₂* ⇨ 仔细地(看) 'carefully (reading)'
很慢 *hěn-màn* 'very slow' + 地 *de₂* ⇨ 很慢地(走) 'very slowly (walking)'
非常早 *fēicháng-zǎo* 'exceptionally ⇨ 非常早地(离开) '(leaving)
  early' + 地 *de₂*   exceptionally early'

Third, the verb complement, indicated by 得 *de₃*. The structure: V-得 *de₃* + complement. The verb uses *de₃* to introduce a complement indicating the manner or degree of the action. When the verb is a verb-object compound, the verb that takes *de₃* must be duplicated. See the examples in 46c. (See also §45.)

46c (看书)看得快极了 *(kàn-shū) kàn-de₃ kuài-jíle* 'read extremely fast'
(吃饭)吃得很少 *(chī-fàn) chī-de₃ hěn shǎo* 'eat very little'
玩儿得真高兴 *wánr-de₃ zhēn gāoxìng* 'have a good time playing' (lit. 'play really happily')
笑得肚子疼 *xiào-de₃ dùzi téng* 'laugh so hard that the stomach hurts'

▶ **Comparative note:** While both 地 *de₂* and 得 *de₃* relate to the manner of an action, the former is more interpretive, i.e. it notes the way the action unfolds, whereas the latter is more descriptive, i.e. it notes the action's character. The adverbial phrase with *de₂* is more likely a speaker's subjective view, whereas the complement introduced by *de₃* is more likely the action's objective nature. Compare sentences 46d–e, and another pair of examples, 46f–g.

46d 王老师喜欢非常快地说话。
Wáng lǎoshī xǐhuan **fēicháng-kuài-de₂** shuō-huà
'Teacher Wang likes to speak really fast.' (He prefers to speak really fast.)

46e 王老师常常说话说得非常快。
Wáng lǎoshī chángcháng shuō-huà **shuō-de₃ fēicháng-kuài**
'Teacher Wang often speaks exceptionally fast.' (The manner in which he speaks is often exceptionally fast.)

46f 我们很早地吃了饭，去看晚场电影。
wǒmen **hěn-zǎo-de₂** chī-le-fàn, qù kàn wǎnchǎng diànyǐng
'We ate early, in order to go to see the evening movie.' (We deliberately ate early in order to see the movie.)

46g 我们吃饭吃得很早。

wǒmen chī-fàn **chī-de₃ hěn-zǎo**

'We eat early.' (Eating early is our habit.)

We summarize the functions of the three homonyms in 46h as a grammatical guide. Based on this guide, the errors in 46i–l can be simply explained and corrected.

46h 的 *de₁* indicates the noun modification: Modifier-的 *de₁* + N

地 *de₂* indicates the verb modification: DA-地 *de₂* + V

得 *de₃* indicates the verb complement: V-得 *de₃* + complement

46i ⊗ 今天我不舒服，因此，我睡觉睡*的很多。

jīntiān wǒ bù shūfu, yīncǐ, wǒ shuì-jiào shuì-**de₁** hěn duō

'I don't feel well today. So I slept a lot.'

▶ **Analysis**: *Hěn duō* 'a lot' is a complement of the verb *shuì* 'sleep.' What follows the verb should be 得 *de₃*.

46j ⊗ 这一带的土地比其他地方肥沃*的多。

zhèi-yídài de tǔdì bǐ qítā dìfang féiwò **de₁** duō

'The soil in this area is much more fertile than other places.'

▶ **Analysis**: In a comparison, the 'much more (adjective)' is DA-得多 *de duō*. Since *duō* is a complement, it follows 得 *de₃*. (See §§6 and 8 for comparisons.)

46k ⊗ 我们春假去旅行，运气*得没有碰到堵车。

wǒmen chūnjià qù lǚxíng, yùnqi-**de₃** méiyǒu pèngdào dǔ-chē

'We traveled during spring break and luckily didn't run into traffic jams.'

▶ **Analysis**: 'Luckily' is an adverb. The descriptive adjective *yùnqi* 'lucky' should take 地 *de₂* to form an adverbial phrase describing the action 'not run into traffic jams.'

46l ⊗ 我还记得你一年前说*得话。

wǒ hái jìde nǐ yì-nián qián shuō-**de₃**-huà

'I still remember what you said a year ago.'

▶ **Analysis**: 'The words you said' is a noun phrase, while 话 *huà* 'words' is modified by 你说 *nǐ shuō* 'you said.' So this case requires 的 *de₁*.

46h summarizes the functions of the three homonyms. The structures are: [Modifier-的 *de₁* + N]; [DA-地 *de₂* + V]; and [V-得 *de₃* + complement].

For related topics, see §§34, 35, and 45.

Exercises

EXERCISE 1. Insert 的 *de₁* in the appropriate place in each phrase/sentence.

1   好吃点心
2   有趣故事
3   大家事
4   我爸爸新车
5   合理制度
6   城西边公路
7   朋友公寓
8   很远地区
9   他买新电脑很贵。
10   我要去那个地方在南美洲。
11   我来介绍一下我旁边这个人。
12   大家都喜欢那个电影我还没看。
13   现在骑自行车人越来越多了。

EXERCISE 2. As appropriate, put 地 *de₂* or 得 *de₃* in the blanks.

1   她儿子十六岁了，长 _____ 很高。
2   李先生总是很客气 _____ 问大家好。
3   客厅比卧室大 _____ 多。
4   他高兴 _____ 说：欢迎欢迎！我们就很随便 _____ 坐下了。
5   你在图书馆不能大声 _____ 说话。
6   妹妹考 _____ 不好，她难过 _____ 哭了。
7   我们不懂，他又耐心 _____ 解释了一次。
8   刘老师说中文说 _____ 很慢，我们都听 _____ 清楚。

§47. 'A little': 一点儿 *yìdiǎnr* vs. 有一点儿 *yǒu yìdiǎnr*

While both 一点儿 *yìdiǎnr* and 有一点儿 *yǒu yìdiǎnr* can be translated as 'a little,' each has its own grammatical function.

Yìdiǎnr is an adjective, indicating an indefinite small quantity. It usually precedes a comparable noun, as in 47a.

47a   买一点儿东西   喝一点儿水   懂一点儿德文
　　　　　mǎi **yìdiǎnr** dōngxi   hē **yìdiǎnr** shuǐ   dǒng **yìdiǎnr** déwén
　　　　　'buy (a little) something'   'drink a little water'   'understand a little German'

Note that the [*yìdiǎnr* + N] phrase is the object of the verb. The noun that *yìdiǎnr* modifies may be omitted when it is clear from the context, as in 47b.

47b   菜很多，你再吃一点儿吧。
　　　　　cài hěn duō, nǐ zài chī-**yìdiǎnr** ba
　　　　　'There is a lot of food, (please) eat a little more.'

The phrase *yǒu yìdiǎnr*, often shortened to 有点儿 *yǒudiǎnr*, functions as an adverb, modifying the descriptive adjective that follows it. The phrase [*yǒu yìdiǎnr* + DA] usually indicates a slight degree of dissatisfaction with the quality represented by the descriptive adjective. See examples 47c–d.

47c   杯子有一点儿脏。
　　　　bēizi yǒu yìdiǎnr zāng
　　　　'The glass is a little dirty.'

47d   老师有一点儿生气。
　　　　lǎoshī yǒu yìdiǎnr shēngqì
　　　　'The teacher is a little upset.'

If the descriptive adjective modified by *yǒu yìdiǎnr* itself has a clearly positive meaning—such as 高兴 *gāoxìng* 'happy,' 满意 *mǎnyì* 'satisfied,' 舒服 *shūfu* 'comfortable,' or 聪明 *cōngming* 'smart'—the negation 不 *bù* 'not' must precede the adjective in the structure [*yǒu yìdiǎnr* + 不 *bù* + DA]. Compare sentences 47e–f with their counterparts 47e′–f′. Without the infixed negation *bù*, sentences 47e–f with clearly positive descriptive adjectives *jiǎngdàolǐ* 'reasonable' and *qīngchu* 'clear' are awkward with *yǒu yìdiǎnr*, as shown in 47e′–f′.

47e   老张有一点儿<u>不</u>讲道理。
　　　　Lǎo Zhāng yǒu yìdiǎnr **bù**-jiǎngdàolǐ
　　　　'Old Zhang is a little unreasonable.'

47e′   ✖ ?老张有一点儿讲道理。
　　　　Lǎo Zhāng yǒu yìdiǎnr jiǎngdàolǐ

47f   黑板上的字有一点儿<u>不</u>清楚。
　　　　hēibǎn shàng-de-zì yǒu yìdiǎnr **bù**-qīngchu
　　　　'The characters on the blackboard are a little unclear.'

47f′   ✖ ?黑板上的字有一点儿清楚。
　　　　hēibǎn shàng-de-zì yǒu yìdiǎnr qīngchu

47g and 47h summarize respectively the structures of the phrases with *yìdiǎnr* and with *yǒu yìdiǎnr* as well as their functions.

47g   一点儿 *yìdiǎnr*
　　　　V + 一点儿 + Obj.: follows a verb and often precedes a noun object.

47h   有一点儿 *yǒu yìdiǎnr*
　　　　有一点儿 + DA: precedes a descriptive adjective usually suggesting a
　　　　　slight dissatisfaction with the quality represented by the adjective
　　　　有一点儿 + 不 + DA~positive~: the negation 不 *bù* must be inserted when the
　　　　　descriptive adjective has a clearly positive meaning.

Since both *yìdiǎnr* and *yǒu yìdiǎnr* can be translated as 'a little,' one may be tempted to regard them as interchangeable and overlook their structural differences. Most errors derive from this misunderstanding.

47i ⊗ 要是你*一点儿累，我们就休息休息。

yàoshì nǐ **yìdiǎnr lèi**, wǒmen jiù xiūxi-xiūxi

'If you are a little tired, we will take a break.'

▶ **Analysis**: *Lèi* 'tired' is a descriptive adjective. It should have *yǒu yìdiǎnr* preceding it.

✓ 要是你有一点儿累，我们就休息休息。

yàoshì nǐ **yǒu yìdiǎnr lèi**, wǒmen jiù xiūxi-xiūxi

47j ⊗ 我喜欢每天早上*喝茶一点儿。

wǒ xǐhuan měitiān zǎoshang **hē-chá yìdiǎnr**

'I like to drink a little tea every morning.'

▶ **Analysis**: *Hē-chá* 'drink tea' is a verb-object phrase. *Yìdiǎnr* comes between the verb and the object (see 47g).

✓ 我喜欢每天早上喝一点儿茶。

wǒ xǐhuan měitiān zǎoshang **hē-yìdiǎnr-chá**

47k ⊗ 我的宿舍地点好，离教室和餐厅都*有一点儿近。

wǒde sùshè dìdiǎn hǎo, lí jiàoshì hé cāntīng dōu **yǒu yìdiǎnr jìn**

'The location of my dorm is good. It's a small distance to both classrooms and the cafeteria.'

▶ **Analysis**: From the context, the descriptive adjective *jìn* 'close' clearly notes a positive view. The sentence thus sounds confusing with *yǒu yìdiǎnr* modifying it (see 47h). One needs to use a more definite adverb, such as 很 *hěn* 'very' or 特别 *tèbié* 'especially,' in this case rather than 'a little.'

✓ 我的宿舍地点好，离教室和餐厅都特别近。

wǒde sùshè dìdiǎn hǎo, lí jiàoshì hé cāntīng dōu **tèbié jìn**

> 一点儿 *yìdiǎnr* lies between the verb and the noun object, whereas 有一点儿 *yǒu yìdiǎnr* always precedes a descriptive adjective. The negation 不 *bù* must be inserted between *yǒu yìdiǎnr* and an adjective that has a clearly positive meaning.

For related topics, see §§1 and 38.

Exercises

EXERCISE 3. Fill in the blanks with 一点儿 *yìdiǎnr* or 有一点儿 *yǒu yìdiǎnr*.

1 我们每天都说 _____ 中文。
2 这双鞋 _____ 小，不舒服。
3 我 _____ 饿，我想吃 _____ 东西。
4 昨天下了 _____ 雨。

5   她在咖啡里放了 ＿＿＿ 牛奶。
6   他忘了我的名字，＿＿＿ 不好意思。
7   箱子 ＿＿＿ 超重。

EXERCISE 4. Translate into Chinese.

1   I am a little thirsty. (So) I want to drink a little water.
2   How about eating a little more?
3   She didn't come. He was a little disappointed.

§48. Conjunctions 和 *hé*/跟 *gēn* vs. adverb 也 *yě*

Both 和 *hé* and 跟 *gēn*, meaning 'and,' are commonly used words for connecting nouns, pronouns, or noun phrases, as shown in 48a–c. The two are interchangeable.

48a   Connecting nouns:

老师和学生	亚洲和非洲	电脑和电话
lǎoshī **hé** xuésheng	Yàzhōu **hé** Fēizhōu	diànnǎo **hé** diànhuà
'teacher and student'	'Asia and Africa'	'computer and telephone'

48b   Connecting pronouns:

他跟她	我们跟你们
tā **gēn** tā	wǒmen **gēn** nǐmen
'he and she'	'we and you (pl.)'

48c   Connecting noun phrases:

红花跟绿叶	姓李的医生和姓王的护士
hóng-huā **gēn** lǜ-yè	xìng Lǐ de yīshēng **hé** xìng Wáng de hùshi
'red flowers and green leaves'	'the doctor named Li and the nurse named Wang'

The adverb 也 *yě* 'also' appears in compound sentences composed of two or more related verb phrases, descriptive adjectives, or clauses. A compound sentence may consist of one subject with more than one predicate, as in 48d, 'drinking coffee and drinking tea,' or with a pair of clauses, each of which has its own subject, as in 48e, 'book' and 'movie.' The adverb *yě* appears before the predicate of the second verb phrase, descriptive adjective, or clause, as in both 48d and 48e.

48d   我喝咖啡，也喝茶。
wǒ hē-kāfēi, **yě** hē-chá
'I drink coffee, and tea too.'

48e   书很有意思，电影也很有意思。

shū hěn yǒuyìsi, diànyǐng **yě** hěn yǒuyìsi

'The book is interesting, and the movie is as well.'

Let us summarize the difference between the functions of *hé/gēn* 'and' on the one hand, and *yě* 'also' on the other. The former are connective words that link nouns, pronouns, or noun phrases, whereas the latter is an adverb that is used before the predicate of a second verb phrase, descriptive adjective, or clause. One may formulate their functions as 48f–g. Note that the asterisks mark the incorrect usages.

48f   [NP 和 *hé*/跟 *gēn* NP] (*[VP/DA/clause 和 *hé*/跟 *gēn* VP/DA/clause])

48g   [Subj. VP₁, 也 *yě* VP₂] or [Subj.₁ VP, Subj.₂ 也 *yě* VP] (*[NP₁ 也 *yě* NP₂])
[Subj. DA₁, 也 *yě* DA₂] or [Subj.₁ DA, Subj.₂ 也 *yě* DA]

Errors overlook the difference between 48f and 48g. Unlike 'and' in English, 和 *hé*/跟 *gēn* do not link clauses, whereas 也 *yě* 'also' does not link noun phrases. These errors also arise from direct translation to Mandarin. See examples 48h–j below. While the English translations may be intelligible, the underlined parts are erroneous in Mandarin.

48h   ❌ 我*也我的家人都喜欢看中国电影。

wǒ **yě** wǒde jiārén dōu xǐhuan kàn Zhōngguó diànyǐng

'My family and I like to watch Chinese movies.'

▶ **Problem**: *Yě* should be replaced with *hé* or *gēn* since *wǒ* 'I' is a pronoun and *wǒde jiārén* 'my family' is a noun phrase.

✅ 我和/跟我的家人都喜欢看中国电影。

48i   ❌ 要是你跟你的同屋谈不来*和你要有一间单人房，请去填一张表。

yàoshi nǐ gēn nǐde tóngwū tán-bù-lái **hé** nǐ yào yǒu yì-jiān-dānrénfáng, qǐng qù tián yì-zhāng-biǎo

'If you can't get along with your roommate and you want a single room, please fill out a form.'

▶ **Problem**: *Hé* should be replaced with a comma. While 'and' can be used in the English sentence, *hé* cannot link two clauses in Mandarin.

✅ 要是你跟你的同屋谈不来，你要有一间单人房，请去填一张表。

48j   ❌ 我的工作时间很灵活，我的工作环境不错，*和我的收入也很公平。

wǒde gōngzuò shíjiān hěn línghuó, wǒde gōngzuò huánjìng búcuò, **hé** wǒde shōurù yě hěn gōngpíng

'My work schedule is flexible; my working environment is good, and my income is also fair.'

▶ **Problem**: *Hé* should be removed. Again, unlike 'and' in the English sentence, *hé* cannot link clauses in Mandarin.

✅ 我的工作时间很灵活，我的工作环境不错，我的收入也很公平。

和 *hé*/跟 *gēn* 'and' link nouns, pronouns, or noun phrases, but never verb phrases, adjectives, or clauses. 也 *yě* 'also' is used before a second verb phrase, adjective, or clause, but never precedes nouns, pronouns or noun phrases.

For related topics, see §§13 and 53.

Exercises

EXERCISE 5. Link the given words/phrases with the conjunctions 和 *hé*/跟 *gēn* or the adverb 也 *yě*.

1   北京大学 哈佛大学
2   妹妹会滑雪 妹妹会游泳
3   上个星期三 这个星期三
4   爸爸高兴极了 妈妈高兴极了
5   红色的大衣 黑色的皮靴
6   他买的饮料 她买的水果
7   姐姐点了冰茶 我点了冰茶
8   她想学文学 她想学历史

EXERCISE 6. Translate into Chinese.

1   The big chair is comfortable, and so is the small one.
2   Both the big and the small chairs are comfortable.
3   We ordered cola; we also ordered beer.

§49. 'Some': 一些 *yìxiē* vs. 有的 *yǒude*

Both 一些 *yìxiē* 'a few, some' and 有的 *yǒude* 'some' modify a noun or a noun phrase. The difference between the two is that the noun or the noun phrase preceded by the former is usually the object of the verb, whereas the noun or the noun phrase preceded by the latter must be the subject.

The word *yìxiē* indicates a small but indefinite quantity, e.g. 一些老师 *yìxiē lǎoshī* 'a few teachers' and 一些水果 *yìxiē shuǐguǒ* 'some fruit.' Since the noun phrase with *yìxiē* has an indefinite reference, it is normally the object of the verb, as *yìxiē xīnshēng* 'some new students' is in 49a. On the other hand, to make the noun phrase with *yìxiē* the subject of a sentence, one needs to replace *yì* with a demonstrative, 这 *zhèi* 'this'/那 *nèi* 'that' or 有 *yǒu* (as in 有的 *yǒude*), to eliminate its indefiniteness, as in 49b (see §37).

49a 我们去机场接了一些新生。

wǒmen qù jīchǎng jiē-le **yìxiē xīnshēng**

'We went to the airport to pick up some new students.'

49b 这/那/有些新生住在那个宿舍里。

zhèi/nèi/yǒu-xiē xīnshēng zhù zài nèi-ge-sùshè li

'These/those/some new students stay in that dorm.'

The meaning of the word *yǒude* is 'some but not all.' It usually indicates a portion of a larger entity. In Mandarin, since the whole stands before the part, the sentence usually begins, 'As for these, some are . . . ,' rather than 'Some of these are . . . .' See example 49c. Note that the noun, *shù* 'tree' in this case, may be omitted after *yǒude* when it is clear from the context. 49c also shows that the noun preceded by *yǒude* is the subject of the short clauses (lit. 'As for these trees, some are tall, some are short').

49c 这些树，有的(树)高，有的(树)矮。

zhèi-xiē-shù, yǒude(shù) gāo, yǒude(shù) ǎi

'Some of these trees are tall, some are short.'

While the noun phrase with *yǒude* can be the subject of a sentence as in 49d, it never follows a verb as the object. Hence 49e is ill-formed. When the noun phrase with *yǒude* is the object of the verb, it must be placed before the verb, such as *yǒude kāfēiguǎnr* 'some coffee shops' in 49e'.

49d 有的咖啡馆儿也卖三明治。

yǒude kāfēiguǎnr yě mài sānmíngzhì

'Some coffee shops also sell sandwiches.'

49e *她喜欢城里有的咖啡馆儿。

tā xǐhuan chénglǐ **yǒude kāfēiguǎnr**

49e' 城里有的咖啡馆儿她喜欢。

chénglǐ **yǒude kāfēiguǎnr** tā xǐhuan

'She likes some of the coffee shops in town.'

 Sentence 49f is erroneous because the noun phrase with 有的 *yǒude* is construed as an object of the verb *fàng* 'to place.' Since a N/NP with *yǒude* can only be the subject but not the object of a sentence, whereas the N/NP with 一些 *yìxiē* usually is the object, in this case use the latter.

49f ✗ 她在台上放了*有的椅子。

tā zài tái-shang fàng-le **yǒude yǐzi**

'She placed some chairs on the stage.'

✓ 她在台上放了一些椅子。

tā zài tái-shang fàng-le **yìxiē yǐzi**

有的 *yǒude* modifies a noun or noun phrase that must be the subject of a sentence, whereas 一些 *yìxiē* routinely modifies a noun or noun phrase that is the object of the sentence.

For related topics, see §37.

Exercises

EXERCISE 7. Fill in the blanks with 一些 *yìxiē* or 有的 *yǒude*.

1 ＿＿＿＿ 便宜货其实质地不错。
2 妈妈去银行取了 ＿＿＿＿ 钱。
3 ＿＿＿＿ 中国菜太辣，我不能吃。
4 他们请了 ＿＿＿＿ 朋友来做客。
5 房间里放着 ＿＿＿＿ 旧家具。

EXERCISE 8. Translate into Chinese.

1 Some of those people are nurses, and some are doctors.
2 Some of the rooms in the dorm are small.
3 She taped some postcards to the door.

§50. 'Each': 每 *měi*-Mea-N vs. 每 *měi*-N

每 *měi* 'each, every' may accompany any noun in either of the two structures shown in 50a–b.

50a 每 *měi* + Mea + N
50b 每 *měi* + N

Now for a quick review of the measures. Mandarin uses a measure word whenever a noun is quantified by a number or linked to a demonstrative, 这 *zhèi* 'this' or 那 *nèi* 'that.' The measure always appears between the number or the demonstrative and the noun. The choice of the measure, however, is determined by the noun. Many nouns require a specific measure. And the same noun may take different measure words in different circumstances, e.g. 一条面包 *yì-tiáo-miànbāo* 'one loaf of bread' or 一片面包 *yí-piàn-miànbāo* 'one slice of bread.' Since the most frequently used measure in Mandarin is 个 *ge*, some nouns may take either *ge* or a specific measure.

We can sort measures into different groups. Here are a few common examples.

50c Standard:
三磅肉 *sān-bàng-ròu* 'three pounds of meat'
十英里路 *shí-yīnglǐ-lù* 'ten miles (of distance)'

50d Specific:
五十张纸 *wǔshí-zhāng-zhǐ* 'fifty sheets of paper'
两颗星 *liǎng-kē-xīng* 'two stars'

50e Collective:
一群人 *yì-qún-rén* 'a group of people'
四套书 *sì-tào-shū* 'four sets of books'

50f Indefinite:
一些桔子 *yì-xiē-júzi* 'some oranges'
一点儿水 *yì-diǎnr-shuǐ* 'a little water'

50g Frequency:
两次讨论 *liǎng-cì-tǎolùn* 'two discussions'
三顿饭 *sān-dùn-fàn* 'three meals'

The word *měi* may replace the number in the phrases that use all these kinds of measures—with the exception of 50f, the indefinite measures—to form phrases such as *měi-bàng-ròu* 'each pound of meat' or *měi-zhāng-zhǐ* 'every sheet of paper.' This structure observes the pattern of 50a: 每 *měi* + Mea + N.

We sometimes, however, may see another structure, 50b: 每 *měi* + N, such as 每天 *měi-tiān* 'every day.' Nouns that appear in this structure amount to measures themselves. In some grammar books they are referred to as 'quasi-measures.' Quasi-measures are small in number and are normally of two kinds: nouns that relate to temporal terms, as listed in 50h, and nouns that represent some types of containers, as sampled in 50i.

50h Temporal nouns:
年 *nián* 'year'　　　小时 *xiǎoshí* 'hour'
月 *yuè* 'month'　　　分钟 *fēnzhōng* 'minute'
星期 *xīngqī* 'week'　秒 *miǎo* 'second'
天 *tiān* 'day'

50i Nouns that represent containers:
碗 *wǎn* 'bowl'　　　袋 *dài* 'bag'
杯 *bēi* 'cup; glass'　瓶 *píng* 'bottle'
盒 *hé* 'box'　　　　罐 *guàn* 'jug'

The word *měi* requires no measure word with the temporal nouns listed in 50h, e.g. *měi-xīngqī* 'every week' or *měi-miǎo* 'every second.' Note that not every temporal noun can be used in this way. 钟头 *zhōngtóu*, another term for 'hour,' cannot be used in this form. Nor can any nouns that represent seasons or portions of a day, such as 中午 *zhōngwǔ* 'noon.' Nouns of the sort in 50i, on the other hand, function as measures for other specific nouns. See 50j below.

50j   每碗饭 *měi-wǎn-fàn* 'each bowl of rice'
     每杯茶 *měi-bēi-chá* 'each cup of tea'
     每盒糖 *měi-hé-táng* 'each box of candy'
     每袋衣服 *měi-dài-yīfu* 'each bag of clothing'
     每瓶酒 *měi-píng-jiǔ* 'each bottle of wine'
     每罐水 *měi-guàn-shuǐ* 'each jug of water'

Errors likely arise from the complexity of quasi-measures.

50k   我*每晚上都在图书馆学习。
     wǒ **měi-wǎnshang** dōu zài túshūguǎn xuéxí
     'I study at the library every evening.'

     ▶ **Analysis**: *Wǎnshang* 'evening' is a noun that does not count as a quasi-measure in Mandarin. Hence there must be a measure between *měi* and *wǎnshang*. 'Every evening' in Mandarin is 每天晚上 *měi-tiān-wǎnshang*, lit. 'every day's evening,' in the structure [每 *měi* + Mea +N]. 天 *tiān* 'day' is the (quasi-)measure in this case.

50l   *每个包她的行李都超重了。
     měi-ge-bāo tāde xíngli dōu chāozhòng le
     'Every bag of her luggage is overweight.'

     ▶ **Analysis**: First, the possessive pronoun *tā-de* 'her' should precede the [每 *měi* + Mea] phrase. Second, *bāo* 'bag' is a quasi-measure itself. It does not need another measure *ge*, and it functions as the (quasi-)measure of the noun *xíngli* 'luggage.'

      她的每包行李都超重了。
     tāde **měi-bāo xíngli** dōu chāozhòng le

As either a number or a demonstrative (这/那 *zhèi/nèi* 'this/that'), 每 *měi* 'each' modifies a noun in the structure [每 *měi* + Mea + N]. But if the noun itself is a 'quasi-measure,' as are those in 50h–i, the structure is: 每 *měi* + N.

For related topics, see §§37 and 49.

Exercises

EXERCISE 9. Where necessary, fill in the blanks with the appropriate measure words: 本 *běn*, 把 *bǎ*, 个 *ge*, 张 *zhāng*, 条 *tiáo*, 辆 *liàng*, 件 *jiàn*, or 只 *zhī*. Some will be used more than once.

1	每 _____ 星期	9	每 _____ 鱼	17	每 _____ 杯
2	每 _____ 汉字	10	每 _____ 纸	18	每 _____ 年
3	每 _____ 书	11	每 _____ 自行车	19	每 _____ 包
4	每 _____ 盒	12	每 _____ 衬衫	20	每 _____ 瓶
5	每 _____ 画儿	13	每 _____ 小时	21	每 _____ 椅子
6	每 _____ 盘	14	每 _____ 天	22	每 _____ 猫
7	每 _____ 月	15	每 _____ 事	23	每 _____ 苹果
8	每 _____ 字典	16	每 _____ 碗	24	每 _____ 问题

EXERCISE 10. Translate into Chinese.

1   She swims three times each week.
2   Every day this week it snowed a bit.
3   Each bottle of wine is expensive.

§51. 'All': adverb 都 *dōu* vs. adjective 所有的 *suǒyǒude*

The English translation for both 都 *dōu* and 所有的 *suǒyǒude* is 'all.' But in Mandarin the former is an adverb, whereas the latter is an adjective. Different parts of speech produce different grammatical functions.

The adverb 'all'

The meaning of 都 'all' is in the sense of 'altogether.' As an adverb it precedes a verb/VP (e.g. another adverb plus the verb). Its meaning of totality usually refers to the plural, or the collective noun/NP standing before it. A noun/NP that precedes *dōu* is usually the subject of its sentence. See examples 51a–b.

51a   学生都睡着了。
        xuésheng dōu shuì-zháo le
        'The students all fell asleep.'

51b   每个人都有名字。
        měi-ge-rén dōu yǒu míngzi
        'Every person has a name.'

On the other hand, if *dōu* is used to refer to the plural object of the verb, this object must be placed at the beginning of the sentence, as *nèi-sān-ge-diànyǐng* 'those three movies,' the object of the verb *kàn* 'watch,' in 51c.

51c   那三个电影她都看过。
    nèi-sān-ge-diànyǐng tā dōu kàn-guo
    'She has watched all three of those movies.'

If both the subject and the transposed object are plural, the sentence may have ambiguous readings. See example 51d. *Dōu* may refer to either the object *zhōngwén hé rìwén* 'Chinese and Japanese' or the subject *tāmen* 'they,' or both. Nonetheless context usually clarifies intention.

51d   中文和日文他们都懂。
    zhōngwén hé rìwén tāmen **dōu** dǒng
    'They understand both Chinese and Japanese.' (*dōu* refers to the Obj.)
    'All of them understand Chinese and Japanese.' (*dōu* refers to the Subj.)
    'All of them understand both Chinese and Japanese.' (*dōu* refers to both
       the Obj. and Subj.)

The adjective 'all'

As an adjective, *suǒyǒude* only modifies nouns. If the noun is polysyllabic, the suffix 的 *de* can be omitted. See a few examples in 51e below.

51e   所有的人 *suǒyǒude rén* 'all of the people'
    所有的钱 *suǒyǒude qián* 'all of the money'
    所有（的）建筑 *suǒyǒu(de) jiànzhù* 'all of the buildings'
    所有（的）问题 *suǒyǒu(de) wèntí* 'all of the problems'

The noun phrase with *suǒyǒude* 'all of the . . .' is most likely the subject of the sentence, and precedes the verb/VP. Since the subject modified by *suǒyǒude* is plural, note that the verb is always preceded by the adverb *dōu* 'altogether,' as in 51f–g. If the noun phrase modified by *suǒyǒude* is the object of the verb, it is usually transposed to the beginning of the sentence, as *suǒyǒude gōngjùshū* 'all the reference books' in 51g.

51f   所有的火车都准时到达了。
    suǒyǒude huǒchē **dōu** zhǔnshí dàodá le
    'All of the trains arrived on time.'

51g   所有的工具书你都可以用。
    suǒyǒude gōngjùshū nǐ dōu kěyǐ yòng
    'You may use all the reference books.'

▶ **Summary**: 51h–i summarize the respective structures of *dōu* and *suǒyǒude* in a sentence pattern. The former is an adverb that precedes the verb phrase, whereas the latter, an adjective, precedes a noun phrase which is usually the subject of the sentence.

51h   Subj.(pl.) + 都 *dōu* VP; or

Obj.(pl.) + Subj.(pl.) + 都 *dōu* VP

51i   所有的 *suǒyǒude*-NP + 都 *dōu* VP

Errors such as 51j–k are most likely caused by the direct translation of 'all' from English to 都 *dōu* in Mandarin. *Dōu* is usually the first word students of Chinese learn for 'all,' and 所有的 *suǒyǒude* usually appears later in their vocabulary. One cannot, however, use *dōu* in these cases, because both *Zhōngguó cài* 'Chinese dishes' in 51j and *xuésheng* 'students' in 51k are nouns. The adverb *dōu* should not be used here since it never precedes nouns (see 51h). The adjective *suǒyǒude* should replace *dōu* in both 51j and 51k. Moreover, the object phrase in 51j, 'almost all Chinese dishes,' must be transposed to the beginning of the clause.

51j   ✖ 从芥兰牛肉到豆腐，我喜欢几乎*都中国菜。
cóng jièlán niúròu dào dòufu, wǒ xǐhuan jīhū **dōu Zhōngguó cài**
'From beef with broccoli to tofu, I like almost all Chinese dishes.'

✔ 从芥兰牛肉到豆腐，几乎所有的中国菜我都喜欢。
cóng jièlán niúròu dào dòufu, jīhū **suǒyǒude Zhōngguó cài** wǒ *dōu* xǐhuan

51k   ✖ *都学生一定得做功课。
dōu xuésheng yídìng děi zuò-gōngkè
'All the students must do their homework.'

✔ 所有的学生 都一定得做功课。
suǒyǒude xuésheng *dōu* yídìng děi zuò-gōngkè

The problem in 51l is that the phrase *suǒyǒude* is placed after the verb *kàn* 'watch.' The phrase with *suǒyǒude*, if it is the object of the verb, must be transposed to the beginning of the sentence (cf. 51g).

51l   ✖ 中国的广告有很好的信息，值得看*所有的。
Zhōngguó-de-guǎnggào yǒu hěnhǎode xìnxī, zhídé kàn **suǒyǒude**
'The Chinese advertisements provide good information. It's worth
watching all (of them).'

✔ . . . , 所有的 都值得看。
. . . , **suǒyǒude** *dōu* zhídé kàn

The adjective 所有的 *suǒyǒude* 'all' modifies nouns, whereas 都 *dōu*, the adverb 'all,' in the sense of 'altogether,' only precedes a V/VP (*dōu* never precedes a N/NP).

For related topics, see §§49 and 52.

Exercises

EXERCISE 11. Fill in the blanks with 都 *dōu* or 所有的 *suŏyŏude*.

1 牛奶，豆浆，茶，我 _____ 喜欢喝。
2 他 _____ 衬衫 _____ 是白色的。
3 楼上 _____ 窗子 _____ 关着。
4 这儿没有外文书。_____ 书 _____ 是英文的。

EXERCISE 12. Translate into Chinese.

1 All the wines are expensive.
2 Each of them shook hands with him.
3 Do all of you work at the university?

§52. The preposition 从 *cóng* and the prepositional phrase 从 *cóng* X 到 *dào* Y

The preposition 从 *cóng* 'from,' followed by a noun/NP, indicates a starting point for the action of the verb. The noun phrase that follows *cóng* may be a time-expression (52a), a location (52b), or a topic (52c). Note that the *cóng* X phrase precedes the verb.

52a 从九点开始上课 *cóng jiŭdiăn kāishĭ shàngkè* 'start class from 9:00'

52b 从中国回来 *cóng Zhōngguó huí-lai* 'return from China'

52c 从小事看出问题 *cóng xiăo-shì kàn-chū wèntí* 'recognize the problem from small things'

Cóng 'from' is often used with 到 *dào* 'to' in the prepositional phrase *cóng* X *dào* Y 'from X to Y' to indicate scope, with X representing the starting point and Y the end. The scope set by this phrase may be temporal, spatial, quantitative, or topical. See examples 52d–g.

52d Temporal, where X and Y are time expressions (and 从 *cóng* is sometimes omitted):

（从）星期一到星期五 *(cóng) xīngqīyī dào xīngqīwŭ* 'from Monday to Friday'

52e Spatial, where X and Y are locations:

从机场到市中心 *cóng jīchăng dào shìzhōngxīn* 'from the airport to downtown'

52f Quantitative, where X and Y are measurements:

从十吨到三十吨 *cóng shí-dūn dào sānshi-dūn* 'from 10 tons to 30 tons'

52g   Material things, degrees, topics, etc.:
从电视到电话 *cóng diànshì dào diànhuà* 'from television to telephone'
从小到大 *cóng xiǎo dào dà* 'from small to large'
从国际贸易到经济发展 *cóng guójì màoyì dào jīngjì fāzhǎn* 'from
    international trading to economic development'

The prepositional phrase *cóng* X *dào* Y grammatically serves as an adverbial modifier of the main verb. There are two possible frameworks for this prepositional phrase. One is in the structure of 52h, where the entire phrase is followed by the adverb 都 *dōu* 'all,' i.e. 'altogether,' and *dōu* likewise precedes the verb, as in examples 52i–k below.

52h   Subj. + 从 *cóng* X 到 *dào* Y + 都 *dōu* + VP

52i   孩子从头到脚都穿得很漂亮。
      háizi **cóng tóu dào jiǎo dōu** chuān-de hěn piàoliang
      'From head to toe, the child is attractively dressed.'

52j   那个地区从十一月到三月都是冬季。
      nèi-ge-dìqū **cóng shíyīyuè dào sānyuè dōu** shì dōngjì
      'From November to March, it is winter in that area.'

52k   菜园里的品种很多，从番茄到南瓜都有。
      càiyuán-lǐ de pǐnzhǒng hěn duō, **cóng fānqié dào nánguā dōu** yǒu
      'There are many kinds of vegetables in the garden. From tomatoes to
        squash, it has everything.'

In the second structure (52l) the duplicated verb appears between *cóng* X and *dào* Y. In distinction from 52h, this structure indicates that the subject carries out an action, from a starting point signified by *cóng* X, all the way to the end signified by *dào* Y. In this case, if the verb is a V-Obj. compound, it first appears before *cóng* X, and the verb then repeats itself before *dào* Y. 52m–n are such examples. On the other hand, if the verb does not display a V-Obj. form, it does not repeat but simply precedes *dào* Y, as in 52o.

52l   Subj. + (V-Obj. +) 从 *cóng* X + V + 到 *dào* Y

52m   我昨天晚上写论文从八点写到夜里两点。
      wǒ zuótiān wǎnshang **xiě-lùnwén** cóng bādiǎn **xiě-dào** yèlǐ liǎngdiǎn
      'Last night I wrote my paper from eight till two in the morning.'

52n   孙老师讲课从丝绸之路讲到罗马帝国。
      Sūn lǎoshī **jiǎng-kè** cóng sīchóu zhī lù **jiǎng-dào** Luómǎ Dìguó
      'Teacher Sun's lectures began with the Silk Road, and ended with the
        Roman Empire.'

52o 我们从第一课<u>学到</u>第十五课。

wǒmen cóng dì-yī-kè **xué-dào** dì-shíwǔ-kè

'We studied (from) Lessons 1 to 15.'

Either 从 *cóng* X 'from X' or 从 *cóng* X 到 *dào* Y 'from X to Y' functions as an adverbial modifier of the verb. *Cóng* X always precedes the verb. In pattern 52h, the *cóng* X *dào* Y phrase also precedes the verb, whereas in the action-oriented pattern 52l, the duplicated verb appears immediately before *dào* Y.

The following errors violate these rules.

52p ⊗ *<u>去学生餐厅</u><u>从我的宿舍</u>很方便。

qù xuésheng cāntīng **cóng wǒde sùshè** hěn fāngbiàn

'Going to the student cafeteria from my dorm is very convenient.'

▶ **Problem**: *Cóng* X follows the verb phrase. *Cóng* X should be moved to the pre-verbal position.

✓ <u>从我的宿舍</u>去学生餐厅很方便。

cóng wǒde sùshè qù xuésheng cāntīng hěn fāngbiàn

52q ⊗ 这个商店*<u>卖从小说到毛衣</u>。

zhèi-ge-shāngdiàn **mài cóng xiǎoshuō dào máoyī**

'This shop sells everything, from fiction to sweaters.'

▶ **Problem**: The *cóng* X *dào* Y phrase follows the verb. The phrase, plus a 都 *dōu* 'all,' should be moved to the pre-verbal position.

✓ 这个商店<u>从小说到毛衣</u>都卖。

zhèi-ge-shāngdiàn **cóng xiǎoshuō dào máoyī** *dōu* **mài**

52r ⊗ 星期二晚上我*<u>上课从七点到十点</u>，很累。

xīngqī'èr wǎnshang wǒ **shàng-kè cóng qīdiǎn dào shídiǎn**, hěn lèi

'On Tuesday evenings I have class from 7 to 10 o'clock. It is tiring.'

▶ **Problem**: An unsplit *cóng* X *dào* Y phrase follows the V-Obj. compound *shàng-kè*. Following pattern 52l, a duplicated verb 上 *shàng* should be inserted between *cóng* X and *dào* Y.

✓ ... 我上课从七点<u>上</u>到十点，很累。

... wǒ **shàng-kè cóng qīdiǎn shàng-dào** shídiǎn, hěn lèi

52l is the pattern that shows the action continuing from X to Y. In this pattern, the duplicated verb appears immediately before the phrase 到 *dào* Y.

For related topics, see §§33 and 51.

Exercises

EXERCISE 13. Translate into Chinese.

1 from February to May
2 from birth to death
3 from country to city
4 drive north from here
5 The winter time-change begins on Sunday.
6 From old to young, everyone likes ice cream.
7 This movie is interesting from the beginning to the end.
8 We walked from the dorm to the cafeteria.
9 They are having a meeting from 4 to 6 o'clock.
10 She is on vacation until Monday.

§53. The position of the adverb: after the subject and before the verb

Listed in 53a are a few frequently used adverbs. These adverbs modify the verb/VP in a Mandarin sentence. Examples 53b–e demonstrate two important traits of Mandarin adverbs: i) they always come **after the subject**, never before it; and ii) they always come **before a verb** or another adverb.

53a 也 *yě* 'also, as well'   先 *xiān* . . . 再 *zài* . . . 'first . . . then . . .'
        却 *què* 'yet, however'   常常 *chángcháng* 'often'

53b 我喝茶，（我）也喝咖啡。
        wǒ hē-chá, (wǒ) **yě** hē-kāfēi
        'I drink tea, also coffee.'

53c 他没复习功课，今天却考得很好。
        tā méi fùxí-gōngkè, jīntiān **què** kǎo-de hěn hǎo
        'He didn't review his homework; yet he did well on his test today.'

53d 你先洗手，再吃饭。
        nǐ **xiān** xǐ-shǒu, **zài** chī-fàn
        'First you wash your hands; then you eat.'

53e 他常常吃快餐。
        tā **chángcháng** chī-kuàicān
        'He often eats fast food.'

Students may be tempted to put the adverb before the subject. 53f–i provide a few such examples. Remember: Mandarin adverbs never precede the subject. Put them **after** the subject.

53f ⊗ 昨天晚上我很累，*却我到三点还没睡。
zuótiān wǎnshang wǒ hěn lèi, **què wǒ** dào sāndiǎn hái méi-shuì
'I was tired last night, even so I still didn't go to bed until 3 o'clock.'

> ▶ **Problem:** The adverb *què* 'even so' precedes the unnecessary subject *wǒ* 'I.'

✓ 昨天晚上我很累，却到三点还没睡。
zuótiān wǎnshang wǒ hěn lèi, **què** dào sāndiǎn hái méi-shuì

53g ⊗ 这个题目对我来说很陌生，*也我不了解任何信息。
zhèi-ge-tímù duì wǒ láishuō hěn mòshēng, **yě wǒ** bù liáojiě rènhé xìnxī
'This topic is very unfamiliar to me. Also I have no information (about it).'

> ▶ **Problem:** The adverb *yě* 'also' precedes the subject *wǒ* 'I.'

✓ 这个题目对我来说很陌生，我也不了解任何信息。
zhèi-ge-tímù duì wǒ láishuō hěn mòshēng, wǒ **yě** bù liáojiě rènhé xìnxī

53h ⊗ *一再他问老师这个问题。
yízài tā wèn lǎoshī zhèi-ge-wèntí
'He repeatedly asked the teacher this question.'

> ▶ **Problem:** The adverb *yízài* 'repeatedly' precedes the subject *tā* 'he.'

✓ 他一再问老师这个问题。
tā **yízài** wèn lǎoshī zhèi-ge-wèntí

53i ⊗ 她春假不回家，*实在她没有钱买机票。
tā chūnjià bù huí-jiā, **shízài tā** méiyǒu qián mǎi-jīpiào
'She is not going home during spring break. The fact is she doesn't have money for the plane ticket.'

> ▶ **Problem:** The adverb *shízài* 'actually' precedes the subject *tā* 'she.'

✓ 她春假不回家，她实在没有钱买机票。
tā chūnjià bù huí-jiā, tā **shízài** méiyǒu qián mǎi-jīpiào

Another common error is using adverbs to modify nouns, as in 53j. Remember: adverbs modify verbs/VP. Put them before a verb or another adverb, never before a noun.

53j 美国人多半儿会说*只英文。
Měiguórén duōbànr huì shuō **zhǐ yīngwén**
'Most Americans only speak English.'

> ▶ **Problem:** The adverb *zhǐ* 'only' precedes the noun *yīngwén* 'English.' It should appear before the verb phrase *huì shuō* 'can speak.'

✓ 美国人多半儿只会说英文。
Měiguórén duōbànr **zhǐ** huì shuō yīngwén

Adverbs precede a verb or another adverb. Consequently they never precede a subject.

For related topics, see §§16, 48, and 54.

Exercises

EXERCISE 14. (§§53–54) Put the parenthetical adverb(s) in the appropriate location(s).

1   他们去星巴克喝咖啡。(常)
2   弟弟很聪明，不用功。(却)
3   你既然不喜欢这件毛衣，别买。(就)
4   李明喜欢运动，喜欢打篮球。(尤其)
5   你只要复习了，一定考得好。(就)
6   我下课以后吃午饭，回宿舍。(先，再)
7   他们知道了，我没听说。(都，却)
8   如果明天不下雨，我们去野餐。(就)
9   我一直想去看画展，可是没有时间。(总是)
10   一年级的学生认识这个字。(都)
11   如果你骑自行车，你得戴安全帽。(就)
12   他昨天没来，不知道。(当然)

§54. The subject and the correlating adverb 就 *jiù*

The adverb 就 *jiù* occurs in compound sentences that possess a pair of complementary words correlating two verb phrases or clauses. *Jiù* is the second word of the complementary pair, meaning 'then' or 'thereupon,' introducing the second verb phrase/clause. See examples 54a–c.

54a   你<u>只要</u>买了票，(你)<u>就</u>可以进去。
      nǐ **zhǐyào** mǎi-le-piào, (nǐ) **jiù** kěyǐ jìnqu
      'Only if you buy a ticket, do you get in.'

54a′   <u>只要</u>你买了票，(你)<u>就</u>可以进去。
       zhǐyào nǐ mǎi-le-piào, (nǐ) **jiù** kěyǐ jìnqu

54b   你<u>既然</u>有病，(你)<u>就</u>好好儿休息吧。
      nǐ **jìrán** yǒu-bìng, (nǐ) **jiù** hǎohāor xiūxi ba
      'Since you are sick, you should get more rest.'

54b' 既然你有病，（你）就好好儿休息吧。

jìrán nǐ yǒu-bìng, (nǐ) **jiù** hǎohāor xiūxi ba

54c 我（一）下了课就回宿舍去睡觉。

wǒ (**yí**) xià-le-kè **jiù** huí-sùshè qù shuìjiào

'(Soon) after the class is over, I'll go back to the dorm to sleep.'

54a–c have a single subject: *nǐ* 'you' in 54a–b and *wǒ* 'I' in 54c. Regarding the position of the subject, 54a–b are different from 54c. First, the subject may appear before or after the first complementary word. Compare 54a–b with 54a'–b'. Second, this single subject may optionally appear at the beginning of the second clause, as the parenthetical subjects show in both examples. These two opinions, however, do not apply to 54c, the pattern of [*yī* VP₁ *jiù* VP₂], where the subject can only appear at the beginning of the sentence.

Compound sentences may also have two subjects—one for each sub-VP/clause, e.g. *háizi* 'child' and *māma* 'mom' in 54d; *shíjiān* 'time' and *wǒmen* 'we' in 54e; and *lǎoshī* 'teacher' and *xuésheng* 'students' in 54f.

54d 只要孩子穿够衣服，妈妈就放心了。

zhǐyào **háizi** chuān-guò-yīfu, **māma jiù** fàng-xīn le

'Only if the child dresses warmly, would the mom be content.'

54d' 孩子只要穿够衣服，妈妈就放心了。

háizi zhǐyào chuān-guò-yīfu, **māma** jiù fàng-xīn le

54e 既然时间还早，我们就再看一场电影。

jìrán **shíjiān** hái zǎo, **wǒmen jiù** zài kàn yì-chǎng-diànyǐng

'Since it is still early, let's watch another movie.'

54e' 时间既然还早，我们就再看一场电影。

shíjiān jìrán hái zǎo, **wǒmen** jiù zài kàn yì-chǎng-diànyǐng

54f 老师（一）解释了语法，学生就明白了。

lǎoshī (yì) jiěshì-le-yǔfǎ, **xuésheng** jiù míngbai le

'(Soon) after the teacher explained the grammar, the students
    understood it.'

In both 54d and 54e, Subj.₁ may appear before or after the first complementary word, as their 54d'–e' counterparts show. Again this is not an option for 54f, the [*yī* VP₁ *jiù* VP₂] pattern, where Subj.₁ can only appear at the beginning of the sentence. Subj.₂ for all of these sentences must appear at the beginning of the second clause, i.e. before the adverb *jiù*.

▶ **Summary**: i) In a compound sentence, the lone subject or Subj.₁ may appear before or after the first complementary word (54a–a', b–b', d–d', and e–e′), whereas Subj.₂ appears at the beginning of the second VP/clause preceding the adverb *jiù*. ii) In the [*yī* VP₁ *jiù* VP₂] pattern, the lone subject or Subj.₁ must appear before the first complementary word (54c & f), whereas Subj.₂ appears at the beginning of the second VP/clause preceding the adverb *jiù*. iii) The cardinal rule: the subject always precedes the correlating adverb *jiù*.

The commonly made error in this case is to place the subject after the correlating adverb 就 *jiù*, as in the erroneous examples 54g–h. Remember: the subject always precedes *jiù*.

54g   ✕ 要是饭有毒，*就我不吃了！
      yàoshì fàn yǒudú, **jiù wǒ** bù chī le
      'If the food is poisoned, (then) I will not eat it.'

      ✓ 要是饭有毒，我就不吃了！
      yàoshì fàn yǒudú, **wǒ jiù** bù chī le

54h   ✕ 你只要有钱，*就你可以买很多东西。
      nǐ zhǐyào yǒu-qián, **jiù nǐ** kěyǐ mǎi hěnduō dōngxi
      'Only if you have money, can you buy many things.'

      ✓ 你只要有钱，你就可以买很多东西。
      nǐ zhǐyào yǒu-qián, **nǐ jiù** kěyǐ mǎi hěnduō dōngxi

The subject always precedes the correlating adverb 就 *jiù*, and never follows it.

For related topics, see §§12, 17, 31, and 32.

§55. Verb-object compound 睡觉 *shuì-jiào* vs. verb-verb compound 睡着 *shuì-zháo*

睡觉 *shuì-jiào* is a verb-object compound, where the verb *shuì* 'sleep' takes the object *jiào*, which is a noun referring to 'a natural condition of rest,' i.e. 'a sleep.' As noted in §39, since Mandarin transitive verbs in most cases do not stand alone, the verb *shuì* 'sleep' has a generic object *jiào*. The verb-object compound *shuì-jiào*, lit. 'sleep a sleep,' functions as a verb, meaning 'sleep' or 'go to bed.'

睡着 *shuì-zháo* is a verb-verb compound, where the verb *shuì* 'sleep' has the verb complement *zháo* 'attain.' As in other V-V compounds, the verb complement expresses the resultant state of the action initiated by the first verb. The verb complement *zháo* here indicates the success of the action *shuì* 'sleep.' The meaning of the entire compound hence comes from both the verb *shuì* and its complement *zháo* 'sleep-attain = fall asleep' (see also §§38, 41, and 42). Since the simple verb *shuì* and the V-V compound *shuì-zháo* convey different meanings, to express the fact that someone 'falls asleep,' one needs to use the V-V compound *shuì-zháo*.

55a below shows the difference between the two verb compounds *shuì-jiào* and *shuì-zháo*. In the first clause, we need to use *shuì-jiào* 'sleep,' whereas in the second clause, we must use the V-V compound to show that the subject tried to sleep but was unable to.

55a　我十点就上床睡觉了，可是两点还没睡着。
wǒ shídiǎn jiù shàng-chuáng **shuì-jiào** le, kěshì liǎngdiǎn hái méi **shuì-zháo**
'I went to bed (to sleep) at ten o'clock, but still lay awake (unable to fall asleep) at two.'

From the context in 55b–c, we realize that each of these two sentences misuses the other sentence's verb compound. To correct these mistakes, we simply reverse the two verb compounds.

55b　 他教训我的时候，我差一点儿*睡觉。
tā jiàoxùn wǒ de shíhou, wǒ chàyìdiǎnr **shuì-jiào**
'While he was lecturing me, I almost ?slept.'

　　　 他教训我的时候，我差一点儿睡着（了）。(I almost fell asleep.)
tā jiàoxùn wǒ de shíhou, wǒ chàyìdiǎnr **shuì-zháo (le)**

55c　 并不是他没有时间帮我的忙，而是他要*睡着。
bìng búshì tā méiyǒu shíjiān bāng wǒde máng, érshì tā yào **shuì-zháo**
'It's not that he lacks time to help me; he simply wants to ?fall aleep.'

　　　 ..., 而是他要睡觉。(He wants to sleep.)
. . . , érshì tā yào **shuì-jiào**

> Differing in structure, the verb-object compound 睡觉 *shuì-jiào* and the verb-verb compound 睡着 *shuì-zháo* express different meanings.

For related topics, see §§38, 39, 41, 42, and 44.

Exercises

EXERCISE 15. Place two parenthetical phrases in their proper locations.

1　他们 _____ ，还没 _____ 喜欢的。(找到，找房子，找不到)
2　妹妹 _____ ，怎么也 _____ 。(学书法，学会了，学不会)

3　学生 ＿＿＿＿＿ 了，可是没 ＿＿＿＿＿。(考好，考得好，考试)

4　她想 ＿＿＿＿＿，可是一直 ＿＿＿＿＿。(睡着，睡觉，睡不着)

5　老师让学生 ＿＿＿＿＿，学生说 ＿＿＿＿＿。(听录音，听不懂，听懂)

6　他们 ＿＿＿＿＿ 点得太多，所以没 ＿＿＿＿＿。(吃完，没吃完，点菜)

§56.　Mandarin variations on the English verb 'ask'

The English verb 'ask' may be used in different senses, as indicated in parentheses at the end of sentences 56a–e. Their respective Mandarin equivalents illustrate how each of these meanings requires a different Mandarin verb (underlined).

56a　The student asked a question. ('inquire')

学生问了一个问题。

xuésheng **wèn**-le yí-ge wèntí

56b　The judge asks the lawyer for an explanation. ('demand')

法官要求律师解释。

fǎguān **yāoqiú** lǜshī jiěshì

56c　The doctor asks the patient to quit smoking. ('urge')

医生让病人戒烟。

yīshēng **ràng** bìngrén jiè-yān

56d　The child asks the parents to buy a toy. ('request a favor')

孩子求/请父母买玩具。

háizi **qiú**/**qǐng** fùmǔ mǎi-wánjù

56e　Friends ask me out for dinner. ('invite')

朋友请我出去吃饭。

péngyou **qǐng** wǒ chūqù chī-fàn

Note that 56a is in a simple structure of [Subj. + V + Obj.], and it is the only one where the English verb 'ask' means simply 'inquire.' The other four examples, 56b–e, require the structure of 56f, as in 'Bill invites Mary to have a coffee,' the subject (N_1) asks N_2 to do something. Note that in this structure, the second noun serves as the object of the first verb and the subject of the second verb phrase.

56f　$N_{1(Subj.)} + V_1 + N_{2(Obj./Subj.)} + VP_2$

Errors occur when students use Mandarin verb 问 *wèn* 'ask (a question)' in the structure of 56f. 56g–i need different Mandarin verbs to express their respective ideas.

56g ✗ 我有问题的时候，*问我爸爸想解决的办法。

wǒ yǒu-wèntí de shíhou, **wèn** wǒ bàba xiǎng jiějú de bànfǎ

'When I have a problem, I ask my dad to come up with a solution.'

▶ **Analysis**: 'Ask' here means 'request help (from dad).' The verb is 请 *qǐng*.

✓ ..., 请我爸爸想解决的办法。

..., **qǐng** wǒ bàba xiǎng jiějú de bànfǎ

56h ✗ 她*问大家去参加她的生日晚会。

tā **wèn** dàjiā qù cānjiā tāde shēngrì wǎnhuì

'She asks everyone to her birthday party.'

▶ **Analysis**: 'Ask' here means 'invite.' The verb is 请 *qǐng*.

✓ 她请大家去参加她的生日晚会。

tā **qǐng** dàjiā qù cānjiā tāde shēngrì wǎnhuì

56i ✗ 老师*问学生每天练习中文。

lǎoshī **wèn** xuésheng měitiān liànxí zhōngwén

'The teacher asks students to practice Chinese everyday.'

▶ **Analysis**: 'Ask' means 'demand' or 'urge.' The verb is 要求 *yāoqiú* or 让 *ràng*.

✓ 老师要求/让学生每天练习中文。

lǎoshī **yāoqiú/ràng** xuésheng měitiān liànxí zhōngwén

> The different meanings of the English verb 'ask' require different Mandarin verbs. 问 *wèn* only refers to 'ask a question.'

Exercises

EXERCISE 16. Choose the correct Chinese translation of each English sentence.

1 We don't know how to get there. We must ask for directions.

    a) 我们不知道怎么去。我们得问一下路。

    b) 我们不知道怎么去。我们得请一下路。

    c) 我们不知道怎么去。我们得要求一下路。

2 He often asks his girlfriend to the movies.

    a) 他常常问女朋友看电影。

    b) 他常常请女朋友看电影。

    c) 他常常让女朋友看电影。

3   The teacher asks students to speak Chinese in class.

    a)   上课的时候，老师问学生说中文。
    b)   上课的时候，老师求学生说中文。
    c)   上课的时候，老师要求学生说中文。

4   Do you want to ask him for help?

    a)   你想问他帮忙吗？
    b)   你想请他帮忙吗？
    c)   你想要求他帮忙吗？

5   The mother asked the child to go to bed early.

    a)   妈妈问孩子早一点儿睡觉。
    b)   妈妈请孩子早一点儿睡觉。
    c)   妈妈让孩子早一点儿睡觉。

6   She asks the waiter whether they have green tea.

    a)   她问服务员有没有绿茶。
    b)   她请服务员有没有绿茶。
    c)   她要求服务员有没有绿茶。

§57. Auxiliary verbs 会 *huì*, 能 *néng*, and 可以 *kěyǐ*

While all of these three auxiliary verbs—会 *huì*, 能 *néng* and 可以 *kěyǐ*—are translated as 'can,' they convey different meanings.

Huì means 'know how to,' referring to a skill, usually acquired through learning or training. See examples 57a–b.

57a   他会说一点儿中文，可是<u>不会</u>写汉字。

      tā **huì** shuō-yìdiǎnr-zhōngwén, kěshì **bú-huì** xiě-hànzì

      'He can speak a little Chinese, but doesn't know how to write Chinese characters.'

57b   我弟弟会吹笛子。

      wǒ dìdi **huì** chuī-dízi

      'My younger brother can play the flute.'

Néng means 'be able to,' referring to ability, the capacity to do something. See 57c–d. 'Be able to' also implies that the situation or conditions allow one to do so. When the meaning veers into 'possibility,' it is interchangeable with 可以 *kěyǐ*, as shown in 57e and 57g.

57c 这个孩子一个夏天能看五十本书。

zhèi-ge-háizi yí-ge-xiàtiān **néng** kàn wǔshí-běn-shū

'This child can read fifty books in a summer.'

57d 你喝了不少酒，不能开车。

nǐ hē-le bùshǎo jiǔ, **bù néng** kāi-chē

'You have drunk a lot. You can't drive.'

57e 完事了。我们能走了。

wán-shì-le. wǒmen **néng** zǒu le

'It's finished. We can leave now.'

Kěyǐ, means 'may,' referring to permission or possibility. See examples 57f–g. Note the similarity between 57g and 57e above.

57f 你可以用我的车。

nǐ **kěyǐ** yòng wǒde chē

'You can/may use my car.'

57g 完事了。我们可以走了。

wán-shì-le. wǒmen **kěyǐ** zǒu le

'It's finished. We can/may leave now.'

To avoid errors such as 57h–j, one needs to be aware of the different meanings these auxiliary verbs respectively convey.

57h ✖ 我到现在还*不可以骑自行车。

wǒ dào xiànzài hái **bù kěyǐ** qí zìxíngchē

'Today I still can't ride a bicycle.'

> ▶ **Analysis**: Knowing how to ride a bicycle is a skill that one has learned. Thus the auxiliary verb should be 会 *huì*.

✔ 我到现在还不会骑自行车。

wǒ dào xiànzài hái **bú huì** qí zìxíngchē

57i ✖ 我没有钱，结果*不会买那个电脑。

wǒ méiyǒu qián, jiéguǒ **bú huì** mǎi nèi-ge-diànnǎo

'I don't have money; so I can't buy that computer.'

> ▶ **Analysis**: It's impossible for me to buy the computer, or I am unable to buy it, because I do not have money. This has nothing to do with skills. So the auxiliary verb should be 能 *néng*.

✔ 我没有钱，结果不能买那个电脑。

wǒ méiyǒu qián, jiéguǒ **bù néng** mǎi nèi-ge-diànnǎo

57j ✖ 在美国，十八岁的人有很多特权，可是*不会喝酒。

zài Měiguó, shíbā suì de rén yǒu hěnduō tèquán, kěshì **bú huì** hē-jiǔ

'In the US, eighteen-year-olds have some privileges. But they can't drink.'

▶ **Analysis**: This case is clearly about permission (and possibility). Again, it has nothing to do with skills. The auxiliary verb therefore should be 可以 *kěyǐ* or 能 *néng*.

✅ 十八岁的人有很多特权，可是<u>不可以/不能</u>喝酒。

shíbā suì de rén yǒu hěnduō tèquán, kěshì **bù kěyǐ/bù néng** hē-jiǔ

> Each auxiliary verb has its own meaning: 会 *huì* means 'know how to'; 能 *néng* means 'be able to'; and 可以 *kěyǐ* means 'may.'

Exercises

EXERCISE 17. Fill in the blanks with an auxiliary verb: 会 *huì*, 能 *néng*, or 可以 *kěyǐ*.

1   我 _____ 说一点儿俄语，也 _____ 看一点儿俄文书。
2   要是你不懂，_____ 问问老师。
3   你在图书馆里不 _____ 大声说话。
4   孩子太小，还不 _____ 走路。
5   上课的时候，老师要我们说中文，不 _____ 说英文。
6   我听说那个美国人 _____ 唱中国民歌。
7   请问我 _____ 在这儿吸烟吗？
8   对不起，我现在很忙，不 _____ 去。

§58.   Cognitive verbs 知道 *zhīdào* and 认识 *rènshi*

While both Mandarin cognitive verbs 知道 *zhīdào* and 认识 *rènshi* are translated as 'know,' they represent different senses of the English verb.

Zhīdào means to know about facts. See examples 58a–b. To express 'know how to do . . . ,' the Mandarin phrase is [知道怎么 *zhīdào zěnme* + VP], as in 58c.

58a   我知道汉语普通话有四声。
      wǒ zhīdào hànyǔ pǔtōnghuà yǒu sì-shēng
      'I know that Mandarin Chinese has four tones.'

58b   我知道丰田是日本车。
      wǒ zhīdào Fēngtián shì Rìběn chē
      'I know that Toyotas are Japanese cars.'

58c 我知道怎么炖羊肉。

wǒ zhīdào zěnme dùn-yángròu

'I know how to make lamb stew.'

Rènshi, representing knowledge as familiarity, has a few denotations, e.g. be acquainted with a person (58d), recognize or be familiar with things (58e–f), and meet someone, even for the first time (58g).

58d 我认识白先生，我们是邻居。

wǒ rènshi Bái xiānsheng, wǒmen shì línju

'I know Mr. Bai. We are neighbors.'

58e 那个学生认识两千多个汉字。

nèi-ge-xuésheng rènshi liǎngqiān duō-ge-hànzì

'That student can handle more than 2,000 Chinese characters.'

58f 他认识路，让他带你去吧。

tā rènshi lù, ràng tā dài nǐ qù ba

'He is familiar with the route. Let him take you there.'

58g 认识你，很高兴。

rènshi nǐ, hěn gāoxìng

'Pleased to meet you.'

 To avoid errors such as 58h–k, one needs to observe the respective denotations that 知道 *zhīdào* and 认识 *rènshi* possess.

58h ⊗ 我*不认识那个学生是谁。

wǒ **bú rènshi nèi-ge-xuésheng shì shéi**

'I don't know who that student is.'

▶ **Analysis**: 'Who that student is' is a fact. The verb here should be *zhīdào*. On the other hand, if the idea is 'I am not acquainted with that student,' remove *shì shéi* 'who it is.'

✓ 我不知道那个学生是谁。

wǒ bù **zhīdào** nèi-ge-xuésheng shì shéi

✓ 我不认识那个学生。

wǒ bú rènshi nèi-ge-xuésheng

58i ⊗ 出租司机*认识我是美国人，他跟我要高价。

chūzū sījī **rènshi** wǒ shì Měiguórén, tā gēn wǒ yào gāo-jià

'The taxi driver knew I was an American, so he asked a higher price.'

▶ **Analysis**: The taxi driver is not acquainted with me. But he knows the fact that I am an American. Thus the verb should be *zhīdào*.

✓ 出租司机知道我是美国人，他跟我要高价。

chūzū sījī **zhīdào** wǒ shì Měiguórén, tā gēn wǒ yào gāo-jià

58j ✗ 高莉莉是我的中文班同学。我当然 *知道她!

Gāo Lìli shì wǒde zhōngwénbān tóngxué. wǒ dāngrán **zhīdào tā**!

'Gao Lili is my classmate in Chinese class. Of course I know her!'

▶ **Analysis**: Since Gao Lili is a classmate, I am certainly her acquaintance. Besides 'she' is not a fact. The verb therefore should be *rènshi*.

✓ 高莉莉是我的中文班同学。我当然认识她!

Gāo Lìli shì wǒde zhōngwénbān tóngxué. wǒ dāngrán **rènshi tā**!

58k ✗ 一年级的学生还 *不知道很多汉字。

yī-niánjí de xuésheng hái **bù zhīdào hěn duō hànzì**

'The first-year students still don't know many Chinese characters.'

▶ **Analysis**: The first-year students are not familiar with many Chinese characters. The verb should be *rènshi*.

✓ 一年级的学生还不认识很多汉字。

yī-niánjí de xuésheng hái **bú rènshi** hěn duō hànzì

知道 *zhīdào* means to know about facts or 'know how to do . . . ,' whereas 认识 *rènshi* represents knowledge in terms of familiarity, such as being acquainted with a person or recognizing things.

For related topics, see §20.

Exercises

EXERCISE 18. From the squared parentheses for each sentence, select 知道 *zhīdào* or 认识 *rènshi*.

1 你[知道，认识]那个女生吗？你[知道，认识]她叫什么名字吗？
2 我[知道，认识]泰山在山东省。
3 请问，你[知道，认识]中国古代的四大发明吗？
4 对不起，我也不[知道，认识]这个字。
5 他们是上大学的时候[知道，认识]的。
6 他[知道，认识]怎么去地铁站。
7 在中国坐火车旅行可以[知道，认识]很多朋友。

Check your grammar

Translate these sentences into Chinese, and then check to see that you have implemented the relevant grammar points. The parenthetical numbers and letters identify the pertinent subsections and examples.

1 I don't feel well today. So I slept a lot. (§46i)
2 The soil in this area is much more fertile than other places. (§46j)

3 We traveled during spring break and luckily didn't run into traffic jams. (§46k)

4 I still remember what you said a year ago. (§46l)

5 If you are a little tired, we will take a break. (§47i)

6 I like to drink a little tea every morning. (§47j)

7 The location of my dorm is good. It's a small distance to both classrooms and the cafeteria. (§47k)

8 My family and I like to watch Chinese movies. (§48h)

9 If you can't get along with your roommate and you want a single room, please fill out a form. (§48i)

10 My work schedule is flexible; my working environment is good, and my income is also fair. (§48j)

11 She placed some chairs on the stage. (§49f)

12 I study at the library every evening. (§50k)

13 Every bag of her luggage is overweight. (§50l)

14 From beef with broccoli to tofu, I like almost all Chinese dishes. (§51j)

15 All the students must do their homework. (§51k)

16 The Chinese advertisements provide good information. It's worth watching all (of them). (§51l)

17 Going to the student cafeteria from my dorm is very convenient. (§52p)

18 This shop sells everything, from fiction to sweaters. (§52q)

19 On Tuesday evenings I have class from 7 to 10 o'clock. It is tiring. (§52r)

20 I was tired last night, even so I still didn't go to bed until 3 o'clock. (§53f)

21 This topic is very unfamiliar to me. Also I have no information (about it). (§53g)

22 He repeatedly asked the teacher this question. (§53h)

23 She is not going home during spring break. The fact is she doesn't have money for the plane ticket. (§53i)

24 Most Americans only speak English. (§53j)

25 If the food is poisoned, (then) I will not eat it. (§54g)

26 Only if you have money, can you buy many things. (§54h)

27 While he was lecturing me, I almost fell asleep. (§55b)

28 It's not that he lacks time to help me; he simply wants to sleep. (§55c)

29 When I have a problem, I ask my dad to come up with a solution. (§56g)

30 She asks everyone to her birthday party. (§56h)

31 The teacher asks students to practice Chinese everyday. (§56i)

32 Today I still can't ride a bicycle. (§57h)

33 I don't have money; so I can't buy that computer. (§57i)

34 In the US, eighteen-year-olds have some privileges. But they can't drink. (§57j)

35 I don't know who that student is. / I am not acquainted with that student. (§58h)

36 The taxi driver knew I was an American, so he asked a higher price. (§58i)

37 Gao Lili is my classmate in Chinese class. Of course I know her! (§58j)

38 The first-year students still don't know many Chinese characters. (§58k)

Answer key to exercises

Part I

EXERCISE 1.
1. 中文语法很容易。zhōngwén yǔfǎ hěn róngyi / 2. 我的朋友都累极了，我却不累。
wǒde péngyou dōu lèi-jíle, wǒ què bú lèi / 3. 天气越来越冷。tiānqì yuèláiyuè lěng /
4. 牛奶不贵。niúnǎi bú guì

EXERCISE 2.
1. 六月有三十天。liùyuè yǒu sānshí tiān / 2. 书桌上有一个电脑。shūzhuō-shàng yǒu
yí-ge-diànnǎo / 3. 宿舍附近有六个网球场吗？ sùshè fùjìn yǒu liù-ge-wǎngqiúchǎng ma /
4. 老师不在她的办公室。lǎoshī bú zài tāde bàngōngshì / 5. 黄河在中国北方。huánghé
zài Zhōngguó běifāng / 6. 孩子们在公园里。háizimen zài gōngyuán-lǐ

EXERCISE 3.
1. 孩子们每天下午在公园里玩儿。háizimen měitiān xiàwǔ zài gōngyuán-li wánr / 2. 很多
美国学生在国外学语言。hěn duō Měiguó xuésheng zài guówài xué yǔyán / 3. 他们在园子
里种了花。tāmen zài yuánzi lǐ zhòng-le-huā / 4. 她喜欢在星巴克喝咖啡。tā xǐhuan zài
xīngbākè hē-kāfēi / 5. 我们在学生餐厅吃午饭。wǒmen zài xuésheng cāntīng chī-wǔfàn

EXERCISE 4.
1. 很多美国学生去中国学中文。hěn duō Měiguó xuésheng qù Zhōngguó xué zhōngwén
/ 2. 我们去山上露营吧。wǒmen qù shānshàng lùyíng ba / 3. 我去邮局寄一封信。wǒ qù
yóujú jì yì-fēng-xìn / 4. 她常去她朋友的房间聊天。tā cháng qù tā péngyou de fángjiān
liáo-tiān / 5. 我们今天没去学生餐厅吃午饭。wǒmen jīntiān méi qù xuésheng cāntīng
chī-wǔfàn

EXERCISE 5.
1. 我和朋友在她家喝咖啡。wǒ hé péngyou zài tā jiā hē-kāfēi / 2. 他们星期五下午在体育馆
打球。tāmen xīngqīwǔ xiàwǔ zài tǐyùguǎn dǎ-qiú / 3. 他们昨天晚饭吃了三个钟头。
tāmen zuótiān chī-wǎnfàn chī-le sān-ge-zhōngtóu / 4. 小马星期二晚上在图书馆工作四个
小时。Xiǎo Mǎ xīngqī'èr wǎnshang zài túshūguǎn gōngzuò sì-ge-xiǎoshí / 5. 小马每个
星期在图书馆工作。Xiǎo Mǎ měi-ge-xīngqī zài túshūguǎn gōngzuò / 6. 我去年学了
九个月的日文。wǒ qùnián xué-le jiǔ-ge-yuè de rìwén / 7. 她不常在电影院看电影。

tā bùcháng zài diànyǐngyuàn kàn-diànyǐng / 8. 他们现在在外面等我呢！tāmen xiànzài zài wàimian děng wǒ ne!

EXERCISE 6.

1. 那个学生去年暑假在超级市场打工。nèi-ge-xuésheng qùnián shǔjià zài chāojí shìchǎng dǎ-gōng / 2. 他们平常吃一个小时的午饭。tāmen píngcháng chī yí-ge-xiǎoshí de wǔfàn; 他们平常吃午饭吃一个小时。tāmen píngcháng chī-wǔfàn chī yí-ge-xiǎoshí / 3. 我们星期二晚上七点上文学课。wǒmen xīngqī'èr wǎnshang qīdiǎn shàng-wénxuékè / 4. 他们每年春天旅行三个星期。tāmen měi-nián chūntiān lǚxíng sān-ge-xīngqī / 5. 她总是在那个地铁站上车。tā zǒngshì zài nèi-ge-dìtiězhàn shàng-chē / 6. 我姐姐在中国教了一个学期的英文。wǒ jiějie zài Zhōngguó jiāo-le yí-ge-xuéqī de yīngwén

EXERCISE 7.

1. 日文语法比中文语法复杂。rìwén yǔfǎ bǐ zhōngwén yǔfǎ fùzá / 2. 箱子比书包重。xiāngzi bǐ shūbāo zhòng / 3. 走路比开车方便。zǒu-lù bǐ kāi-chē fāngbiàn / 4. 哥哥比弟弟高一点儿。gēge bǐ dìdi gāo yìdiǎnr / 5. 北京比承德大得多。Běijīng bǐ Chéngdé dà-de duō / 6. 桔子比苹果贵一块钱。júzi bǐ píngguǒ guì yí-kuài-qián / 7. 我的室友比我早起一个钟头。wǒde shìyǒu bǐ wǒ zǎo qǐ yí-ge-zhōngtóu / 8. 他比我多看三本书。tā bǐ wǒ duō kàn sān-běn-shū

EXERCISE 8.

1. 茶杯和酒杯一样大。chábēi hé jiǔbēi yíyàng dà / 2. 地铁站和汽车站一样近。dìtiězhàn hé qìchēzhàn yíyàng jìn / 3. 蓝色的和绿色的一样好看。lánsè-de hé lǜsè-de yíyàng hǎokàn / 4. 那本书没有这本书（这么）有意思。nèi-běn-shū méiyǒu zhèi-běn-shū (zhème) yǒuyìsi / 5. 中学生没有大学生忙。zhōngxuéshēng méiyǒu dàxuéshēng máng / 6. 今天没有昨天（那么）冷。jīntiān méiyǒu zuótiān (nème) lěng

EXERCISE 9.

1. 手表比钟贵。shǒubiǎo bǐ zhōng guì / 2. 新电脑比旧电脑快。xīn diànnǎo bǐ jiù diànnǎo kuài / 3. 西瓜比桃子好吃。xīguā bǐ táozi hǎochī / 4. 这个星期的功课比上个星期的多。zhèi-ge-xīngqī de gōngkè bǐ shàng-ge-xīngqī de duō / 5. 看书比看电视有意思。kàn-shū bǐ kàn-diànshì yǒuyìsi / 6. 滑冰比滑雪容易学。huá-bīng bǐ huá-xuě róngyi xué

EXERCISE 10.

1. 我妈妈唱歌唱得比我好得多。wǒ māma chàng-gē chàng-de bǐ wǒ hǎo-de duō; 我妈妈比我唱歌唱得好得多。wǒ māma bǐ wǒ chàng-gē chàng-de hǎo-de duō; 我妈妈唱歌比我唱得好得多。wǒ māma chàng-gē bǐ wǒ chàng-de hǎo-de duō / 2. 弟弟跑步跑得跟哥哥一样快。dìdi pǎo-bù pǎo-de gēn gēge yíyàng kuài; 弟弟跟哥哥跑步跑得一样快。dìdi gēn gēge pǎo-bù pǎo-de yíyàng kuài; 弟弟跑步跟哥哥跑得一样快。dìdi pǎo-bù gēn gēge pǎo-de yíyàng kuài / 3. 大人睡觉睡得没有孩子多。dàrén shuì-jiào shuì-de méiyǒu háizi duō; 大人没有孩子睡觉睡得多。dàrén méiyǒu háizi shuì-jiào shuì-de duō; 大人睡觉没有孩子睡得多。dàrén shuì-jiào méiyǒu háizi shuì-de duō

EXERCISE 11.

1. 他比他妹妹高三英寸。tā bǐ tā mèimei gāo sān yīngcùn / 2. 四月比三月暖和一点儿。sìyuè bǐ sānyuè nuǎnhuo yìdiǎnr / 3. 他的手机和我的一样新。tāde shǒujī hé wǒde yíyàng xīn / 4. 山东菜没有四川菜（那么）辣。Shāndōng cài méiyǒu Sìchuān cài (nème) là / 5. 女儿比爸爸下棋下得好。nǚ'ér bǐ bàba xià-qí xià-de hǎo / 6. 他吃得跟我一样多，可是没有我（这么）胖。tā chī-de gēn wǒ yíyàng duō, kěshì méiyǒu wǒ (zhème) pàng

EXERCISE 12.

1. 我把我的旧车卖了。wǒ bǎ wǒde jiù-chē mài le / 2. 你今天一定得把这个练习做完。nǐ jīntiān yídìng děi bǎ zhèi-ge-liànxí zuò-wán / 3. 你把这件事告诉谁了？nǐ bǎ zhèi-jiàn-shì gàosù shuí le? / 4. Cannot be changed. / 5. 请你把电视打开，好不好？qǐng nǐ bǎ diànshì dǎ-kāi, hǎo bù hǎo? / 6. Cannot be changed. / 7. 如果有问题，请你把手举起来。rúguǒ yǒu wèntí, qǐng nǐ bǎ shǒu jǔ-qǐlái / 8. 你明天把你的功课交给老师吧。nǐ míngtiān bǎ nǐde gōngkè jiāo gěi lǎoshī ba / 9. Cannot be changed. / 10. 我喜欢把上课的笔记记在书上。wǒ xǐhuan bǎ shàngkè de bǐjì jì zài shūshang / 11. 他们把所有的新影碟都借走了。tāmen bǎ suǒyǒude xīn yǐngdié dōu jiè-zǒu le / 12. 商店把老人买的东西送来了。shāngdiàn bǎ lǎorén mǎi de dōngxi sòng-lái le

EXERCISE 13.

1. 他们不想把窗子打开。tāmen bù xiǎng bǎ chuāngzi dǎ-kāi / 2. 请（你）把椅子搬出去。qǐng (nǐ) bǎ yǐzi bān-chūqù / 3. 她已经把我的电话号码忘了。tā yǐjīng bǎ wǒde diànhuà hàomǎ wàng le / 4. 你不能把车停在这儿。nǐ bù néng bǎ chē tíng zài zhèr / 5. 我把这个问题看得太简单了。wǒ bǎ zhèi-ge-wèntí kàn-de tài jiǎndān le / 6. 我没把电脑带回家。wǒ méi bǎ diànnǎo dài-huí jiā

EXERCISE 14.

1. 他的钱被小偷偷了。tāde qián bèi xiǎotōu tōu le / 2. 玩具常常被孩子弄坏。wánjù chángcháng bèi háizi nòng-huài / 3. 蛋糕叫他吃了。dàngāo jiào tā chī le / 4. 我没有伞，衣服都被雨淋湿了。wǒ méiyǒu sǎn, yīfu dōu bèi yǔ lín-shī le / 5. 书已经被他还给图书馆了。shū yǐjīng bèi tā huán gěi túshūguǎn le / 6. 房间让小毛打扫得很干净。fángjiān ràng Xiǎo Máo dǎsǎo de hěn gānjìng

Part II

EXERCISE 1.

1. 如果你今天晚上有空，我们就去看电影。rúguǒ nǐ jīntiān wǎnshang yǒu kòng, wǒmen jiù qù kàn-diànyǐng / 2. 要是我知道，我就告诉你。yàoshi wǒ zhīdào, wǒ jiù gàosu nǐ / 3. 如果你忘了她的名字，你一定会觉得不好意思。rúguǒ nǐ wàng-le tāde míngzi, nǐ yídìng huì juéde bùhǎoyìsi

EXERCISE 2.

1. 学生不但得上课，而且得做功课。xuésheng búdàn děi shàng-kè, érqiě děi zuò-gōngkè / 2. 她不但喜欢看故事，而且喜欢给我们讲（她看的）故事。tā búdàn xǐhuan kàn-gùshi, érqiě xǐhuan gěi wǒmen jiǎng (tā kàn de) gùshi / 3. 不但男孩子踢足球，而且女孩子也踢。búdàn nán háizi tī-zúqiú, érqiě nǚ háizi yě tī

EXERCISE 3.

1. 虽然我的朋友有电视，可是他很少看。suīrán wǒde péngyou yǒu diànshì, kěshi tā hěnshǎo kàn / 2. 虽然我会说一点儿中文，却说得不好。suīrán wǒ huì shuō yìdiǎnr zhōngwén, què shuō-de bùhǎo / 3. 虽然（正在）下雪，天气却不冷。suīrán (zhèngzài) xià-xuě, tiānqì què bù lěng

EXERCISE 4.

1. a / 2. a / 3. b / 4. a / 5. b / 6. b

EXERCISE 5.
1. 学中文，你先学拼音，再学汉字。xué-zhōngwén, nǐ xiān xué-pīnyīn, zài xué-hànzì /
2. 小孩子先学走路，再学跑。xiǎoháizi xiān xué-zǒulù, zài xué-pǎo / 3. 下车的人先下，
上车的人再上。xiàchē-de rén xiān xià, shàngchē-de-rén zài shàng / 4. 你先坐下，
我们再谈。nǐ xiān zuò-xia, wǒmen zài tán

EXERCISE 6.
1. 她决定先吃午饭，再回家。tā juédìng xiān chī-wǔfàn, zài huí-jiā / 2. 你先查查地图，
再去。nǐ xiān chácha-dìtú, zài qù / 3. 你先说，我再答。nǐ xiān shuō, wǒ zài dá

EXERCISE 7.
1. 他一毕业就找到一个很好的工作。tā yí bìyè jiù zhǎo-dào yí-ge hěnhǎo de gōngzuò /
2. 她今天一回到宿舍就睡觉了。tā jīntiān yì huí-dào sùshè jiù shuìjiào le / 3. 天一变冷，
他就容易感冒。tiān yí biàn lěng, tā jiù róngyì gǎnmào / 4. 他们一上车，火车就开了。
tāmen yí shàng-chē, huǒchē jiù kāi le

EXERCISE 8.
1. 那个运动员一喝冰茶就肚子疼。nèi-ge-yùndòngyuán yì hē-bīngchá jiù dùzi téng /
2. 她一有点儿钱就花掉。tā yì yǒu-diǎr-qián jiù huā-diào / 3. 他一解释，我们就懂了。
tā yì jiěshì, wǒmen jiù dǒng le

EXERCISE 9.
1. 樱花美不美？yīnghuā měi-bù-měi? / 2. 他的话有没有道理？tāde-huà yǒu-méi-yǒu
dàolǐ? / 3. 那个法国人会不会说英文？nèi-ge-Fǎguórén huì-bú-huì shuō-yīngwén? / 4. 你喝不
喝啤酒？nǐ hē-bù-hē píjiǔ? / 5. 你看得懂看不懂中文书？nǐ kàn-de-dǒng kàn-bù-dǒng
zhōngwén-shū? / 6. 他们买没买房？tāmen mǎi-méi-mǎi fáng? / 7. 你们周末睡得晚不晚？
nǐmen zhōumò shuì-de wǎn-bù-wǎn?

EXERCISE 10.
1. 你会开车吗？nǐ huì kāi-chē ma?; 你会不会开车？nǐ huì-bú-huì kāi-chē? / 2. 你今天
下午碰得到他吗？nǐ jīntiān xiàwǔ pèng-de-dào tā ma?; 你今天下午碰得到碰不到他？
nǐ jīntiān xiàwǔ pèng-de-dào pèng-bú-dào tā? / 3. 你昨天晚上看新闻了吗？nǐ zuótiān
wǎnshang kàn-xīnwén le ma?; 你昨天晚上看没看新闻？nǐ zuótiān wǎnshang
kàn-méi-kàn xīnwén? / 4. 汤很热吗？tāng hěn rè ma?; 汤热不热？tāng rè-bú-rè?

EXERCISE 11.
1. 那个女孩儿是谁？nèi-ge-nǚháir shì shéi? / 2. 这是谁的电话号码？zhèi shì shéi-de
diànhuà hàomǎ? / 3. 比尔是哪国人？Bǐ'ěr shì nǎ-guó rén? / 4. 你们常常去哪儿？
nǐmen chángcháng qù nǎr? / 5. 你们什么时候开会？nǐmen shénme shíhou kāi-huì? /
6. 裙子（卖）多少钱？qúnzi (mài) duōshǎo qián? / 7. 她是什么专业？tā shì shénme
zhuānyè? / 8. 中文班有多少个学生？zhōngwénbān yǒu duōshǎo ge xuésheng? /
9. 哪辆车是老李的？nǎ-liàng-chē shì Lǎo Lǐ de? / 10. 他们怎么去机场？tāmen zěnme
qù jīchǎng?

EXERCISE 12.
1. 一年有多少天？yì-nián yǒu duōshǎo tiān? / 2. 这是谁的手机？zhèi shì shéide shǒujī? /
3. 她常在哪儿吃晚饭？tā cháng zài nǎr chī-wǎnfàn? / 4. 你今天有什么课？nǐ jīntiān yǒu
shénme kè? / 5. 你最喜欢哪首歌？nǐ zuì xǐhuan nǎ-shǒu-gē?

EXERCISE 13.
1. 他父母知道他喜欢不喜欢那个工作。tā fùmǔ zhīdào tā xǐhuan-bù-xǐhuan nèi-ge-gōngzuò / 2. 学生知道大考难不难。xuésheng zhīdào dàkǎo nán-bù-nán / 3. 我们不知道水暖工来不来。wǒmen bù zhīdào shuǐnuǎngōng lái-bù-lái / 4. 我们也不知道水暖工什么时候来。wǒmen yě bù zhīdào shuǐnuǎngōng shénme shíhou lái / 5. 她不知道她为什么选了中文课。tā bù zhīdào tā wèishénme xuǎn-le zhōngwénkè / 6. 你知道他喝茶还是喝咖啡吗？nǐ zhīdào tā hē-chá háishì hē-kāfēi ma?; 你知道不知道他喝茶还是喝咖啡？nǐ zhīdào-bù-zhīdào tā hē-chá háishì hē-kāfēi? / 7. 你知道不知道我们应该点什么菜？nǐ zhīdào-bù-zhīdào wǒmen yīnggāi diǎn shénme cài?

EXERCISE 14.
1. A: 还是 háishì; B: 或者 huòzhě / 2. 或者 huòzhě / 3. 还是 háishì / 4. 或者 huòzhě

EXERCISE 15.
1. 你喜欢红色的还是蓝色的？nǐ xǐhuān hóngsè-de háishì lánsè-de? / 2. 你觉得报纸贵还是杂志贵？nǐ juéde bàozhǐ guì háishì zázhì guì? / 3. 你早上或者晚上吃这个药都可以。nǐ zǎoshang huòzhě wǎnshang chī zhèi-ge-yào dōu kěyǐ / 4. 她想学一门东亚语言，中文或者日文都行。tā xiǎng xué yì-mén-dōngyà yǔyán, zhōngwén huòzhě rìwén dōu xíng / 5. 李先生今年夏天去中国还是去印度？Lǐ xiānsheng jīnnián xiàtiān qù Zhōngguó háishì qù Yìndù? / 6. 对我来说，住宿舍或者住校外，都一样。duì wǒ lái shuō, zhù-sùshè huòzhě zhù-xiàowài, dōu yíyàng / 7. 我们吃米饭或者面条都好。wǒmen chī-mǐfàn huòzhě miàntiáo dōu hǎo

Part III

EXERCISE 1.
Chronological time: 2; 3; 6; 8; 10; 11 / Durational time: 1; 4; 5; 7; 9; 12

EXERCISE 2.
1. 中午十二点 zhōngwǔ shí'èr-diǎn / 2. 这个星期 zhèi-ge-xīngqī / 3. 两个小时十分钟 liǎng-ge-xiǎoshí shí fēnzhōng / 4. 星期一上午十点 xīngqīyī shàngwǔ shí-diǎn / 5. 一七八九年七月十四日 yī qī bā jiǔ nián qīyuè shísì rì / 6. 半年 bàn nián / 7. 五个月 wǔ-ge-yuè / 8. 晚上七点十分 wǎnshang qī-diǎn shí-fēn / 9. 夜里两点半 yèlǐ liǎng-diǎn-bàn / 10. 一年以后 yì-nián yǐhòu / 11. 七天 qī-tiān / 12. 昨天早晨／早上六点 zuótiān zǎochén/zǎoshang liù-diǎn

EXERCISE 3.
1. 他早上六点出去跑步，风雨无阻。tā <u>zǎoshang liù-diǎn</u> chūqù pǎo-bù, fēngyǔ wúzǔ / 2. 我们休息十分钟。wǒmen xiūxi <u>shí-fēnzhōng</u> / 3. 张老先生每天打一个钟头（的）太极拳。Zhāng lǎo xiānsheng měitiān dǎ <u>yí-ge-zhōngtóu</u> (de) tàijíquán / 4. 我弟弟下个星期六过生日。wǒ dìdi <u>xià-ge-xīngqīliù</u> guò-shēngrì / 5. 他昨天太累了，睡了整整一天（的）觉。tā zuótiān tài lèi le, shuì-le <u>zhěngzhěng yì-tiān</u> (de) jiào / 6. 她明年春天大学毕业。tā <u>míngnián chūntiān</u> dàxué bìyè / 7. 他们十月打算结婚。tāmen shíyuè dǎsuàn jié-hūn (*decision made in October*); 他们打算十月结婚。tāmen dǎsuàn shíyuè jié-hūn (*wedding to be held in October*) / 8. 我们已经认识多久了？wǒmen yǐjīng rènshi <u>duōjiǔ</u> le? / 9. 他们去年在非洲旅行了两个月。tāmen <u>qùnián</u> zài Fēizhōu lǚxíng-le <u>liǎng-ge-yuè</u> / 10. 几个孩子今天在外面玩儿了三个多小时。jǐ-ge-háizi <u>jīntiān</u> zài wàimian wánr-le <u>sān-ge duō xiǎoshí</u> / 11. 他以前学过六个星期（的）中文。tā <u>yǐqián</u> xué-guò

liù-ge-xīngqī (de) zhōngwén / 12. 邻居周末请了一天（的）客。línjū zhōumò qǐng-le yì-tiān (de) kè

EXERCISE 4.
1. 今年夏天 jīnnián xiàtiān / 2. 上个星期 shàng-ge-xīngqī / 3. 两个钟头 liǎng-ge zhōngtóu / 4. 十二个月 shí'èr-ge-yuè / 5. 九点二十分 jiǔ diǎn èrshi fēn / 6. 夜里 yèlǐ

EXERCISE 5.
1. 我们每天晚上六点看新闻。wǒmen měitiān wǎnshang liù-diǎn kàn-xīnwén / 2. 他演讲了二十分钟。tā yǎnjiǎng-le èr'shi-fēnzhōng / 3. 我们在这儿等了三个钟头了！wǒmen zài-zhèr děng-le sān-ge-zhōngtóu le? / 4. 秋季学期九月开始。qiūjì xuéqī jiǔyuè kāishǐ / 5. 老人每天下午午睡半个钟头。lǎo-rén měitiān xiàwǔ wǔshuì bàn-ge-zhōngtóu / 6. 那个售货员一个星期工作六天。nèi-ge-shòuhuòyuán yí-ge-xīngqī gōngzuò liù-tiān

EXERCISE 6.
1. 开车的时候，有些人用手机。kāi-chē de shíhou, yǒuxiē rén yòng-shǒujī / 2. 问路的时候，他很客气。wèn-lù de shíhou, tā hěn kèqi / 3. 我们第一次见面的时候，她留着长发。wǒmen dìyīcì jiàn-miàn de shíhou, tā liú-zhe chángfà / 4. 在非洲旅行的时候，我碰到了一个老同学。zài Fēizhōu lǚxíng de shíhou, wǒ pèng-dào-le yí-ge-lǎo tóngxué

EXERCISE 7.
1. 她以前吸烟。tā yǐqián xī-yān / 2. 早上七点以前请别给我打电话。zǎoshang qī-diǎn yǐqián qǐng bié gěi wǒ dǎ-diànhuà / 3. 我们以前不认识。wǒmen yǐqián bú rènshi / 4. 你以前住在哪儿？nǐ yǐqián zhù zài nǎr? / 5. 看课文以前，我们最好先学生词。kàn-kèwén yǐqián, wǒmen zuìhǎo xiān xué-shēngcí / 6. 你出国旅行以前需要换一些钱吗？nǐ chū-guó lǚxíng yǐqián xūyào huàn yìxiē qián ma?

EXERCISE 8.
1. 以前 yǐqián / 2. 的时候 de shíhou / 3. 时时刻刻 shíshíkèkè / 4. 以前 yǐqián / 5. 的时候 de shíhou / 6. 时时刻刻 shíshíkèkè / 7. 的时候 de shíhou / 8. 以前 yǐqián / 9. 以前 yǐqián / 10. 的时候 de shíhou

EXERCISE 9.
1. A₁: 我在咖啡里放牛奶了。wǒ zài kāfēi li fàng-niúnǎi le; A₂: 我没（有）在咖啡里放牛奶。wǒ méi(you) zài kāfēi li fàng-niúnǎi / 2. A₁: 他的话，我听懂了。tāde huà wǒ tīng-dǒng le; A₂: 他的话，我没（有）听懂。tāde huà, wǒ méi(you) tīng-dǒng / 3. A₁: 我说完了。wǒ shuō-wán le; A₂: 我没（有）说完。wǒ méi(you) shuō-wán / 4. A₁: 进来以前，我敲门了。jìnlai yǐqián, wǒ qiāo-mén le; A₂: 进来以前，我没（有）敲门。jìnlai yǐqián, wǒ méi(you) qiāomén

EXERCISE 10.
1. 她两天以前去看了医生。tā liǎng-tiān yǐqián qù kàn-le yīshēng / 2. 他没（有）看昨天晚上的新闻。tā méi(you) kàn zuótiān wǎnshang de xīnwén / 3. 上个星期天天下雨。shàng-ge-xīngqī tiāntiān xià-yǔ / 4. 晚饭的时候，他们喝了一瓶红酒。wǎnfàn de shíhou, tāmen hē-le yì-píng-hóngjiǔ / 5. 我们不知道你去年在国外。wǒmen bù zhīdào nǐ qùnián zài guówài / 6. 那个学生做完功课了吗？nèi-ge-xuésheng zuò-wán gōngkè le ma; 那个学生做完功课了没有？nèi-ge-xuésheng zuò-wán gōngkè le méiyou?

EXERCISE 11.

1. 她父母是昨天晚上回去的。tā fùmǔ shì zuótiān wǎnshang huíqù de / 2. 他们是坐出租车去郊外的。tāmen shì zuò-chūzūchē qù jiāowài de / 3. 是她妈妈把这件事告诉她的。shì tā māma bǎ zhèi-jiàn-shì gàosù tā de / 4. 我去中国是学中文的。wǒ qù Zhōngguó shì xué-zhōngwén de / 5. 我是上中学的时候去中国学的中文。wǒ shì shàng-zhōngxué de shíhou qù-Zhōngguó xué de zhōngwén / 6. 他是花了两千块钱买的新电脑。tā shì huā-le liǎngqiān-kuài-qián mǎi de xīn diànnǎo / 7. 那个孩子是在墨西哥出生的。nèi-ge-háizi shì zài Mòxīgē chūshēng de / 8. 妹妹是从学校回来的。mèimei shì cóng xuéxiào huílai de / 9. 弟弟是跟我们一起去滑雪的。dìdi shì gēn wǒmen yìqǐ qù huá-xuě de

EXERCISE 12.

1. 她父母是昨天晚上回去的吗？tā fùmǔ shì zuótiān wǎnshang huíqù de ma?; 她父母是不是昨天晚上回去的？tā fùmǔ shì-bú-shì zuótiān wǎnshang huíqù de? / 2. 他们是怎么去郊外的？tāmen shì zěnme qù jiāowài de? / 3. 是谁把这件事告诉她的？shì shéi bǎ zhèi-jiàn-shì gàosù tā de? / 4. 你是什么时候去中国学的中文？nǐ shì shénme shíhou qù-Zhōngguó xué de zhōngwén? / 5. 他是花了多少钱买的新电脑？tā shì huā-le duōshǎoqián mǎi de xīn diànnǎo? / 6. 那个孩子是在哪儿出生的？nèi-ge-háizi shì zài nǎr chūshēng de? / 7. 妹妹是从学校回来的吗？mèimei shì cóng xuéxiào huílai de ma?; 妹妹是不是从学校回来的？mèimei shì-bú-shì cóng xuéxiào huílai de? / 8. 弟弟是跟我们一起去做什么的？dìdi shì gēn wǒmen yìqǐ qù zuò-shénme de?

EXERCISE 13.

1. b / 2. a / 3. a / 4. a / 5. b / 6. a / 7. b / 8. a / 9. a / 10. b / 11. a

EXERCISE 14.

1. 才 cái / 2. 就 jiù / 3. 就 jiù; 才 cái / 4. 就 jiù / 5. 就 jiù / 6. 才 cái / 7. 才 cái / 8. 就 jiù

EXERCISE 15.

1. 他们下个星期才来。tāmen xià-ge-xīngqī cái lái / 2. 我们有了钱才能买电视。wǒmen yǒu-le-qián cái néng mǎi-diànshì / 3. 她上午十一点就吃午饭了。tā shàngwǔ shíyī-diǎn jiù chī-wǔfàn le / 4. 你付了钱，我们就走。nǐ fù-le-qián, wǒmen jiù zǒu

EXERCISE 16.

1. 等到 děngdào / 2. 到 dào / 3. 两点钟 liǎng-diǎn zhōng / 4. 八点 bā-diǎn

EXERCISE 17.

1. 我们每星期二上课上到下午四点。wǒmen měi xīngqī'èr shàng-kè shàng-dào xiàwǔ sìdiǎn / 2. 他等你等到九点半。tā děng-nǐ děng-dào jiǔ-diǎn bàn / 3. 他们看电视看到半夜两点。tāmen kàn-diànshì kàn-dào bànyè liǎng-diǎn / 4. 这儿的冬天很长。下雪下到四月。zhèr de dōngtiān hěn cháng. xià-xuě xià-dào sìyuè

Part IV

EXERCISE 1.

的 *de* is necessary: 2; 3; 5; 8; 11; 12 / 的 *de* is unnecessary: 1; 4; 6; 7; 9; 10

EXERCISE 2.

1. 她常用的字典 tā cháng yòng de zìdiǎn / 2. 姓王的工程师 xìng Wáng de gōngchéngshī / 3. 我上星期看的书 wǒ shàng-xīngqī kàn de shū / 4. 坐火车去上班的人 zuò-huǒchē qù shàng-bān de rén / 5. 他最近买的车 tā zuìjìn mǎi de chē / 6. 他最近买

的车是丰田车。tā zuìjìn mǎi de chē shì fēngtián chē / 7. 坐火车去上班的(那个)人很高。
zuò-huǒchē qù shàng-bān de (nèi-ge) rén hěn gāo / 8. 她真喜欢我们上星期看的电影。
tā zhēn xǐhuan wǒmen shàng-xīngqī kàn de diànyǐng

EXERCISE 3.
1. a / 2. b / 3. b / 4. a / 5. b / 6. a / 7. a / 8. b

EXERCISE 4.
1. 山顶上有一个小房子。shān dǐngshang yǒu yí-ge-xiǎo fángzi / 2. 公园里到处是花草。
gōngyuán li dàochù shì huācǎo / 3. 我(的)左边儿的位子空着。wǒ (de) zuǒbiānr de
wèizi kòng-zhe / 4. 公路的旁边是农田。gōnglù de pángbiān shì nóngtián / 5. 图书馆的
外面停着很多自行车。túshūguǎn de wàimiàn tíng-zhe hěn duō zìxíngchē / 6. 校区就在
湖的附近。xiàoqū jiù zài hú de fùjìn / 7. 他们在饭馆的后面装车。tāmen zài fànguǎn de
hòumiàn zhuāng-chē / 8. 孙子坐在爷爷和奶奶的中间(儿)。sūnzi zuò zài yéye hé nǎinai
de zhōngjiān(r)

EXERCISE 5.
1. 一个苹果 yí-ge-píngguǒ / 2. 这一个苹果 zhèi-yí-ge-píngguǒ / 3. 这些车 zhèi-xiē-chē /
4. 这五辆车 zhèi-wǔ-liàng-chē / 5. 九件衣服 jiǔ-jiàn-yīfu / 6. 哪一家商店？něi-yì-jiā-
shāngdiàn? / 7. 那张地图 nèi-zhāng-dìtú / 8. 那些树 nèi-xiē-shù / 9. 那八棵树 nèi-bā-kē-shù /
10. 这封信 zhèi-fēng-xìn / 11. 那一份报 nèi-yí-fèn-bào / 12. 哪条路？něi-tiáo-lù?

EXERCISE 6.
1. 我买了一张大地图。wǒ mǎi-le yì-zhāng dà dìtú / 2. 那三辆车都是蓝色的。nèi-sān-
liàng-chē dōu shì lánsè de / 3. 这个桔子真甜。zhèi-ge-júzi zhēn tián / 4. 那些游客是
韩国人。nèi-xiē-yóukè shì Hánguórén / 5. 他想吃这些葡萄。tā xiǎng chī zhèi-xiē-pútao /
6. 这条街上有五个小饭馆。zhèi-tiáo-jiē shang yǒu wǔ-ge xiǎo fànguǎn / 7. 她有两个孩子，
一个女儿和一个儿子。tā yǒu liǎng-ge-háizi, yí-ge-nǚ'ér hé yí-ge ér'zi / 8. 他们订了四张
去中国的机票。tāmen dìng-le sì-zhāng qù Zhōngguó de jīpiào / 9. 我们没看那个电影。
wǒmen méi kàn nèi-ge-diànyǐng / 10. 哪只狗是你的？něi-zhī-gǒu shì nǐde?

EXERCISE 7.
Polysyllabic intransitive verbs: 1; 7; 10; 13 / V-Obj. compounds: 2; 4; 6; 8; 11; 15 / V-V
compounds: 3; 5; 9; 12; 14

EXERCISE 8.
1a. 喝绿茶 hē lǜ chá; 1b. 喝一杯热茶 hē yì-bēi rè chá; 1c. 喝朋友送的茶 hē péngyou
sòng de chá / 2a. 坐公交车 zuò gōngjiāochē; 2b. 坐出租车 zuò chūzūchē; 2c. 坐中午
的火车 zuò zhōngwǔ de huǒchē; 2d. 坐去纽约的火车 zuò qù Niǔyuē de huǒchē /
3a. 唱一首歌 chàng yì-shǒu-gē; 3b. 唱日本歌 chàng Rìběngē; 3c. 唱好听的歌 chàng
hǎotīng-de gē; 3d. 唱他写的歌 chàng tā-xiě de gē; 3e. 唱我最喜欢的歌 chàng wǒ
zuì-xǐhuan de gē / 4a. 做几个菜 zuò jǐ-ge-cài; 4b. 做中国菜 zuò Zhōngguócài;
4c. 做风味菜 zuò fēngwèicài; 4d. 做我们喜欢吃的菜 zuò wǒmen-xǐhua-chī de cài

EXERCISE 9.
1. 妈妈做了一个水果蛋糕。māma zuò-le yí-ge-shuǐguǒ dàngāo / 2. 我们这个星期听了
五个演讲。wǒmen zhèi-ge-xīngqī tīng-le wǔ-ge-yǎnjiǎng / 3. 那个孩子正在学画画儿。
nèi-ge-háizi zhèngzài xué-huàhuàr / 4. 李先生今天从图书馆借了两本书。Lǐ xiānsheng
jīntiān cóng túshūguǎn jiè-le liǎng-běn-shū / 5. 他们只买美国制造的商品。tāmen zhǐ

mǎi Měiguó zhìzào de shāngpǐn / 6. 我们点了她最喜欢吃的菜。wǒmen diǎn-le tā zuì xǐhuan chī de cài / 7. 我妹妹很少给父母写信。她总是给他们打电话。wǒ mèimei hěnshǎo gěi fùmǔ xiě-xìn。tā zǒngshi gěi tāmen dǎ-diànhuà / 8. 她很想跟他结婚。 tā hěn xiǎng gēn tā jié-hūn / 9. 售货员每天跟顾客打交道。shòuhuòyuán měitiān gēn gùkè dǎ-jiāodào / 10. 他喜欢跟朋友开玩笑。tā xǐhuan gēn péngyou kāi-wánxiào

EXERCISE 10.
1. 学 xué / 2. 学会 xué-huì / 3. 想到 xiǎng-dào / 4. 想 xiǎng / 5. 看 kàn / 6. 看 kàn / 7. 看到 kàn-dào / 8. 吃完 chī-wán / 9. 学完 xué-wán / 10. 关上 guān-shang / 11. 洗 xǐ / 12. 写清楚 xiě-qīngchu

EXERCISE 11.
1. 下 xià / 2. 回 huí / 3. 去 qù / 4. 进 jìn; 出 chū / 5. 来 lái / 6. 起 qǐ

EXERCISE 12.
1. 看不懂 kàn-bù-dǒng / 2. 坐得下 zuò-de-xià / 3. 吃不完 chī-bù-wán / 4. 听得见 tīng-de-jiàn / 5. 想不起来 xiǎng-bù-qǐlái / 6. 记不住 jì-bú-zhù / 7. 听得懂 tīng-de-dǒng / 8. 买不到 mǎi-bú-dào / 9. 搬得出去 bān-de-chūqù / 10. 做得完 zuò-de-wán

EXERCISE 13.
1. 我们没看见他回来。wǒmen méi kàn-jian tā huílai / 2. 你今天看得完这本书吗？nǐ jīntiān kàn-de-wán zhèi-běn-shū ma?; 你今天看得完看不完这本书？nǐ jīntiān kàn-de-wán kàn-bù-wán zhèi-běn-shū? / 3. 门坏了，关不上了。mén huài le, guān-bú-shàng le / 4. 他们今天买到了新鲜的鱼。tāmen jīntiān mǎi-dào le xīnxiān de yú / 5. 张太太看不懂英文。Zhāng tàitai kàn-bù-dǒng yīngwén / 6. 全家都听到了这个消息。quánjiā dōu tīng-dào le zhèi-ge xiāoxi / 7. 这个题目很复杂，你说不清楚。zhèi-ge-tímù hěn fùzá, nǐ shuō-bù-qīngchu / 8. 王护士已经搬出去了。Wáng hùshi yǐjīng bān-chūqù le / 9. 对不起，我没听懂你说的话。duìbuqǐ, wǒ méi tīng-dǒng nǐ shuō de huà / 10. 这是地址。你想我们在这儿找得到他吗？zhèi shì dìzhǐ。nǐ xiǎng wǒmen zài-zhèr zhǎo-de-dào tā ma? / 11. 你说对了，她就是我妹妹。nǐ shuō-duì le, tā jiù shì wǒ mèimei / 12. 他点了太多的菜，我们没吃完。tā diǎn-le tài duō de cài, wǒmen méi chī-wán

EXERCISE 14.
1. 老师写字写得很好看。lǎoshī xiě-zì xiě-de hěn hǎokàn / 2. 老先生起来得很早。 lǎo xiānsheng qǐlai-de hěn zǎo / 3. 爸爸喝啤酒喝得多不多？bàba hē-píjiǔ hē-de duō-bù-duō? / 4. 你打字打得真慢！nǐ dǎ-zì dǎ-de zhēn màn! / 5. 我游泳游得不太好。 wǒ yóu-yǒng yóu-de bú tài hǎo / 6. 姐姐走路走得很快。jiějie zǒu-lù zǒu-de hěn kuài / 7. 大厨做菜做得怎么样？dàchú zuò-cài zuò-de zěnmeyàng? / 8. 你吃水果吃得太少。 nǐ chī-shuǐguǒ chī-de tài shǎo

Part V

EXERCISE 1.
1. 好吃的点心 hǎochī de₁ diǎnxin / 2. 有趣的故事 yǒuqù de₁ gùshi / 3. 大家的事 dàjiā de₁ shì / 4. 我爸爸的新车 wǒ bàba de₁ xīn chē / 5. 合理的制度 hélǐ de₁ zhìdù / 6. 城西边的公路 chéng xībiān de₁ gōnglù / 7. 朋友的公寓 péngyou de₁ gōngyù / 8. 很远的地区 hěn yuǎn de₁ dìqū / 9. 他买的新电脑很贵。tā mǎi de₁ xīn diànnǎo hěn guì / 10. 我要去的那个地方在南美洲。wǒ yào qù de₁ nèi-ge dìfang zài Nán Měizhōu / 11. 我来介绍一下

我旁边的这个人。wǒ lái jièshào yíxià wǒ pángbiān *de*₁ zhèi-ge-rén / 12. 大家都喜欢的
那个电影我还没看。dàjiā dōu xǐhuan *de*₁ nèi-ge-diànyǐng wǒ hái méi kàn / 13. 现在骑
自行车的人越来越多了。xiànzài qí-zìxíngchē *de*₁ rén yuèláiyuè duō le

EXERCISE 2.
1. 得 *de*₃ / 2. 地 *de*₂ / 3. 得 *de*₃ / 4. 地 *de*₂; 地 *de*₂ / 5. 地 *de*₂ / 6. 得 *de*₃; 得 *de*₃ /
7. 地 *de*₂ / 8. 得 *de*₃; 得 *de*₃

EXERCISE 3.
1. 一点儿 yìdiǎnr / 2. 有一点儿 yǒu yìdiǎnr / 3. 有一点儿 yǒu yìdiǎnr; 一点儿 yìdiǎnr /
4. 一点儿 yìdiǎnr / 5. 一点儿 yìdiǎnr / 6. 有一点儿 yǒu yìdiǎnr / 7. 有一点儿 yǒu yìdiǎnr

EXERCISE 4.
1. 我有一点儿渴，我想喝一点儿水。wǒ yǒu yìdiǎnr kě, wǒ xiǎng hē yìdiǎnr shuǐ /
2. 再吃一点儿，怎么样？zài chī yìdiǎnr, zěnmeyàng? / 3. 她没来。他有一点儿失望。
tā méi lái. tā yǒu yìdiǎnr shīwàng

EXERCISE 5.
1. 北京大学跟哈佛大学 Běijīng dàxué gēn Hāfó dàxué / 2. 妹妹会滑雪，也会游泳。
mèimei huì huá-xuě, yě huì yóuyǒng / 3. 上个星期三跟这个星期三 shàng-ge xīngqīsān
gēn zhèi-ge xīngqīsān / 4. 爸爸高兴极了，妈妈也高兴极了。bàba gāoxìng jíle, māma
yě gāoxìng jíle / 5. 红色的大衣和黑色的皮靴 hóngsè de dàyī hé hēisè de píxuē /
6. 他买的饮料和她买的水果 tā mǎi de yǐnliào hé tā mǎi de shuǐguǒ / 7. 姐姐点了冰茶，
我也点了冰茶。jiějie diǎn-le bīngchá, wǒ yě diǎn-le bīngchá / 8. 她想学文学，也想学历史。
tā xiǎng xué-wénxué, yě xiǎng xué-lìshǐ

EXERCISE 6.
1. 大椅子很舒服，小椅子也很舒服。dà yǐzi hěn shūfu, xiǎo yǐzi yě hěn shūfu / 2. 大椅子
和小椅子都很舒服。dà yǐzi hé xiǎo yǐzi dōu hěn shūfu / 3. 我们点了可乐，也点了啤酒。
wǒmen diǎn-le kělè, yě diǎn-le píjiǔ

EXERCISE 7.
1. 有的 yǒude / 2. 一些 yìxiē / 3. 有的 yǒude / 4. 一些 yìxiē / 5. 一些 yìxiē

EXERCISE 8.
1. 那些人，有的是护士，有的是医生。nèi-xiē-rén, yǒude shì hùshi, yǒude shì yīshēng /
2. 宿舍里有的房间很小。sùshè lǐ yǒude fángjiān hěn xiǎo / 3. 她在门上贴了一些明信片。
tā zài mén-shang tiē-le yìxiē míngxìnpiàn

EXERCISE 9.
Phrases that do not need a measure word: 1; 4; 6; 7; 13; 14; 16; 17; 18; 19; 20
Phrases that need a measure word: 2) 每个汉字 měi-ge-hànzì; 3) 每本书 měi-běn-shū;
5) 每张画儿 měi-zhāng-huàr; 8) 每本字典 měi-běn-zìdiǎn; 9) 每条鱼 měi-tiáo-yú;
10) 每张纸 měi-zhāng-zhǐ; 11) 每辆自行车 měi-liàng-zìxíngchē; 12) 每件衬衫
měi-jiàn-chènshān; 15) 每件事 měi-jiàn-shì; 21) 每把椅子 měi-bǎ-yǐzi; 22) 每只猫
měi-zhī-māo; 23) 每个苹果 měi-ge-píngguǒ; 24) 每个问题 měi-ge-wèntí

EXERCISE 10.
1. 她每星期游三次泳。tā měi xīngqī yóu-sāncì-yǒng / 2. 这个星期每天都下了一点儿雪。
zhèi-ge-xīngqī měitiān dōu xià-le yìdiǎnr xuě / 3. 每瓶酒都很贵。měi-píng-jiǔ dōu hěn guì

EXERCISE 11.
1. 都 dōu / 2. 所有的 suǒyǒude; 都 dōu / 3. 所有的 suǒyǒude; 都 dōu / 4. 所有的 suǒyǒude; 都 dōu

EXERCISE 12.
1. 所有的酒都很贵。suǒyǒude jiǔ dōu hěn guì / 2. 他们每个人都跟他握了手。tāmen měi-ge-rén dōu gēn tā wǒ-le shǒu / 3. 你们都在大学工作吗？nǐmen dōu zài dàxué gōngzuò ma?

EXERCISE 13.
1. 从二月到五月 cóng èryuè dào wǔyuè / 2. 从生到死 cóng shēng dào sǐ / 3. 从农村到城市 cóng nóngcūn dào chéngshì / 4. 从这儿往北开 cóng zhèr wàng běi kāi / 5. 冬季时间从星期天开始。dōngjì shíjiān cóng xīngqītiān kāishǐ / 6. 从老到少，人人都喜欢冰激凌。cóng lǎo dào shào, rénrén dōu xǐhuan bīngjīlíng / 7. 这个电影从头到尾都很有意思。zhèi-ge-diànyǐng cóng tóu dào wěi dōu hěn yǒuyìsi / 8. 我们从宿舍走到餐厅。wǒmen cóng sùshè zǒu-dào cāntīng / 9. 他们开会从四点开到六点。tāmen kāi-huì cóng sìdiǎn kāi-dào liùdiǎn / 10. 她放假放到星期一。tā fàng-jià fàng-dào xīngqīyī

EXERCISE 14.
1. 他们常去星巴克喝咖啡。tāmen *cháng* qù xīngbākè hē-kāfēi / 2. 弟弟很聪明，却不用功。dìdi hěn cōngming, *què* bú yònggōng / 3. 你既然不喜欢这件毛衣，就别买。nǐ jìrán bù xǐhuan zhèi-jiàn-máoyī, *jiù* bié mǎi / 4. 李明喜欢运动，尤其喜欢打篮球。Lǐ Míng xǐhuan yùndòng, *yóuqí* xǐhuan dǎ-lánqiú / 5. 你只要复习了，就一定考得好。nǐ zhǐyào fùxí le, *jiù* yídìng kǎo-de-hǎo / 6. 我下课以后先吃午饭，再回宿舍。wǒ xià-kè yǐhòu *xiān* chī-wǔfàn, *zài* huí-sùshè / 7. 他们都知道了，我却没听说。tāmen *dōu* zhīdào le, wǒ *què* méi tīngshuō / 8. 如果明天不下雨，我们就去野餐。rúguǒ míngtiān bú xià-yǔ, wǒmen *jiù* qù yěcān / 9. 我一直想去看画展，可是总是没有时间。wǒ yìzhí xiǎng qù kàn-huàzhǎn, kěshi *zǒngshi* méiyǒu shíjiān / 10. 一年级的学生都认识这个字。yī-niánjí de xuésheng *dōu* rènshi zhèi-ge-zì / 11. 如果你骑自行车，你就得戴安全帽。rúguǒ nǐ qí-zìxíngchē, nǐ *jiù* děi dài-ānquánmào / 12. 他昨天没来，当然不知道。tā zuótiān méi lái, *dāngrán* bù zhīdào

EXERCISE 15.
1. 找房子 zhǎo-fángzi; 找到 zhǎo-dào / 2. 学书法 xué-shūfǎ; 学不会 xué-bú-huì / 3. 考试 kǎo-shì; 考好 kǎo-hǎo / 4. 睡觉 shuì-jiào; 睡不着 shuì-bù-zháo / 5. 听录音 tīng-lùyīn; 听不懂 tīng-bù-dǒng / 6. 点菜 diǎn-cài; 吃完 chī-wán

EXERCISE 16.
1. a / 2. b / 3. c / 4. b / 5. c / 6. a

EXERCISE 17.
1. 会 huì; 能 néng / 2. 可以 kěyǐ / 3. 能 néng or 可以 kěyǐ / 4. 会 huì / 5. 能 néng / 6. 会 huì / 7. 可以 kěyǐ / 8. 能 néng

EXERCISE 18.
1. 认识 rènshi; 知道 zhīdào / 2. 知道 zhīdào / 3. 知道 zhīdào / 4. 认识 rènshi / 5. 认识 rènshi / 6. 知道 zhīdào / 7. 认识 rènshi

Appendix
Examples in traditional characters

§1

1a	電影很有意思。	diànyǐng hěn yǒuyìsi
1b	張先生非常忙。	Zhāng xiānsheng fēicháng máng
1c	張先生越來越忙。	Zhāng xiānsheng yuèláiyuè máng
1d	張先生(真是)忙極了。	Zhāng xiānsheng (zhēnshì) máng jí le
1e	張先生不忙。	Zhāng xiānsheng bù máng
1f	張先生不怎麼忙。	Zhāng xiānsheng bù zěnme máng
1g	張先生忙。	Zhāng xiānsheng máng

§2

2a	我父親在家，他剛從德國回來。	wǒ fùqin zài jiā, tā gāng cóng Déguó huílai
2b	公共圖書館在第一銀行的對面。	gōnggòng túshūguǎn zài dìyī yínháng de duìmiàn
2c	*三個快餐店在第一銀行的附近。	*sān-ge kuàicāndiàn zài dìyī yínháng de fùjìn
2d	第一銀行的附近有三個快餐店。	dìyī yínháng de fùjìn yǒu sān-ge kuàicāndiàn
2e	第一銀行的對面有一個公共圖書館。	dìyī yínháng de duìmiàn yǒu yí-ge gōnggòng túshūguǎn
2f	第一銀行的對面有*公共圖書館。	dìyī yínháng de duìmiàn yǒu *gōnggòng túshūguǎn
2g	公共圖書館不在第一銀行的對面。	gōnggòng túshūguǎn bú zài dìyī yínháng de duìmiàn
2h	這兒沒有很多樹。	zhèr méiyǒu hěnduō shù

§3

3b	王先生在大學教書；王太太在銀行工作。	Wáng xiānsheng zài dàxué jiāo-shū; Wáng tàitai zài yínháng gōngzuò
3c	她常常在超級市場買東西。	tā chángcháng zài chāojí shìchǎng mǎi dōngxi
3d	他們每天下午在公園下棋。	tāmen měitiān xiàwǔ zài gōngyuán xià-qí

3e   她不（常）在超級市場買東西。tā bù(cháng) zài chāojí shìchǎng mǎi dōngxi

3f   她在超級市場沒買東西。tā zài chāojí shìchǎng méi mǎi dōngxi

3g   ?她常常在超級市場不買東西。?tā chángcháng zài chāojí shìchǎng bù mǎi dōngxi

§4

4a   他們（常）在快餐店吃飯。tāmen (cháng) zài kuàicāndiàn chī-fàn

4b   李太太（有的時候）去農貿市場買東西。Lǐ tàitai (yǒude shíhou) qù nóngmào shìchǎng mǎi-dōngxi

4c   他畢業以後去中國工作。tā bìyè yǐhòu qù Zhōngguó gōngzuò

4d   他畢業以後不去中國工作。tā bìyè yǐhòu bú qù Zhōngguó gōngzuò

4e   他畢業以後沒去中國工作。tā bìyè yǐhòu méi qù Zhōngguó gōngzuò

§5

5b   王家每星期五吃餃子。Wáng jiā měi xīngqīwǔ chī-jiǎozi

5c   王家常常吃餃子。Wáng jiā chángcháng chī-jiǎozi

5d   王先生在外面吃午飯。Wáng xiānsheng zài wàimian chī-wǔfàn

5e   王先生吃午飯吃一個小時。Wáng xiānsheng chī-wǔfàn chī yí-ge xiǎoshí

5f   王先生常常在外面吃午飯。Wáng xiānsheng chángcháng zài wàimian chī-wǔfàn

5g   王先生每天吃午飯吃一個小時。Wáng xiānsheng měitiān chī-wǔfàn chī yí-ge xiǎoshí

5h   王太太星期三下午在超級市場買菜。Wáng tàitai xīngqīsān xiàwǔ zài chāojí shìchǎng mǎi-cài

5i   王先生王太太總是晚飯以後散半個鐘頭步。Wáng xiānsheng Wáng tàitai zǒngshì wǎnfàn yǐhòu sàn bàn-ge zhōngtóu bù

5j   王太太每星期二在大學上三個小時（的）繪畫課。Wáng tàitai měi xīngqí'èr zài dàxué shàng sān-ge xiǎoshí (de) huìhuà kè

§6

6a   咖啡比茶貴。kāfēi bǐ chá guì

6b   這條街上的房子比鄰街的老。zhèi-tiáo-jiē shang de fángzi bǐ línjiē de lǎo

6c   說中文比寫漢字容易。shuō-zhōngwén bǐ xiě-hànzì róngyi

6d   說中文不比寫漢字容易。shuō-zhōngwén bù bǐ xiě-hànzì róngyi

6e   手機比座機小一點兒。shǒujī bǐ zuòjī xiǎo yìdiǎnr

6f   她的汽車比我的貴得多。tāde qìchē bǐ wǒde guì-de duō

6g   咖啡比茶貴一毛錢。kāfēi bǐ chá guì yì-máo-qián

6h   張老師比林老師多教一門課。Zhāng lǎoshī bǐ Lín lǎoshī duō jiāo yì-mén-kè

6i   我室友比我晚睡兩個鐘頭。wǒ shìyǒu bǐ wǒ wǎn shuì liǎng-ge-zhōngtóu

§7

7b   這個房間跟那個房間一樣。zhèi-ge fángjiān gēn nèi-ge fángjiān yíyàng

7c   蘋果跟橘子一樣嗎？píngguǒ gēn júzi yíyàng ma

7e   我妹妹跟我一樣高。wǒ mèimei gēn wǒ yíyàng gāo

7g   課本有字典那麼貴。kèběn yǒu zìdiǎn nème guì

7h   我妹妹不跟我一樣高。wǒ mèimei bù gēn wǒ yíyàng gāo

7i   我妹妹跟我不一樣高。wǒ mèimei gēn wǒ bù yíyàng gāo

7j   兒子有父親那麼高，可是沒有父親（那麼）胖。érzi yǒu fùqin nème gāo, kěshi
      méiyǒu fùqin (nème) pàng

7k   說中文沒有寫漢字（這麼）難。shuō-zhōngwén méiyǒu xiě-hànzì (zhème) nán

§8

8d   她說中文說得比我好。tā shuō zhōngwén shuō-de bǐ wǒ hǎo

8e   她比我說中文說得好。tā bǐ wǒ shuō zhōngwén shuō-de hǎo

8f   她說中文比我說得好。tā shuō zhōngwén bǐ wǒ shuō-de hǎo

8g   她說中文說得比我好一點兒/得多。tā shuō zhōngwén shuō-de bǐ wǒ hǎo
      yìdiǎnr/-de duō

8h   學生寫字寫得跟老師一樣快。xuésheng xiě-zì xiě-de gēn lǎoshī yíyàng kuài

8i   學生跟老師寫字寫得一樣快。xuésheng gēn lǎoshī xiě-zì xiě-de yíyàng kuài

8j   學生寫字跟老師寫得一樣快。xuésheng xiě-zì gēn lǎoshī xiě-de yíyàng kuài

8k   我們看書看得沒有他多。wǒmen kàn-shū kàn-de méiyǒu tā duō

8l   我們沒有他看書看得多。wǒmen méiyǒu tā kàn-shū kàn-de duō

8m   我們看書沒有他看得多。wǒmen kàn-shū méiyǒu tā kàn-de duō

§9

9a   他打破了他的茶杯。tā dǎ-pò-le tāde chábēi

9b   他把他的茶杯打破了。tā bǎ tāde chábēi dǎ-pò-le

9c   來 lái; 去 qù; 離開 líkāi; 喜歡 xǐhuan; 怕 pà; 覺得 juéde; 像 xiàng;
      知道 zhīdào; 認識 rènshi; 記得 jìde; 是 shì; 在 zài; 有 yǒu

9d   他們把書桌搬出去了。tāmen bǎ shūzhuō bān-chūqu le

9e   請你把信交給李先生。qǐng nǐ bǎ xìn jiāo-gěi Lǐ xiānsheng

9f   乘客把箱子放在行李架上。chéngkè bǎ xiāngzi fàng-zài xínglijià shang

§10

10b   我不把事情辦完，不能回家。wǒ bù bǎ shìqing bàn-wán, bù néng huí-jiā

10c   你應該把他們送到機場。nǐ yīnggāi bǎ tāmen sòng-dào jīchǎng

10d   我先把事情辦完，再回家。wǒ xiān bǎ shìqing bàn-wán, zài huí-jiā

10e   她今天上午把數據整理好了。tā jīntiān shàngwǔ bǎ shùjù zhěnglǐ-hǎo le

10f   老師沒把這一章解釋清楚。lǎoshī méi bǎ zhèi-yì-zhāng jiěshì-qīngchu

10g   你可以把東西搬進來。nǐ kěyǐ bǎ dōngxi bān-jìnlai

10h   客人想把他們的車停在路邊兒。kèren xiǎng bǎ tāmen-de chē tíng zài lùbiānr

10i   小王把朋友的自行車騎到學校去了。Xiǎo Wáng bǎ péngyou-de zìxíngchē qí dào
      xuéxiào qù le

10j   我把功課交給老師了。wǒ bǎ gōngkè jiāo gěi lǎoshī le

10k   我把他的名字忘了。wǒ bǎ tāde míngzi wàng le

§11

11b 衣服被（雨）淋濕了。yīfu bèi (yǔ) lín-shī le

11c 錢讓賊偷走了。qián ràng zéi tōu-zǒu le

11d 老蔡叫老婆罵了一頓。Lǎo Cài jiào lǎopo mà-le yí-dùn

11e 位子沒被佔去，我真高興。wèizi méi bèi zhàn-qù, wǒ zhēn gāoxìng

11f 衣服馬上讓雨淋濕了。yīfu mǎshàng ràng yǔ lín-shī le

11g 冰箱裡的食物都叫他吃光了。bīngxiāng-lǐ de shíwù dōu jiào tā chī-guāng le

11h 車子叫他洗得乾乾淨淨。chēzi jiào tā xǐ de gāngānjìngjìng

11i 走丟了的孩子讓警察找回來了。zǒu-diū-le de háizi ràng jǐngchá zhǎo-huílai le

§12

12a 如果/要是他有問題，就來問我。rúguǒ/yàoshì tā yǒu wèntí, jiù lái wèn wǒ

12b 如果/要是他不去，誰去？rúguǒ/yàoshì tā bú qù, shéi qù?

12c 他有問題，就來問我。tā yǒu wèntí, jiù lái wèn wǒ

12d 如果/要是你有問題，一定來問我。rúguǒ/yàoshì nǐ yǒu wèntí, yídìng lái wèn wǒ

12e 如果/要是你有問題，也來問我。rúguǒ/yàoshì nǐ yǒu wèntí, yě lái wèn wǒ

12f 如果/要是我有錢，就買那條船。rúguǒ/yàoshì wǒ yǒu qián, jiù mǎi nèi-tiáo-chuán

§13

13a 我們的功課不但多，而且難。wǒmen-de gōngkè búdàn duō, érqiě nán

13b 張老師不但看書看得多，並且看得很快。Zhāng lǎoshī búdàn kàn-shū kàn-de duō, bìngqiě kàn-de hěn kuài

13c 不但我去，而且我們全家人都去。búdàn wǒ qù, érqiě wǒmen quán jiārén dōu qù

13d 不但公園裡，並且街道兩旁都種著花。búdàn gōngyuán-lǐ, bìngqiě jiēdào liǎngpáng dōu zhòng-zhe huā

§14

14a 這張桌子雖然小，可是很貴。zhèi-zhāng-zhuōzi suīrán xiǎo, kěshì hěn guì

14b 老王雖然抽煙，可是不喝酒。Lǎo Wáng suīrán chōu-yān, kěshì bù hē-jiǔ

14c 雖然李太太喜歡看電視，可是李先生不喜歡看。suīrán Lǐ tàitai xǐhuan kàn diànshì, kěshì Lǐ xiānsheng bù xǐhuan kàn

14d 這張桌子小，可是很貴。zhèi-zhāng-zhuōzi xiǎo, kěshì hěn guì

14e 老王雖然抽煙，?不喝酒。Lǎo Wáng suīrán chōu-yān, ?bù hē-jiǔ

14f 雖然圖書館有不少書，但是字典不多。suīrán túshūguǎn yǒu bùshǎo shū, dànshì zìdiǎn bù duō

14g 雖然圖書館有不少書，字典卻不多。suīrán túshūguǎn yǒu bùshǎo shū, zìdiǎn què bù duō

§15

15b 我們一邊(兒)唱歌，一邊(兒)跳舞。wǒmen yìbiān(r) chàng-gē, yìbiān(r) tiào-wǔ

15c 他一邊(兒)吃飯，一邊(兒)喝啤酒，一邊(兒)看新聞。tā yìbiān(r) chī-fàn, yìbiān(r) hē-píjiǔ, yìbiān(r) kàn-xīnwén

15e 我給他打電話的時候，他正在睡覺。wǒ gěi tā dǎ-diànhuà de shíhou, tā zhèngzài shuì-jiào

15f 他到教室的時候，老師正在回答問題。tā dào-jiàoshì de shíhou, lǎoshī zhèngzài huídá-wèntí

§16

16a 我先洗手，再吃飯。wǒ xiān xǐ-shǒu, zài chī-fàn

16b 我們先學生詞，再讀課文。wǒmen xiān xué-shēngcí, zài dú-kèwén

16c 她先吃飯，然後看新聞。tā xiān chī-fàn, ránhòu kàn-xīnwén

16d 吃中餐的時候，先吃涼菜，再吃熱菜，然後喝湯。chī-zhōngcān de shíhou, xiān chī-liángcài, zài chī-rècài, ránhòu hē-tāng

16e 我們先吃涼菜，再吃熱菜，然後喝湯，最後吃甜點。wǒmen xiān chī-liángcài, zài chī-rècài, ránhòu hē-tāng, zuìhòu chī-tiándiǎn

16f 先吃涼菜，再吃熱菜，我們然後喝湯，我們最後吃甜點。xiān chī-liángcài, zài chī-rècài, wǒmen ránhòu hē-tāng, wǒmen zuìhòu chī-tiándiǎn

§17

17a 他一從國外回來就去看王先生了。tā yì cóng guówài huí-lai jiù qù kàn Wáng xiānsheng le

17b 電話一響，他就接了。diànhuà yì xiǎng, tā jiù jiē le

17c 雨一停，太陽就出來了。yǔ yì tíng, tàiyang jiù chū-lai le

17d 你開到下一個路口，往右一拐就到了。nǐ kāi-dào xià yí-ge-lùkǒu, wàng yòu yì guǎi jiù dào le

17e 你一打聽就知道了。nǐ yì dǎting jiù zhīdao le

17f 她一有錢就給朋友買禮物。tā yì yǒu-qián jiù gěi péngyou mǎi-lǐwù

17g 七點一到，電影就開始了。qīdiǎn yí dào, diànyǐng jiù kāishǐ le

17h 我一敲，你就把門開開。wǒ yì qiāo, nǐ jiù bǎ mén kāi-kai

§18

18a 這兩個學生明年去中國。zhèi liǎng-ge-xuésheng míngnián qù Zhōngguó
⇨這兩個學生明年去中國嗎？ zhèi liǎng-ge-xuésheng míngnián qù Zhōngguó ma

18b 他今天做得完功課。tā jīntiān zuò-de-wán gōngkè
⇨他今天做得完功課嗎？ tā jīntiān zuò-de-wán gōngkè ma

18c 新建的機場很大。xīnjiàn de jīchǎng hěn dà
⇨新建的機場很大嗎？ xīnjiàn de jīchǎng hěn dà ma?

18d　附近有沒有菜市場？ fùjìn yǒu-méi-yǒu càishìchǎng?

18d′　附近有菜市場沒有？ fùjìn yǒu càishìchǎng méi-yǒu?

18e　你們晚上看不看電視？ nǐmen wǎnshang kàn-bú-kàn diànshì?

18e′　你們晚上看電視不看？ nǐmen wǎnshang kàn diànshì bú-kàn?

18f　你找得到找不到那本書？ nǐ zhǎo-de-dào zhǎo-bú-dào nèi-běn-shū?

18f′　你找得到那本書找不到？ nǐ zhǎo-de-dào nèi-běn-shū zhǎo-bú-dào?

18g　這個箱子重不重？ zhèi-ge-xiāngzi zhòng-bú-zhòng?

18h　Q:　他今天做得完功課嗎？ tā jīntiān zuò-de-wán gōngkè ma?

　　　A:　做得完。zuò-de-wán / 他做得完。tā zuò-de-wán / 他今天做得完。
　　　　　tā jīntiān zuò-de-wán / 他做得完功課。tā zuò-de-wán gōngkè

18i　Q:　那個電影有意思嗎？ nèi-ge diànyǐng yǒuyìsi ma?

　　　A:　有意思。yǒuyìsi / 很有意思。hěn yǒuyìsi / 有意思極了。yǒuyìsi jí le / 不太有
　　　　　意思。bú tài yǒuyìsi

§19

19a　什麼 shénme; 什麼地方 / 哪兒 shénme dìfang/nǎr; 什麼時候 shénme shíhou;
　　　哪 něi(nǎ); 多少/幾 duōshǎo/jǐ; 多少錢 duōshǎoqián; 誰 shéi(shuí);
　　　誰的 shéide(shuíde); 多 duō + Adj.; 為什麼 wèishénme; 怎麼 zěnme

19b　Q:　草上有什麼？ cǎo-shàng yǒu shénme? /

　　　A:　草上有露水。cǎo-shàng yǒu lùshuǐ

19c　Q:　你去哪兒買東西？ nǐ qù nǎr mǎi-dōngxi? /

　　　A:　我去農貿市場買東西。wǒ qù nóngmào shìchǎng mǎi-dōngxi

19d　Q:　你什麼時候去？ nǐ shénme shíhou qù? /

　　　A:　我中午去。wǒ zhōngwǔ qù

19e　Q:　哪杯茶是你的？ něi-bēi-chá shì nǐde? /

　　　A:　左邊這杯是我的。zuǒ-biān zhèi-bēi shì wǒde

19f　Q:　這本字典多少錢？ zhèi-běn-zìdiǎn duōshǎoqián? /

　　　A:　這本字典三十塊。zhèi-běn-zìdiǎn sānshí-kuài

19g　Q:　誰去？ shéi qù? / A: 我去。wǒ qù

19h　Q:　他是誰的朋友？ tā shì shéide péngyou? /

　　　A:　他是老張的朋友。tā shì Lǎo Zhāng de péngyou

19i　Q:　學校離他家多遠？ xuéxiào lí tā-jiā duō yuǎn? /

　　　A:　學校離他家一英里。xuéxiào lí tā-jiā yì-yīnglǐ

19j　Q:　他為什麼不睡覺？ tā wèishénme bú shuìjiào? /

　　　A:　因為他得復習功課。yīnwèi tā děi fùxí gōngkè

19j′　Q:　他怎麼不睡覺？ tā zěnme bú shuìjiào? /

　　　A:　因為他得復習功課。yīnwèi tā děi fùxí gōngkè

§20

20a　他在家還是出去了？ tā zài-jiā háishì chūqù le?

20b　我 (不) 知道他在家還是出去了。wǒ (bù) zhīdào tā zài-jiā háishì chūqù le

20c　你知道不知道他在家還是出去了？ nǐ zhīdào bù zhīdào tā zài-jiā háishì chūqù le?

20d　我 (不) 知道他們喝不喝咖啡。wǒ (bù) zhīdào tāmen hē-bù-hē kāfēi

20e 我(不)知道郵局離這兒遠不遠。wǒ (bù) zhīdào yóujú lí zhèr yuǎn-bù-yuǎn

20f 我(不)知道她今天看得完看不完那本書。wǒ (bù) zhīdào tā jīntiān kàn-de-wán kàn-bù-wán nèi-běn-shū

20g 我(不)知道那個人是誰。wǒ (bù) zhīdào nèi-ge-rén shì shéi

20h 我(不)知道你弟弟叫什麼名字。wǒ (bù) zhīdào nǐ dìdi jiào shénme míngzi

20i 我(不)知道他們什麼時候回來。wǒ (bù) zhīdào tāmen shénme shíhou huílai

20j 我(不)知道你為什麼選這門課。wǒ (bù) zhīdào nǐ wèishéme xuǎn zhèi-mén-kè

20k 我(不)知道這種車賣多少錢。wǒ (bù) zhīdào zhèi-zhǒng-chē mài duōshǎoqián

§21

21a Q: (是)我洗碗還是你洗碗？ (shì) wǒ xǐ-wǎn háishì nǐ xǐ-wǎn? /
A: 我洗。wǒ xǐ.

21b Q: 我們(是)下棋還是看電影？ wǒmen (shì) xià-qí háishì kàn-diànyǐng? /
A: 看電影。kàn-diànyǐng.

21c Q: 我們喝什麼？(是)茶還是咖啡？ wǒmen hē shénme? (shì) chá háishì kāfēi? /
A: 茶。chá.

21d 那是一輛日本車還是一輛法國車？ nèi shì yí-liàng Rìběn chē háishì yí-liàng Fǎguó chē

21e 我洗碗或者你洗碗，都可以。wǒ xǐ-wǎn huòzhě nǐ xǐ-wǎn, dōu kěyǐ

21f 下棋或者看電影，都行。xià-qí huòzhě kàn-diànyǐng, dōu xíng

21g 茶或者咖啡，都好。chá huòzhě kāfēi, dōu hǎo

21h 我們下棋，或者看電影，或者聊天，都行。wǒmen xià-qí, huòzhě kàn-diànyǐng, huòzhě liáo-tiān, dōu xíng

§22

22a 二〇〇八年 èr líng líng bā nián; 明年 míng nián

22b 春天 chūntiān; 去年夏天 qùnián xiàtiān

22c 二月 èryuè; 這個月 zhèi-ge yuè

22d 星期天 xīngqītiān; 上星期二 shàng xīngqī'èr

22e 十七號 shíqī hào; 昨天 zuótiān

22f 早上 zǎoshang; 下午 xiàwǔ

22g 中午十二點一刻 zhōngwǔ shí'èr-diǎn yí-kè

22h 從前 cóngqián; 剛才 gāngcái; 三天以後 sān-tiān yǐhòu; 畢業的時候 bìyè de shíhou

22i 二〇一〇年一月一號中午十二點五分 èr líng yī líng nián yīyuè yīhào zhōngwǔ shí'èr-diǎn wǔ-fēn

22j 二〇〇八年夏天 èr líng líng bā nián xiàtiān

22k 明年九月 míngnián jiǔyuè

22l 兩年 liǎng-nián; 半年 bàn-nián

22m 三個夏天 sān-ge xiàtiān

22n 六個月 liù-ge yuè

22o 四個星期 sì-ge xīngqī

22p 三十天 sānshi-tiān; 幾天 jǐ-tiān

22q 一(個)上午 yí (ge) shàngwǔ; 一夜 yí yè

22r   二十四（個）小時 èrshísì-(ge) xiǎoshí; 三十分鐘 sānshi-fēnzhōng

22s   一會兒 yìhuǐr; 一些日子 yìxiē rìzi; 很久 hěnjiǔ

22t   三年三個月零五天 sān-nián sān-ge yuè líng wǔ-tiān; 八個小時（零）二十分鐘
bā-ge xiǎoshí (líng) èrshi-fēnzhōng

§23

23a   凌晨 língchén

23b   清晨 qīngchén

23c   早晨/早上 zǎochén/zǎoshang

23d   上午 shàngwǔ

23e   中午 zhōngwǔ

23f   下午 xiàwǔ

23g   傍晚 bàngwǎn

23h   晚上 wǎnshang

23i   夜裡 yèlǐ

23j   半夜/午夜 bànyè/wǔyè

§24

24a   他們九點上課。tāmen jiǔdiǎn shàngkè

24b   上個星期我病了，沒上班。shàng-ge xīngqī wǒ bìng le, méi shàng-bān

24c   你什麼時候走？nǐ shénme shíhou zǒu? /（我）下個月（走）。(wǒ) xià-ge yuè (zǒu)

24d   我姐姐昨天晚上十一點半生了一個女兒。wǒ jiějie zuótiān wǎnshang shíyī-diǎn
bàn shēng-le yí-ge nǚ'er.

24e   美國一七七六年七月四號宣告獨立。Měiguó yī qī qī liù nián qīyuè sì hào
xuāngào dúlì

24f   她看電視看了兩個小時。tā kàn-diànshì kàn-le liǎng-ge-xiǎoshí

24g   她看了兩個小時（的）電視。tā kàn-le liǎng-ge-xiǎoshí (de) diànshì

24h   我們每天工作八個小時，中午休息一個小時。wǒmen měitiān gōngzuò
bā-ge-xiǎoshí, zhōngwǔ xiūxi yí-ge-xiǎoshí

24i   你每天工作多長時間？nǐ měitiān gōngzuò duōcháng shíjiān? / 八個小時。
bā-ge xiǎoshí

24j   她學中文學了多久了？tā xué-zhōngwén xué-le duō jiǔ le? /
（學了）三年了。(xué-le) sān-nián le

24k   上個星期這兒下雨下了三天。shàng-ge xīngqī zhèr xià-yǔ xià-le sān-tiān

24l   王老師去年夏天教了兩個月（的）中文。Wáng lǎoshī qù nián xiàtiān jiāo-le liǎng-ge
yuè (de) zhōngwén

§25

25a   上中文課的時候，學生一定得說中文。shàng-zhōngwénkè de shíhou, xuésheng
yídìng děi shuō-zhōngwén

25b   講課的時候，老師用了幻燈圖片。jiǎng-kè de shíhou, lǎoshī yòng-le huàndēng túpiàn

25c 在電影院看電影的時候，很多人吃爆米花。zài diànyǐngyuàn kàn-diànyǐng de shíhou, hěnduō rén chī-bàomǐhuā

25d 媽媽不在家的時候，孩子吃了很多巧克力。māma bú zàijiā de shíhou, háizi chī-le hěnduō qiǎokèlì

§26

26a 以前我不懂中文。yǐqián wǒ bù dǒng-zhōngwén

26b 他們以前住在費城。tāmen yǐqián zhù zài Fèichéng

26c 我們學校比以前大多了。wǒmen xuéxiào bǐ yǐqián dà duō le

26d 你十點（以）前可以在辦公室找到老師。nǐ shídiǎn (yǐ)qián kěyǐ zài bàngōngshì zhǎo-dào lǎoshī

26e 她兩年（以）前還是一個中學生。tā liǎng-nián (yǐ)qián háishì yí-ge zhōngxuéshēng

26f 吃飯（以）前，你應該洗手。chī-fàn (yǐ)qián, nǐ yīnggāi xǐ-shǒu

26g 我每天去醫院上班（以）前遛狗。wǒ měitiān qù yīyuàn shàng-bān (yǐ)qián liù-gǒu

§27

27a 他時時刻刻提醒自己要冷靜。tā shíshíkèkè tíxǐng zìjǐ yào lěngjìng

27b 財迷時時刻刻想發財。cáimí shíshíkèkè xiǎng fā-cái

§28

28a 我們昨天去了動物園。wǒmen zuótiān qù-le dòngwùyuán

28b 他們買了一個冰箱。tāmen mǎi-le yí-ge bīngxiāng

28c 明年我的中國朋友畢了業可能回國。míngnián wǒde Zhōngguó péngyou bì-le-yè kěnéng huíguó

28d 我一九九八年在中國旅行。wǒ yī jiǔ jiǔ bā nián zài Zhōngguó lǚxíng

28e 我沒（有）從圖書館借書。wǒ méi(yǒu) cóng túshūguǎn jiè-shū

28f 你看那個電影了嗎？nǐ kàn nèi-ge diànyǐng le ma?

28g 你看沒看那個電影？nǐ kàn-méi-kàn nèi-ge diànyǐng?

28h 你看那個電影了沒有？nǐ kàn nèi-ge diànyǐng le méiyou?

28h′ 你看了那個電影沒有？nǐ kàn-le nèi-ge diànyǐng méiyou?

§29

29a 他們（是）昨天晚上到的。tāmen (shì) zuótiān wǎnshang dào de

29b 他們（是）從上海來的。tāmen (shì) cóng Shànghǎi lái de

29c 我們（是）坐火車來的。wǒmen (shì) zuò-huǒchē lái de

29d 我們（是）跟父母一起來的。wǒmen (shì) gēn fùmǔ yìqǐ lái de

29d′ 我們不是跟父母一起來的。wǒmen bú shì gēn fùmǔ yìqǐ lái de

29e 她（是）去那兒學法律的。tā (shì) qù-nàr xué-fǎlǜ de

29e′ 她不是去那兒學法律的。tā bú shì qù-nàr xué-fǎlǜ de

29f （是）我鎖的門。(shì) wǒ suǒ de mén

29f′   不是我鎖的門。 bú shì wǒ suǒ de mén
29g   我是在中國買的這張畫兒。 wǒ shì zài Zhōngguó mǎi de zhèi-zhāng-huàr
29g′   這張畫兒，我是在中國買的。 zhèi-zhāng-huàr, wǒ shì zài Zhōngguó mǎi de
29h   我是開車去機場接她的。 wǒ shì kāi-chē qù jīchǎng jiē tā de
29h′   我是開車去機場接的她。 wǒ shì kāi-chē qù jīchǎng jiē de tā
29i   他是去年畢業的嗎？ tā shì qùnián bì-yè de ma?
29j   他是不是去年畢業的？ tā shì-bú-shì qùnián bì-yè de?
29k   Q: 他是什麼時候來的？ tā shì shénme shíhou lái de? /
       A: 他是昨天來的。 tā shì zuótiān lái de
29l   Q: 他是怎麼來的？ tā shì zěnme lái de? /
       A: 他是坐飛機來的。 tā shì zuò-fēijī lái de
29m   Q: 他是從哪兒來的？ tā shì cóng nǎr lái de? /
       A: 他是從紐約來的。 tā shì cóng Niǔyuē lái de

§30

30a   他們去年結婚了。 tāmen qùnián jié-hūn le
30b   他們是去年結婚的。 tāmen shì qùnián jié-hūn de
30c′   他們去年結婚了嗎？ tāmen qùnián jié-hūn le ma? / 對，他們去年結婚了。
       duì, tāmen qùnián jié-hūn le
30d′   他們是什麼時候結婚的？ tāmen shì shénme shíhòu jié-hūn de? /
       他們是去年結婚的。 tāmen shì qùnián jié-hūn de
30e   她下班以後從辦公室開車去機場接先生了。 tā xiàbān yǐhòu cóng bàngōngshì
       kāi-chē qù-jīchǎng jiē xiānsheng le
30f   她是什麼時候去機場的？ tā shì shénme shíhòu qù-jīchǎng de? / 她是下班以後去的。
       tā shì xiàbān yǐhòu qù de
30g   她是從哪兒去機場的？ tā shì cóng nǎr qù-jīchǎng de? / 她是從辦公室去的。
       tā shì cóng bàn'gōngshì qù de
30h   她是怎麼去機場的？ tā shì zěnme qù-jīchǎng de? / 她是開車去的。
       tā shì kāi-chē qù de
30i   她是為什麼去機場的？ tā shì wèishénme qù-jīchǎng de? / 她是去接先生的。
       tā shì qù jiē xiānsheng de

§31

31a   我明天才回去。 wǒ míngtiān cái huíqu
31b   我明天就回去。 wǒ míngtiān jiù huíqu
31d   電影七點開始，李先生七點一刻才來。 diànyǐng qīdiǎn kāishǐ, Lǐ xiānsheng qīdiǎn
       yíkè cái lái
31e   電影七點開始，王先生六點半就來了。 diànyǐng qīdiǎn kāishǐ, Wáng xiānsheng
       liùdiǎn bàn jiù lái le
31g   我排了三個小時(的)隊才買到球票。 wǒ pái-le sān-ge-xiǎoshí (de) duì cái mǎi-dào
       qiúpiào
31h   我等了五分鐘他就來了。 wǒ děng-le wǔ-fēnzhōng tā jiù lái le

§32

32b 孩子洗完/了手才吃飯。háizi xǐ-wán/le-shǒu cái chī-fàn
32c 孩子洗完/了手就吃飯。háizi xǐ-wán/le-shǒu jiù chī-fàn
32d 我看了小說才知道誰是殺手。wǒ kàn-le-xiǎoshuō cái zhīdào shéi shì shāshǒu
32e 她演講完，觀眾才開始提問。tā yǎnjiǎng-wán, guānzhòng cái kāishǐ tíwèn
32f 她寫完信就去寄。tā xiě-wán-xìn jiù qù jì
32g 他們吃了午飯就去上課了。tāmen chī-le-wǔfàn jiù qù shàng-kè le

§33

33b 昨天晚上她們聊天兒聊到十二點。zuótiān wǎnshang tāmen liáo-tiānr liáo-dào shí'èr diǎn
33c 今天下午中文班考試要考到五點。jīntiān xiàwǔ zhōngwénbān kǎo-shì yào kǎo-dào wǔ diǎn
33d 張先生動了手術，得在醫院住到星期三。Zhāng xiānsheng dòng-le shǒushù, děi zài yīyuàn zhù-dào xīngqīsān

§34

34a 高山 gāo shān / 大河 dà hé / 小城 xiǎo chéng / 好書 hǎo shū / 老人 lǎo rén / 懶貓 lǎn māo / 新車 xīn chē / 舊地址 jiù dìzhǐ
34b 有意思的故事 yǒuyìsi-de gùshi / 容易的考試 róngyì-de kǎoshì / 好看的衣服 hǎokàn-de yīfu 舒服的椅子 shūfu-de yǐzi / 和藹的老師 hé'ǎi-de lǎoshī / 用功的學生 yònggōng-de xuésheng
34c 不重要的事 bú zhòngyào-de shì / 很忙的人 hěn máng-de rén / 貴極了的東西 guì jíle-de dōngxi / 最大的河 zuì dà-de hé
34d 聰明人 cōngming rén / 有錢人 yǒuqián rén / 便宜貨 piányi huò

§35

35a 喝咖啡的人 hē-kāfēi de rén
35b 會說中文的美國學生 huì-shuō-zhōngwén de Měiguó xuésheng
35c 在書店工作的女孩兒 zài shūdiàn-gōngzuò de nǚháir
35d 她寫的信 tā-xiě de xìn
35e 我在中國認識的朋友 wǒ-zài Zhōngguó-rènshi de péngyou
35f （他們）去年買的房子（tāmen) qùnián-mǎi de fángzi
35g 那個喝咖啡的人是我的朋友。nèi-ge hē-kāfēi de rén shì wǒde péngyou
35h 我認識那個喝咖啡的人。wǒ rènshi nèi-ge hē-kāfēi de rén

§36

36a 東 dōng / 西 xī / 南 nán / 北 běi / 上 shàng / 下 xià / 左 zuǒ / 右 yòu / 前 qián / 後 hòu / 裡 lǐ / 外 wài / 對 duì / 旁 páng / 中 zhōng

36b 東面; 東邊(兒) dōngmiàn; dōngbiān(r) / 西面; 西邊(兒) xīmiàn;
xībiān(r) / 南面; 南邊(兒) nánmiàn; nánbiān(r) / 北面; 北邊(兒) běimiàn;
běibiān(r) / 上面; 上邊(兒); 上頭 shàngmiàn; shàngbiān(r); shàngtou / 下面;
下邊(兒); 下頭 xiàmiàn; xiàbiān(r); xiàtou / 左面; 左邊(兒) zuǒmiàn;
zuǒbiān(r) / 右面; 右邊(兒) yòumiàn; yòubiān(r) / 前面; 前邊(兒);
前頭 qiánmiàn; qiánbiān(r); qiántou / 後面; 後邊(兒); 後頭 hòumiàn;
hòubiān(r); hòutou / 裡面; 裡邊(兒); 裡頭 lǐmiàn; lǐbiān(r); lǐtou / 外面; 外邊(兒);
外頭 wàimiàn; wàibiān(r); wàitou / 對面 duìmiàn / 旁邊(兒) pángbiān(r) /
中間(兒) zhōngjiān(r)

36c 附近 fùjìn / 樓上 lóushàng / 樓下 lóuxià / 頂上 dǐngshang / 底下 dǐxia / 當中
dāngzhōng / 東北 dōngběi / 東南 dōngnán / 西北 xīběi / 西南 xīnán

36d 圖書館(的)對面 túshūguǎn (de) duìmiàn / 袋子(的)裡邊(兒) dàizi (de) lǐbiān(r) /
書櫃(的)頂上 shūguì (de) dǐngshang / 床(的)底下 chuáng (de) dǐxia / 學校(的)
附近 xuéxiào (de) fùjìn / 城(的)西北 chéng (de) xīběi

36e 桌上 zhuō-shang / 報上 bào-shang / 牆上 qiáng-shang / 地上 dì-shang / 街上
jiē-shang / 家裡 jiā-li / 窗外 chuāng-wài

§37

37a 書 shū
37b 一本書 yì-běn-shū
37c 這十本書 zhèi-shí-běn-shū
37d 這本書 zhèi-běn-shū
37e 這些書 zhèi-xiē-shū
37f 我們學校開中文課。wǒmen xuéxiào kāi zhōngwénkè
37g 中文課不難。zhōngwénkè bù nán

§38

38a 生長 shēngzhǎng / 活動 huódòng / 休息 xiūxi / 工作 gōngzuò / 出現 chūxiàn /
顫抖 chàndǒu
38b 我們現在休息休息。wǒmen xiànzài xiūxi-xiūxi
38c 他們在冷風中不停地顫抖。tāmen zài lěngfēng zhōng bùtíngde chàndǒu
38d 朝陽出現在地平線上。zhāoyáng chūxiàn zài dìpíngxiàn shang
38e 說話 shuō-huà / 看書 kàn-shū / 吃飯 chī-fàn
38f 說謊 shuō-huǎng / 看電視 kàn-diànshì / 吃葡萄 chī-pútao
38g 說定 shuō-dìng / 看見 kàn-jiàn / 吃完 chī-wán / 推遲 tuī-chí /
長大 zhǎng-dà / 解散 jiě-sàn
38h 王先生推遲了行期。Wáng xiānsheng tuī-chí le xíngqī
38i 王先生把行期推遲了。Wáng xiānsheng bǎ xíngqī tuī-chí le

§39

39a 看書 kàn-shū / 寫字 xiě-zì / 唱歌 chàng-gē / 跳舞 tiào-wǔ / 吃飯 chī-fàn / 做事 zuò-shì /
畫畫兒 huà-huàr / 買東西 mǎi-dōngxi / 喝酒 hē-jiǔ / 開車 kāi-chē

39b 看報 kàn-bào / 寫信 xiě-xìn / 唱戲 chàng-xì / 跳水 diào-shuǐ / 吃素 chī-sù /做飯 zuò-fàn / 畫圖 huà-tú / 買房子 mǎi-fángzi / 喝水 hē-shuǐ / 開飛機 kāi-fēijī

39c 看兩本書 kàn-liǎng-běn-shū / 看德文書 kàn-déwén-shū / 看暢銷書 kàn-chàngxiāo-shū / 看有趣的書 kàn-yǒuqùde-shū / 看昨天買的書 kàn-zuótiān mǎide-shū

§40

40a 喝酒 hē-jiǔ

40b 喝法國酒 hē-Fǎguó-jiǔ / 喝一杯酒 hē-yì-bēi-jiǔ / 喝朋友送的酒 hē péngyou sòng de-jiǔ

40c 我常常＊發短信我的朋友。wǒ chángcháng *fā-duǎnxìn wǒde péngyou / 我常常＊發我的朋友短信。wǒ chángcháng *fā wǒde péngyou duǎnxìn

40d 說話 shuō-huà / 聊天 liáo-tiān / 寫信 xiě-xìn / 打電話 dǎ-diànhuà / 開玩笑 kāi-wánxiào / 結婚 jié-hūn / 離婚 lí-hūn / 上當 shàng-dàng / 照像 zhào-xiàng

40e 我常常給父母寫信/打電話/發短信/照像。wǒ chángcháng gěi fùmǔ xiě-xìn/dǎ-diànhuà/ fā-duǎnxìn/zhào-xiàng

40f 王先生在跟鄰居說話/聊天/開玩笑。Wáng xiānsheng zài gēn línjū shuō-huà/liáo-tiān/kāi-wánxiào / 比爾跟莎麗結婚/離婚了。Bǐ'ěr gēn Shālì jié-hūn/ lí-hūn le

40g 那個商人總是讓顧客上當。nèi-ge shāngren zǒngshì ràng gùkè shàng-dàng

§41

41a 寫信 xiě-xìn / 寫完 xiě-wán / 寫完信 xiěwán-xìn

41b 看 kàn / 看見 kàn-jian

41c 看 kàn / 看懂 kàn-dǒng

41d 找 zhǎo / 找到 zhǎo-dào

41e 買 mǎi / 買到 mǎi-dào

41f 喝 hē / 喝完 hē-wán

41g 帶 dài / 帶回 dài-huí

41h 我們得去找李先生。wǒmen děi qù zhǎo Lǐ xiānsheng

41i 我們得去找到李先生。wǒmen děi qù zhǎo-dào Lǐ xiānsheng

41j 我們八點就開始找李先生，到十點才找到。wǒmen bādiǎn jiù kāishǐ zhǎo Lǐ xiānsheng, dào shídiǎn cái zhǎo-dào

§42

42a 聽見 tīng-jiàn / 唱完 chàng-wán / 夠著 gòu-zháo / 想到 xiǎng-dào / 抓住 zhuā-zhù / 長成 zhǎng-chéng / 做好 zuò-hǎo / 猜對 cāi-duì / 聽錯 tīng-cuò / 寫清楚 xiě-qīngchu

42b 她總是星期六上午洗衣服。tā zǒngshì xīngqīliù shàngwǔ xǐ-yīfu

42c 她星期六一定得洗乾淨衣服才能做別的事。tā xīngqīliù yídìng děi xǐ-gānjing-yīfu cái néng zuò biéde shì

§43

43a   來 lái; 飛來 fēi-lái / 去 qù; 送去 sòng-qù

43b   上 shàng; 提上 tí-shàng / 下 xià; 放下 fàng-xià / 進 jìn; 搬進 bān-jìn / 出 chū; 賣出 mài-chū / 起 qǐ; 拿起 ná-qǐ / 回 huí; 收回 shōu-huí / 過 guò; 推過 tuī-guò

43c   上來 shànglái; 上去 shàngqù / 下來 xiàlái; 下去 xiàqù / 進來 jìnlái; 進去 jìnqù / 出來 chūlái; 出去 chūqù / 起來 qǐlái / 回來 huílái; 回去 huíqù / 過來 guòlái; 過去 guòqù

43d   送上來 / 上去 sòng-shànglái/-shàngqù // 拿下來 / 下去 ná-xiàlái/-xiàqù // 走進來 / 進去 zǒu-jìnlái/-jìnqù // 搬出來 / 出去 bān-chūlái/-chūqù // 站起來 zhàn-qǐlái // 跑回來 / 回去 pǎo-huílái/-huíqù // 跳過來 / 過去 tiào-guòlái/-guòqù

43e   姐姐拿出一條漂亮的圍巾。jiějie ná-chū yì-tiáo piàoliang de wéijīn

43f   學生把中文字典帶來了。xuésheng bǎ zhōngwén zìdiǎn dài-lái le

43g   馬先生送過來一瓶酒。Mǎ xiānsheng sòng-guòlái yì-píng-jiǔ

43h   馬先生送過一瓶酒來。Mǎ xiānsheng sòng-guò yì-píng-jiǔ lái

43i   他把車開回城去了。tā bǎ chē kāi-huí chéng-qù le

43i′   他把車 * 開回去城了。tā bǎ chē *kāi-huíqù chéng le

§44

44a   警察抓到了小偷。jǐngchá zhuā-dào le xiǎotōu

44b   警察沒(有)抓到小偷。jǐngchá méi(yǒu) zhuā-dào xiǎotōu

44c   警察把小偷抓到了。jǐngchá bǎ xiǎotōu zhuā-dào le

44d   警察把小偷帶回來了。jǐngchá bǎ xiǎotōu dài-huílai le

44d′   警察把小偷帶了回來。jǐngchá bǎ xiǎotōu dài-le-huílai

44e   看得完 kàn-de-wán / 看不完 kàn-bù-wán / 做得好 zuò-de-hǎo / 做不好 zuò-bù-hǎo / 回得來 huí-de-lái / 回不來 huí-bù-lái

44f   請你把話說清楚。qǐng nǐ bǎ huà shuō-qīngchu

44g   請你把話*說得清楚。qǐng nǐ bǎ huà *shuō-de-qīngchu

§45

45a   王老師說話說得很快。Wáng lǎoshī shuō-huà shuō-de hěn kuài

45b   她妹妹唱歌唱得真是好極了。tā mèimei chàng-gē chàng-de zhēnshì hǎo-jíle

45c   我昨天喝咖啡喝得太多，晚上睡不著。wǒ zuótiān hē-kāfēi hē-de tài duō, wǎnshang shuì-bù-zháo

45d   那首歌，她唱得不錯。nèi-shǒu-gē, tā chàng-de búcuò

45e   天氣太熱，我們休息得不好。tiānqì tài rè, wǒmen xiūxi-de bù hǎo

45f   你來得不巧，她剛走。nǐ lái-de bù qiǎo, tā gāng zǒu

45g   你看書看得多不多？nǐ kàn-shū kàn-de duō-bù-duō?

45h   他學中文學得怎麼樣？tā xué-zhōngwén xué-de zěnmeyàng

§46

46a   老師的辦公室 lǎoshī-de₁ bàngōngshì / 圖書館的書 túshūguǎn-de₁ shū / 她的房間 tā-de₁ fángjiān / 我們的主意 wǒmen-de₁ zhúyi / 成功的商人 chénggōng-de₁ shāngren / 很新的電腦 hěnxīn-de_1 diànnǎo / 我昨天買的車 wǒ zuótiān mǎi-de_1 chē / 他講的故事 tā jiǎng-de_1 gùshi

46b 高興地(唱) gāoxìngde_2 (chàng) / 仔細地(看) zǐxìde_2 (kàn) / 很慢地(走) hěn-mànde₂ (zǒu) / 非常早地(離開) fēicháng-zǎode₂ (líkāi)

46c (看書)看得快極了 (kàn-shū) kàn-de_3 kuài-jíle /(吃飯)吃得很少 (chī-fàn) chī-de_3 hěn shǎo / 玩兒得真高興 wánr-de_3 zhēn gāoxìng / 笑得肚子疼 xiào-de_3 dùzi téng

46d 王老師喜歡非常快地說話。Wáng lǎoshī xǐhuan fēicháng-kuài-de_2 shuō-huà

46e 王老師常常說話說得非常快。Wáng lǎoshī chángcháng shuō-huà shuō-de_3 fēicháng-kuài

46f 我們很早地吃了飯,去看晚場電影。wǒmen hěn-zǎo-de_2 chī-le-fàn, qù kàn wǎnchǎng diànyǐng

46g 我們吃飯吃得很早。wǒmen chī-fàn chī-de_3 hěn-zǎo

§47

47a 買一點兒東西 mǎi yìdiǎnr dōngxi / 喝一點兒水 hē yìdiǎnr shuǐ / 懂一點兒德文 dǒng yìdiǎnr déwén

47b 菜很多,你再吃一點兒吧。cài hěn duō, nǐ zài chī-yìdiǎnr ba

47c 杯子有一點兒髒。bēizi yǒu yìdiǎnr zāng

47d 老師有一點兒生氣。lǎoshī yǒu yìdiǎnr shēngqì

47e 老張有一點兒不講道理。Lǎo Zhāng yǒu yìdiǎnr bù-jiǎngdàoli

47e′ ?老張有一點兒講道理。?Lǎo Zhāng yǒu yìdiǎnr jiǎngdàoli

47f 黑板上的字有一點兒不清楚。hēibǎn shàng-de-zì yǒu yìdiǎnr bù-qīngchu

47f′ ?黑板上的字有一點兒清楚。?hēibǎn shàng-de-zì yǒu yìdiǎnr qīngchu

47g 一點兒 yìdiǎnr

47h 有一點兒 yǒu yìdiǎnr

§48

48a 老師和學生 lǎoshī hé xuésheng / 亞洲和非洲 Yàzhōu hé Fēizhōu / 電腦和電話 diànnǎo hé diànhuà

48b 他跟她 tā gēn tā / 我們跟你們 wǒmen gēn nǐmen

48c 紅花跟綠葉 hóng-huā gēn lǜ-yè / 姓李的醫生和姓王的護士 xìng Lǐ de yīshēng hé xìng Wáng de hùshi

48d 我喝咖啡,也喝茶。wǒ hē-kāfēi, yě hē-chá

48e 書很有意思,電影也很有意思。shū hěn yǒuyìsi, diànyǐng yě hěn yǒuyìsi

§49

49a 我們去機場接了一些新生。wǒmen qù jīchǎng jiē-le yìxiē xīnshēng

49b 這/那/有些新生住在那個宿舍裡。zhèi/nèi/yǒu-xiē xīnshēng zhù zài nèi-ge-sùshè li

49c 這些樹,有的(樹)高,有的(樹)矮。zhèi-xiē-shù, yǒude(shù) gāo, yǒude(shù) ǎi

49d 有的咖啡館兒也賣三明治。yǒude kāfēiguǎnr yě mài sānmíngzhì

49e *她喜歡城裡有的咖啡館兒。*tā xǐhuan chénglǐ yǒude kāfēiguǎnr

49e′ 城裡有的咖啡館兒她喜歡。chénglǐ yǒude kāfēiguǎnr tā xǐhuan

§50

50c 三磅肉 sān-bàng-ròu / 十英里路 shí-yīnglǐ-lù

50d 五十張紙 wǔshí-zhāng-zhǐ / 兩顆星 liǎng-kē-xīng

50e 一群人 yì-qún-rén / 四套書 sì-tào-shū

50f 一些橘子 yì-xiē-júzi / 一點兒水 yì-diǎnr-shuǐ

50g 兩次討論 liǎng-cì-tǎolùn / 三頓飯 sān-dùn-fàn

50h 年 nián / 月 yuè / 星期 xīngqī / 天 tiān / 小時 xiǎoshí / 分鐘 fēnzhōng / 秒 miǎo

50i 碗 wǎn / 杯 bēi / 盒 hé / 袋 dài / 瓶 píng / 罐 guàn

50j 每碗飯 měi-wǎn-fàn / 每杯茶 měi-bēi-chá / 每盒糖 měi-hé-táng /
每袋衣服 měi-dài-yīfu / 每瓶酒 měi-píng-jiǔ / 每罐水 měi-guàn-shuǐ

§51

51a 學生都睡著了。 xuésheng dōu shuì-zháo le

51b 每個人都有名字。 měi-ge-rén dōu yǒu míngzi

51c 那三個電影她都看過。 nèi-sān-ge-diànyǐng tā dōu kàn-guo

51d 中文和日文他們都懂。 zhōngwén hé rìwén tāmen dōu dǒng

51e 所有的人 suǒyǒude rén / 所有的錢 suǒyǒude qián / 所有（的）建築 suǒyǒu(de)
jiànzhù / 所有（的）問題 suǒyǒu(de) wèntí

51f 所有的火車都準時到達了。 suǒyǒude huǒchē dōu zhǔnshí dàodá le

51g 所有的工具書你都可以用。 suǒyǒude gōngjùshū nǐ dōu kěyǐ yòng

§52

52a 從九點開始上課 cóng jiǔdiǎn kāishǐ shàngkè

52b 從中國回來 cóng Zhōngguó huí-lai

52c 從小事看出問題 cóng xiǎo-shì kàn-chū wèntí

52d （從）星期一到星期五 (cóng) xīngqīyī dào xīngqīwǔ

52e 從機場到市中心 cóng jīchǎng dào shìzhōngxīn

52f 從十噸到三十噸 cóng shí-dūn dào sānshi-dūn

52g 從電視到電話 cóng diànshì dào diànhuà / 從小到大 cóng xiǎo dào dà /
從國際貿易到經濟發展 cóng guójì màoyì dào jīngjì fāzhǎn

52i 孩子從頭到腳都穿得很漂亮。 háizi cóng tóu dào jiǎo dōu chuān-de hěn
piàoliang

52j 那個地區從十一月到三月都是冬季。 nèi-ge-dìqū cóng shíyīyuè dào sānyuè dōu
shì dōngjì

52k 菜園裡的品種很多，從番茄到南瓜都有。 càiyuán-lǐ de pǐnzhǒng hěn duō, cóng
fānqié dào nánguā dōu yǒu

52m 我昨天晚上寫論文從八點寫到夜裡兩點。 wǒ zuótiān wǎnshang xiě-lùnwén cóng
bādiǎn xiě-dào yèlǐ liǎngdiǎn

52n 孫老師講課從絲綢之路講到羅馬帝國。 Sūn lǎoshī jiǎng-kè cóng sīchóu zhī lù
jiǎng-dào Luómǎ Dìguó

52o 我們從第一課學到第十五課。 wǒmen cóng dì-yī-kè xué-dào dì-shíwǔ-kè

§53

53a 也 yě / 卻 què / 先 xiān . . . 再 zài . . . / 常常 chángcháng

53b 我喝茶，(我)也喝咖啡。wǒ hē-chá, (wǒ) yě hē-kāfēi

53c 他沒復習功課，今天卻考得很好。tā méi fùxí-gōngkè, jīntiān què kǎo-de hěn hǎo

53d 你先洗手，再吃飯。nǐ xiān xǐ-shǒu, zài chī-fàn

53e 他常常吃快餐。tā chángcháng chī-kuàicān

§54

54a 你只要買了票，(你)就可以進去。nǐ zhǐyào mǎi-le-piào, (nǐ) jiù kěyǐ jìnqu

54a′ 只要你買了票，(你)就可以進去。zhǐyào nǐ mǎi-le-piào, (nǐ) jiù kěyǐ jìnqu

54b 你既然有病，(你)就好好兒休息吧。nǐ jìrán yǒu-bìng, (nǐ) jiù hǎohāor xiūxi ba

54b′ 既然你有病，(你)就好好兒休息吧。jìrán nǐ yǒu-bìng, (nǐ) jiù hǎohāor xiūxi ba

54c 我(一)下了課就回宿舍去睡覺。wǒ (yí) xià-le-kè jiù huí-sùshè qù shuìjiào

54d 只要孩子穿夠衣服，媽媽就放心了。zhǐyào háizi chuān-guò-yīfu, māma jiù fàng-xīn le

54d′ 孩子只要穿夠衣服，媽媽就放心了。háizi zhǐyào chuān-guò-yīfu, māma jiù fàng-xīn le

54e 既然時間還早，我們就再看一場電影。jìrán shíjiān hái zǎo, wǒmen jiù zài kàn yì-chǎng-diànyǐng

54e′ 時間既然還早，我們就再看一場電影。shíjiān jìrán hái zǎo, wǒmen jiù zài kàn yì-chǎng-diànyǐng

54f 老師(一)解釋了語法，學生就明白了。lǎoshī (yì) jiěshì-le-yúfǎ, xuésheng jiù míngbai le

§55

55a 我十點就上床睡覺了，可是兩點還沒睡著。wǒ shídiǎn jiù shàng-chuáng shuì-jiào le, kěshì liǎngdiǎn hái méi shuì-zháo

§56

56a 學生問了一個問題。xuésheng wèn-le yí-ge wèntí

56b 法官要求律師解釋。fǎguān yāoqiú lǜshī jiěshì

56c 醫生讓病人戒煙。yīshēng ràng bìngrén jiè-yān

56d 孩子求 / 請父母買玩具。háizi qiú/qǐng fùmǔ mǎi-wánjù

56e 朋友請我出去吃飯。péngyou qǐng wǒ chūqù chī-fàn

§57

57a 他會說一點兒中文，可是不會寫漢字。tā huì shuō-yìdiǎnr-zhōngwén, kěshì bú-huì xiě-hànzì

57b 我弟弟會吹笛子。wǒ dìdi huì chuī-dízi

57c 這個孩子一個夏天能看五十本書。zhèi-ge-háizi yí-ge-xiàtiān néng kàn wǔshí-běn-shū

57d 你喝了不少酒，不能開車。nǐ hē-le bùshǎo jiǔ, bù néng kāi-chē

57e 完事了。我們能走了。wán-shì-le. wǒmen néng zǒu le

57f 你可以用我的車。nǐ kěyǐ yòng wǒde chē

57g 完事了。我們可以走了。wán-shì-le. wǒmen kěyǐ zǒu le

§58

58a 我知道漢語普通話有四聲。wǒ zhīdào hànyǔ pǔtōnghuà yǒu sì-shēng

58b 我知道豐田是日本車。wǒ zhīdào Fēngtián shì Rìběn chē

58c 我知道怎麼炖羊肉。wǒ zhīdào zěnme dùn-yángròu

58d 我認識白先生，我們是鄰居。wǒ rènshi Bái xiānsheng, wǒmen shì línju

58e 那個學生認識兩千多個漢字。nèi-ge-xuésheng rènshi liǎngqiān duō-ge-hànzì

58f 他認識路，讓他帶你去吧。tā rènshi lù, ràng tā dài nǐ qù ba

58g 認識你，很高興。rènshi nǐ, hěn gāoxìng

Bibliography

Chao, Yuen-ren. 1948. *Mandarin Primer*. Cambridge, MA: Harvard University Press.
——. 1968. *A Grammar of Spoken Chinese*. Berkeley: University of California Press.
Cheung, Hung-nin Samuel (et al.) 1994. *A Practical Chinese Grammar*. Hong Kong: Chinese University Press.
DeFrancis, John. 1946. *Beginning Chinese*. New Haven, CT: Yale University Press.
—— (ed.) 1996. *ABC Chinese–English Dictionary*. Honolulu: University of Hawaii Press.
Han, Dezhi. 1993. *Fifty Patterns of Modern Chinese*. Hong Kong: Chinese University Press.
Li, Charles N. & Sandra A. Thompson. 1981. *Mandarin Chinese: A function reference grammar*. Berkeley: University of California Press.
Lin, Helen T. 1981. *Essential Grammar for Modern Chinese*. Boston: Cheng & Tsui Company.
Marney, John. 1977. *A Handbook of Modern Chinese Grammar*. San Francisco: Chinese Materials Center.
Mickel, Stanley L. 1999. *Dictionary for Readers of Modern Chinese Prose*. New Haven, CT: Yale University Press.
Norman, Jerry. *Chinese*. 1988. Cambridge: Cambridge University Press.
Ross, Claudia. 2004. *Schaum's Outlines of Chinese Grammar*. New York: McGraw-Hill.
Ross, Claudia & Jing-heng Sheng Ma. 2006. *Modern Mandarin Chinese Grammar*. London and New York: Routledge.
Sun, Chaofen. 2006. *Chinese: A linguistic introduction*. Cambridge: Cambridge University Press.
Syrokomla-Stefanowska, A. D. & Mabel Lee. 1986. *Basic Chinese Grammar and Sentence Patterns*. Sydney, Australia: Wild Peony.
Tiee, Henry Hung-Yeh. 1990. *A Reference Grammar of Chinese Sentences*. Tucson: University of Arizona Press.
Yip, Po-Ching & Don Rimmington. 1997. *Chinese: An essential grammar*. London and New York: Routledge.
——. 1998. *Intermediate Chinese: A grammar and workbook*. London and New York: Routledge.

——. 2009. *Basic Chinese: A grammar and workbook*, 2nd edition. London and New York: Routledge.

Yong, Shin. 1997. 'Grammatical functions of verb-complements in Mandarin Chinese,' *Linguistics* 35(1): 1–24.

陈玉洁．2007. '量词结构与量词的定语标记功能,'《中国语文》2007.6: 516–30.

龚千炎．2000.《汉语的时相, 时制, 时态》商务印书馆。

兰宾汉邢向东主编．2006.《现代汉语》中华书局。

刘月华等．1983.《实用现代汉语语法》外语教学与研究出版社。

吕叔湘主编．2000.《现代汉语八百词》商务印书馆。

——. 2006.《语法学习》复旦大学出版社。

王灿龙．2006. '存现句句法结构动因的多角度考察,'《语法研究和探索》（十三）, 商务印书馆, 214–19.

张伯江．2006. '存现句里的专有名词宾语,'《语法研究和探索》（十三）, 商务印书馆, 128–45.

张豫峰．2006.《现代汉语句子研究》学林出版社。

朱德熙．1999.《语法讲义》商务印书馆。

Index